THE ADVENTURE

JIMMY "J.R." CALHOUN

PublishAmerica
Baltimore

First printing

ISBN: 1-4137-9158-1
PUBLISHED BY PUBLISHAMERICA, LLLP
www.publishamerica.com
Baltimore

Printed in the United States of America

DEDICATION

To all of the men and women in the armed forces and the Federal Aviation Administration (FAA) engaged in the profession of air traffic control and to their often-ignored families. In my opinion the honor of being an air traffic controller marks one as a proud, bold, and maybe a little foolish, but I would not be anything else.

ACKNOWLEDGMENTS

It would be totally impossible to acknowledge all of the individuals and events that made my career possible. The foundation was laid by the dedicated attention of all of my teachers and classmates in school. This was enforced by the example provided to me by my parents. Each step of my career was guided by dedicated professionals, starting with the chief petty officers and ending with all of the flag officers I was privileged to serve. Other than the initial foundation, my career was marked by the constant observation of the sacrifices made by the men and women placed under my charge. Despite the pressures generated as the result of limited income, family concerns, long periods of separation, and the actual stress of air traffic control, they never let me down. Often, my expectations far exceeded their capability, but for almost forty years, they gave me more than I deserved. This story is a reflection of their sacrifices and has been told in an effort to gain them the credit they have earned.

CHAPTER I

THE ADVENTURE BEGINS

After graduating from High School, I sat down with a classmate, my best friend Jerry Mason. Our conversation focused on what we were going to do with the rest of our lives. Options were slim; neither of us had the money or frankly the grades to go to college, no jobs in the immediate area, my Dad was in the VA hospital and my mom attempting to make a living for the family (she succeeded), by running a little hamburger joint named the Panther Den. We debated the issue for hours, and while a number of options were discussed, we could not make any type of decision. In frustration we decided to go to the nearest town with a movie theater to see a show. This proved to be the defining decision in my life, as the movie showing was *Mr. Roberts*. After seeing that movie, watching sailors chase native girls down the pier, there was no doubt where the future lay. For me it was the Navy. My friend agreed to go with me with the understanding that he would not be a cook while in the Navy. As you can imagine, upon graduation from boot camp his orders read transfer to Cook and Bakers School.

The next day I contacted a recruiter and made an appointment for myself and my friend. We were interviewed, took a physical and the basic GCT/ARI exam, and were accepted for enlistment. About two weeks later, we caught a Trailways Bus and traveled to the big city of New Orleans where we were sworn in and joined the rest of the recruits for our first trip in airplane, from the Big Easy to the Navy Recruit Training Center (NRTC) in San Diego, California. This was my first flight, and I kept waiting for the wind to hit me in the face. We were over the Sabine River, the boundary between Texas and Louisiana, before I realized we had taken off. The only significant event on the flight was a layover in El Paso. That is where I bought my first pack of cigarettes (Parliaments as I recall), the first of many bad decisions I have made.

Since many of you went through boot camp, I will leave out the routine stuff. Needless to say, it was a learning experience. I still get chills when I remember the venereal disease (VD) movies. First significant event, after initial fear and confusion was the classification. You must know that all I knew about the Navy was what I saw in the movie. I did not know the Navy had airplanes, and I had never personally known anyone in the Navy; thus, my role model was my company commander Boatswain's Mate Chief (BMC) Vernon Calvary. When the classifier, a personnel man second class (PN2) as I recall, asked me if I wanted to be an electronic technician (ET), aviation electronic technician (AT) or fire control technician (FT), based on my GCT/ARI scores, I asked him what that was. He said well they work on radios and stuff like that. That did not sound interesting to me, so I responded with the request to be a Boatswain's Mate. (I thought BM's wore khaki clothing and kicked the crap out of recruits, and felt I would be happy with that.) He responded with the statement, "You can be anything in the Navy, and you want to be a Boatswain." I said yes, and he said, "I am going to do you a favor and make you an aviation boatswain's mate." I said okay, since I did not know what that meant.

One of the interesting developments that happened in boot camp was my being appointed as a squad leader. After the first two weeks our company was in last place in the honor company competition. The chief was mad. He called an all-hands meeting and said he was restructuring the leadership of the company. He had reviewed our records and determined that I probably knew less about organization and the military than anyone else in the company, so he made me a squad leader. That was a big deal. After the reorganization we really began to shape up and climb up the list in the company competition.

The end result of this reorganization was a more-focused approach to following directions, leading to the designation of our company, company 297 of 1956, being designated as the honor company. We owed our success to the drive, talent, and stubbornness of our company commander. He told us if we did win Honor Platoon, he would get a recruit haircut. At the end of the eighth week, it was obvious that we were going to win, so he went to San Diego with us on our first liberty and got his head shaved. Additionally, we ran head first into some folks from an all-Texas company while downtown. One insult led to another, and before I knew it, our chief was leading the charge to kick their butts. (I believe that was the initial foundation for the respect and admiration I developed for the Navy chief during my career.)

One of the things a recruit must do when enrolled in Navy boot camp is to successfully demonstrate the ability to swim. I was somewhat amazed that a number of folks in our company could not pass this relatively simple test. My friend Jerry Mason was appointed as the non-swim petty officer for the company. His responsibility was to muster the non-swimmers and march them to the pool. They would then practice until all personnel either passed or were dropped from recruit training. We had one guy from Salt Lake. The first time he entered the pool he sank like a rock. Not only did he sink, he lay on the bottom of the pool and never moved. The petty officer in charge of swimming qualification finally noticed that this guy was drowning. He ran over and captured him with a sheep's hook, which was a long pole with a curve on the end. After laying him on the pool apron, he gave him mouth-to-mouth recitation until he fully recovered. Once the recruit from Salt Lake had recovered, he was asked by the instructor if he had ever been in the water before. He said, "Yes, my family and I often went to the Great Salt Lake for vacation. I had never had any difficulty in swimming before; in fact, you cannot sink in the Great Salt Lake." (You learn a lot of stuff in boot camp.)

When we graduated we had a situation. During the ten weeks of boot camp we had pitched in and bought a lot of stuff. (This was not a voluntary participation.) The items included two steam irons, two ironing boards, two radios, and some similar stuff. Since this material was bought with funds solicited from every member of the company, no one actually had claim to the merchandise. We finally decided to donate all of this equipment to our company commander. Twenty-five years later I was at a meeting in San Diego. The business was concluded in the early afternoon. I decided to see if my old company commander had retired in the San Diego area. I checked the phone book, found his name, and gave him a call. Obviously he did not remember me, but when I invited him and his wife out to dinner he accepted the invitation. When I arrived at their modest home, he came out to greet me. He had aged gracefully, and I would have recognized him anywhere. Company commanders make a great impression on their recruits. We went out to dinner and began to exchange sea stories. When we got to the part about him getting a recruit haircut and having a fight with the folks from Texas, the memories clicked in and we really had a good talk. He was delighted that I had received a commission, and when I told him he had been the first positive example in my Navy career, and I could tell he really appreciated my comment. I finally gathered the courage to ask him what he did with all of those irons, radios, etc. He laughed and said that most of the companies did what we did by giving the stuff to their company commanders. He said they all had a deal with a hock shop. When classes graduated, they all took the stuff down and cashed it in. He said that was a company commander's proficiency pay.

Upon graduation since there was a quota system in place, instead of going directly to Lakehurst NJ for Aviation Boatswain School, I was sent for six-months temporary duty at the Naval Auxiliary Air Station (NAAS) Ream Field located south of San Diego on the Mexican Border. Since I had heard stories about Tijuana I felt that had to be a pretty good deal.

The first stop I made after leaving boot camp on the way to the bus station to go home on two weeks graduation leave was the Seven Seas in San Diego. Since I still did not really know anything about the Navy. I bought some 36-inch bell bottom trousers, dragons on the cuff of my jumper, a double-rolled neckerchief, and since I had seen folks on the base wearing some ribbons, which I thought dressed up the uniform somewhat, I picked out three based on the color and added them to the list. You can imagine the hit I made when I arrived home (population 800, all rigged out up in tailor-mades with three ribbons, and I had only been gone for ten weeks.) In the first three days I was home I recruited five guys for the Navy but that is another story. (Got lots of dates also. This is another story also, but most of it would be considered bullshit.)

After boot leave, I made the long bus trip back to the San Diego area and reported for duty. I arrived at my new duty station late in the evening, after Taps and the duty Master at Arms put me in a 12-man room. When I woke up the next morning, I was in a room with 11 African Americans and was scared to death. (Remember this was 1956, and I was fresh out of Louisiana.) I survived the shock and traveled to personnel to check in and get my assignment. I was assigned to be a mess cook and given the rest of the day off to get my gear stowed, check in to permanent quarters, etc.

To kill some time, I went over to the Gedunk (Navy Exchange Coffee Shop) to get some coffee. Naturally, I was homesick (had been gone three days, and did not know anyone on the base so basically, I was looking for a friend.) A third-class petty officer sat down at the table next to me and he had Louisiana stenciled on his dungaree shirt. That was the connection I had been looking for. I walked over and introduced myself. He asked me where I was going to work and told him I had been assigned to mess cooking but would really like to work in the Gedunk as my folks had a little old hamburger joint and I felt I could do well there. He turned out to be a master at arms assigned to the Navy Exchange and took me to Personnel. Had a conversation with the chief and my assignment was changed to be in the Special Services Department with an assignment as short order cook in the Gedunk.

The work was easy and I did well, even considered changing to strike for Ship Serviceman but I had a problem. The folks running the place would not let me go to chow as when chow was being served the Gedunk was busy. Since I only made $17.00 a payday, I could not buy much so I was reduced to sliding hamburger patties off the back of the grill into the grease pit and wiping them off when no one was looking. I also stole a lot of slices of pie when no one was looking, chocolate cream as I recall. I went hungry a lot and decided the Ship Service rating was not for me. (The 12 years at sea vs. two years ashore rotation may have played a factor in that decision also.)

After about three months working in the Gedunk which included my first exposure to a floor buffer (another story), I had to go over to Personnel for some reason. When I walked in they had a sign posted that said, "Be an Air Controller Early Warning (ACW) and fly, $55.00 a month flight pay. Do you qualify? They had listed the basic qualifications, i.e., flight physical, not color blind, GCT/ARI combination of 110 or more. After reading, I asked to talk to the chief. He listened to me as I indicated that I was qualified and very interested. He checked my records, set up a flight physical and when the results were provided sent off a speed letter to the bureau. In about ten days, I received an orders modification changing my orders from Aviation Boatswain Class A school to Airman Preparatory School (AN/P) in Norman Oklahoma for further transfer to ACW A School at the Naval Air Technical Training Center (NATTC) Glynco, Brunswick, Georgia.

After receiving my orders modification I continued to work in the Gedunk until my transfer a period of approximately three months. During this period of time, my basic wise-ass attitude almost ended my career. For the folks that went to Navy Boot Camp during the mid 1950s you will recall that we had to wash our uniforms and hang them to dry using clothes stops. Now for you folks that don't know, a clothes stop was a piece of string approximately 12 inches long. We had to affix our clothing with these pieces of string to a rope (line.) If you did not tie a square knot, you got a demerit. I thought this was a bit much and made a decision to buy two dozen clothes pins and send them to the commanding officer of the Naval Recruit Training Command along with a note indicating the contents of the package had been invented at least one hundred years earlier, was used in rural America to affix clothing to lines and recommend that the Navy consider adopting this technology. I was a bit proud of myself until about a week later. My boss called me into his office and told me I had a phone call from a chief petty officer at the Recruit Training Command. I answered the phone in a military manner and the chief asked me if I was Airman Apprentice J.R. Calhoun, 438 57 2345. I answered, yes sir. He said, "I work for the commanding officer, and we received your package. I would like for you to know that we get a package similar to the one you sent about once a week. I have been on the job for almost three years and you are the first person dumb enough to not only sent the package but to put your correct return address on the package." I knew my career was over before it started, but the chief said, "Good note, and good attitude; just don't be fool enough to advertise who you are when you pull a stunt like this in the future."

After that close call, I concentrated on Tijuana liberty, studying for the Airman's test and essentially trying to keep my nose clean until I was transferred. To this day, I have not returned to the Naval Training Center in San Diego for fear that someone will stop me and put me in the brig for being disrespectful to the base commander.

I feel obligated to share the buffer story I referenced earlier. You must understand that things like floor buffers were unknown to folks in Merryville, Louisiana, at that time. We had a bunch of folks assigned to the Gedunk that had the responsibility of keeping the place neat and clean. (I believe, at that time, the Navy had lots of folks whose only job was to keep things neat, clean and freshly painted.) I observed this clean-up crew waxing and polishing the floors with a machine they called a buffer. When the place was closed for business, these guys would move all of the tables and chairs against the walls (bulkheads), swab the decks, lay down a coat of wax, let it dry, turn up the jukebox to a Little Richard song and have a grand old time. I observed this very closely and could not wait until I could get my hands on one of those buffers. It looked really simple, but as I found out, looks can be deceptive. Instead of an open floor to demonstrate my prowess with a buffer, I chose the narrow aisle within the Navy Exchange retail store. In fact, the place I chose was the display area for shaving lotion and similar glass containers. Needless to say, since I did not understand that all I had to do to stop the machine was to turn it loose, I kept trying to bulldog the sucker. Results were $54.00 worth of broken merchandise. Since my paycheck again was only $17.00 every two weeks a serious dent was placed upon my liberty opportunities for the next six weeks.

Since this is my story, I would be remiss in skimming over the Tijuana liberty reference referenced herein. I cannot begin to describe the shock this old country boy experienced on his first visit to this fine and upstanding location. You could never have made me believe what I saw, experienced, and lived through in the bars and shops along the main drag of that town. A number of year's later, similar experiences in the Philippines made the TJ experiences relatively tame in comparison but the shock of first exposure to the various temptations available to a young sailor far from home was a memorable experience.

One story about Tijuana worth repeating is my experience is smuggling booze. You must understand that the paycheck for a young Airman was approximately $17.00 every two weeks. After basic essentials, soap, shaving gear, cigarettes, haircuts, etc., there wasn't much left to spend on liberty. In Tijuana, you could buy hard booze in ½ pint bottles for between 50 and 75 cents. You could take that across the border and sell it to the kids in recruit training for $3.50 per bottle, that is if you could get away with it. My experience consisted of buying four half-pints for 60 cents per bottle, placing the bottles in my socks and very carefully walking across the bridge that connected Tijuana to the border crossing. What I did not know was on the American end of that bridge was a bunch of folks called Shore Patrol. These folks were there to essentially come to the aid of sailors that were not able to run fast enough to escape the trouble they were in, either because of wounds, broken bones, or an excess load of the fine beverages dispensed by friendly bartenders, without reference to age or state of drunkenness. One additional responsibility of the shore patrol was to assure that sailors returning from Tijuana did not bring back cheep booze with the intent of either drinking it themselves or selling it to shipmates deprived of the opportunity to cross that bridge and engage in dispensing foreign aid in return for services in kind. The leader of the shore patrol detachment was a well-seasoned chief petty officer. Obviously, this guy had seen everything and very possibly had tried out all of the tricks himself in his younger, irresponsible days. I carefully walked up to the chief and when he asked me I was bringing back anything across the border, I looked him straight in the eye and replied, "No, sir." He said, "Well, I don't want you to get into any trouble. With that, he carefully taped each side of both ankles with his nightstick, breaking all four bottles. Obviously, I could not acknowledge this disaster, not only to my investment but to my plans for wealth. I carefully walked away from the shore patrol detachment, with two socks full of broken glass and leaking booze like a 1940 Ford Coupe with a broken radiator hose. Looking back, I am sure the chief had a great laugh when relating this story to his peers over coffee.

CHAPTER II

AIRMAN PREPARATORY SCHOOL

After spending my two weeks leave at home after graduating from Recruit Training, I caught a bus to the big city of Norman Oklahoma to attend the five week indoctrination into Naval Aviation. Because of the six months I had spent at Ream Field and my promotion to Airman (E-3) I was the Platoon Leader of the Clerical Branch of the class. You must understand that was a big deal. Not only did I march the platoon to the classes, I was responsible for mustering the folks, attempting to maintain good order and discipline, etc. Because of these vast responsibilities, I was allowed to go on overnight liberty on Friday and Saturdays while the other class members had to return from liberty by 11 P.M. (2300) on Fridays and Saturdays.

I took my responsibilities very seriously and frankly became a pain in the ass. Since I rated overnight liberty, I did not have to get up at six A.M. reveille on Saturday and Sundays but could sleep in. The chief in charge of our platoon recognized that power had gone to my head and set a trap for me with the weekend duty master at arms (MAA.)

One Saturday morning the MAA came through the barracks hitting each bunk and stating, Reveille, Reveille, Reveille, drop your cocks and grab your socks. First time I wake you up, next time I write you up, reveille, reveille, reveille. When he came by my bunk, since I knew that did not apply to me, I just turned over and went back to sleep. The next time he came by, he bounced my butt out of the rack and I woke up lying on the floor. (I was sleeping on the top bunk.) I was totally confused and attempted to explain that I was a wheel and the early rising did not apply to me. He asked me if I was a student in the AN P School. When I said, yes sir, he said, there are no wheels in that school. You have a choice. I can write your ass up and you will go to the brig for 30 days (The brig in Norman was known through out the Navy as being a tuff brig), or you can use the steel wool that I provide to make every shit can in this barracks look like new. Since I was scared to death of going to the brig, the choice was easy. I spent that Saturday and Sunday going through a month's supply of steel wool. My class mates spent the weekend making fun of me which taught me a lesson. On Monday when the chief came to work, the first question he asked was where the wheel was. That is when I realized I had been set up but looking back, the lesson was timely and stayed with me throughout my career.

The education we received in AN P School was thorough, broad and interesting. The liberty in Norman, a small town adjacent to Oklahoma City, area was outstanding. The fact that the Navy installation was adjacent to the University of Oklahoma may explain the opportunities available for a bunch of young sailors away from home for the first time. Mess cooks and compartment cleaners were selected from class members every two weeks. If selected, the individual was guaranteed an additional three month assignment. I actually saw folks paying shipmates to trade with them, thus staying in the area. Since most of us were without transportation, the folks with wheels were very popular. Hitchhiking was a popular mode of transportation, and the good folks from Oklahoma were most gracious in sharing rides.

At graduation five personnel in my class were transferred to Glynco for training as ACWs. I was still the senior man resulting in my assignment as leader of the Glynco draft. We rode a train from Norman down to Georgia and once again my enthusiastic attitude about being in charge became an issue.

As the individual responsible for the draft, I had all of the records and most importantly, all of the meal chits. Our first meal was in the evening. I mustered my troops in the dining car and broke out the menu. Our dinner chit was valued at $1.65. The only thing on the menu that cost $1.65 was chicken croquets. I had never heard of chicken croquets and because I was in charge, I would never have asked any of my troops for an explanation, besides three of the guys were Yankees and the other was from Oklahoma, so I assumed they did not know. I finally asked the steward, an elderly black gentleman, if he could tell me what part of a chicken a croquet was. He almost fell down laughing, said they were not very good and indicated that he would feed us roast beef, mashed potatoes and green beans for the same price. Looking back, that might have been one of the best meals I have ever been served.

After dinner, I herded the gang to the sleeper car the Navy had reserved for our overnight travel. Got everyone tucked in and went to sleep. About midnight, I woke up and noticed that the train had stopped. I got up and went to the door just as the conductor arrived. He told me that someone had made a mistake and booked some other folks for our sleeper and we would have to get up and go to the day car for the rest of the night. This incident was, as I recall the first time the *Mr. Roberts* style of leadership, as I understood it, kicked in. I told the conductor that the U.S. Government had paid for my folks to have a sleeper, and we were not going to be moved. With that, I closed the door and went back to bed. A number of hours later I woke up and noticed that the train was not moving. All of the rest of the troops were still asleep, so I opened the door to the sleeper car and gazed out on the switching yard in Mobile Alabama. I did not know where we were but after getting the folks up, we walked across the yard and the folks running the place informed me that the conductor had unhooked our car and replaced it with another. They told me that we would be hooked up to another train leaving the yard at one P.M. so we had a five-hour layover. Guess my first attempt at aggressive leadership was not exactly a success, but I must say that I was taking care of my troops.

With the five-hour layover we decided to find a place for breakfast. I mention this because all of the folks in my charge with the exception of one guy from Oklahoma were Yankees. Much to my surprise, they did not know what grits were. The Okie and I told them that they should put sugar and cream in the little grits bowl and eat it like Cream of Wheat. I do not think they liked grits very much and could not understand why we mashed our eggs in our grits along with pepper and ate like we had not had a meal in about a week.

Late that afternoon, the folks running the train finally acknowledged our presence and allowed us to catch a train with a final destination of Brunswick, Georgia. After an all-night trip, in the day coach, I might add, the train stopped in the middle of what we referrer to in Louisiana, as the Piney Woods. The only thing there was a turn around for the train, a bunch of empty cars, and a large pile of short pine logs called pulp wood. I finally found the conductor and asked him where we were. He said this is the last stop, Brunswick Georgia. I said there is supposed to be a Navy base around here somewhere. He said yes, you have to call the base and ask them to send out transportation. I said where is the phone? He said you have to walk about a mile and a half up that road to the first house on the right. Those folks, if they are home, will let you borrow their phone for the call. (I really thought this was a bit primitive, and if you are from Merryville, it takes a lot to be thought of as primitive.) My troops and I made the 1 ½ mile walk, borrowed the phone and I made the call. In about an hour, a cargo van dispatched from the base showed up and gave us a ride to NATTC Glynco, Brunswick Georgia.

CHAPTER III

EDUCATION OF AN
AIRBORNE AIR CONTROLLER

Little did I know when we checked into this base dominated by pine trees, pine straw, old buildings and two of the largest buildings I had ever seen (blimp hangers), that I would spend a great deal of my life during the next 14 years at that location. After being dropped off at the officer of the day's (OOD), we checked in and were assigned billeting in barracks number four. This was an open-bay building with everyone living in open spaces separated by banks of lockers used to store our extra clothing and uniforms. Each floor (Deck) had one large bathroom (head) with a capacity of approximately twenty folks. The group of folks that came with me from Norman attempted to obtain billeting in close proximity to each other, but we ended up scattered throughout both floors of the building.

The day after our arrival we all mustered in the Training Building (T), and were introduced to the officer in charge (OIC) and the staff of instructors that were going to educate us for the next twelve weeks. I cannot remember the officer's name but some of those instructors, I will never forget. One of the guys was a second class petty officer (E-5) by the name of Jim Corner. Even at that stage of his career he was a legend, not only with the ladies, but for his capacity to get outside of lots of booze. Another was a radar man first class (E-6.) He was comparable to our home-room teacher and had a side-line business. He made leather goods. While I cannot attest to this, but rumor had it, that if you purchased a wallet and matching belt, your grade would reflect your commitment to learning. As a minimum you were encouraged to purchase a leather key chain holder or your chances of success were reduced dramatically. The third key player in our instructor cadre was a chief petty officer named Al White. He was a typical chief petty officer, totally professional, hard-nosed and dedicated to turning a group of fresh-out-of-High-School kids, into Airborne Air Controllers.

Classwork began, and frankly it was not difficult. We learned about navigation, relative motion, radar, plotting and basic facts about what the mission of Airborne Controllers was all about, the aircraft that we would fly in as crewmembers, etc. I was making really good progress until we got to the subject of Identification Friend or Foe (IFF.) Chief White was the instructor, and I could not understand how one aircraft could challenge another and get a response without anyone talking to each other. Since I knew we were going to be tested on this stuff, I would not let Chief White proceed until I understood the concept. Believe that was one of the first times I really pissed a chief off. It got so bad that he started to ask me about my family, where I was raised, mother's name, etc. Bottom line, after being grilled about personal stuff, he explained that we were distant relatives. He knew that we had to be kin to each other because of my stubbornness and inability to understand or at least accept simple explanations. He finally satisfied my curiosity by explaining that one black box in one aircraft talked to another and either got a positive or negative response. I really did not understand black boxes talking to each other but felt that I could answer any question they might ask on the subject.

As we continued through the curriculum things were going pretty well in the classroom but in the barracks, I was constantly being moved from cubical to cubical without explanation. This was irritating but acceptable until the afternoon when I got in from school and was told by the Barracks master at arms (MAA) to take my gear and move to another barracks. Obviously, I did what I was told, but when I found out that I was the only student in that barracks I was, to say the least, disturbed.

The next day, I complained to everyone that I thought was in charge of anything but to no avail. The class was working in the radar labs by now and we ran over time, thus missing the bus back to the barracks area. Three of us went to the pick up point to catch a ride back to main side. After about a 15-minute wait, an older gentleman in a convertible with the top down, stopped and offered us a ride. During the trip, he asked all of us how things were going. We responded that we were enjoying the school and learning a lot of stuff. I popped off that while the school was great, they were really screwing with my mind by moving me around from cubical to cubical and finally out of the student barracks to a barracks occupied by Ship's Company (permanently stationed personnel.) He asked me for my name and why I was being moved around and I responded that I did not know. I had asked the folks in charge, and no one had bothered to give me an answer.

The next morning when we arrived for class, Petty Officer Bernakie told me to go to the leading chief's office. (Folks, if you are not familiar with the Navy, when a non-rated person is told to go to the leading chief's office, it can be compared to being sent to the principal's office.) Since I had never met the leading chief, had no idea where his office was. (Someone told me.) I was scared to death. I could not remember doing anything wrong, was carrying good grades, and did not have a clue.

When I finally found the office, I walked in, stood at attention and reported that Airman Calhoun was reporting as ordered. The chief acknowledged my presence with a loud, "What the fuck are you doing violating the chain of command and going direct to the commanding officer with a bitch?" I was totally shocked as frankly, I did not know what the chain of command was, and had no idea who was the commanding officer. I attempted to share my ignorance with the chief but he was not in a listening mood. He said, "I got my ass chewed out this morning by the OIC because one of my students went directly to the commanding officer complaining about his billeting and being moved around a lot." The light came on! I asked the chief if the CO drove a convertible. He said yes. I then related the story about what actually happened and he cooled down somewhat. He said, he had talked to the chief master at arms (CMAA) and told him, at the direction of the commanding officer, to find me a bunk in the student barracks and make sure I was not moved again until, either I flunked out or graduated from school. Needless to say, this made me extremely popular with the MAA staff but after relocating, I did not have to move again until I graduated from school. (This was the first, but by no means the last time, I got in trouble by talking to someone I did not know that ultimately I found out was someone important.)

The class was making good progress in the classroom and the laboratories. Finally we were ready for our first training flight. Not only were we going to get to fly in a real airplane, we would get flight pay for the first time. The excitement was similar to that one experiences prior to a football or basketball game. We knew we were ready, the instructors were confident so we boarded the flight with high expectations. The training flight was scheduled for four hours and after takeoff, we went to the training area which was located about 50 miles off the Eastern Coast of Georgia. After climbing to altitude (about eight thousand feet), the radar was turned on, communications checks were made, and we were ready to go to work. After about 30 minutes I began to sense tension growing in the instructors. All of the students had their heads down desperately looking for Bogies (aircraft), or Skunks (ships.) (We had learned all of that terminology in the classroom.) After about 45 minutes, Petty Officer Bernakie came over to my operation position, leaned down and said, "Calhoun, what the fuck are you guys doing?"

I replied, "I cannot speak for everyone else, but I am searching for a plane or a ship. This must be a bad place to look."

He said, "Do you remember the problem you had in Chief White's class about IFF?"

I said yes.

He reached over to the IFF switch and selected Mode III. The return from the scope was so bright; my vision was affected for about 30 seconds. He said, "You dumb shit, don't you see all of those targets?"

I replied, "Yes, I see all of those little specks, but nothing that looks like a ship or an airplane."

He went nuts! After a brief conversation with the senior instructor, Chief White, a call was made to the cockpit and the remainder of the flight was cancelled. We returned to base and all of us were marched from the flight line back to the school house (a distance of three miles) where extra instruction was provided for about ten hours. Never again did folks in my class confuse scope clutter with actual targets. The next and subsequent training flights went off without a hitch, and I believe we made our instructors proud. The lesson learned about assuming the student knowing the obvious when in fact, they do not have a clue, served me well in a subsequent tour as an instructor in the Advanced Air Traffic Control School (Class B.)

The class continued to progress through the course of instruction. We all began to anticipate our orders upon successful completion of the school. Our options for duty were well known. The ACWs were destined to be assigned to either Early Warning Squadrons home ported out of Barber's Point, Hawaii, on the West Coast or Pax River Maryland on the East coast. The squadrons in Hawaii deployed to Midway Island and flew missions between Midway and Adak, Alaska, while the squadrons at Pax River deployed to Newfoundland and flew barrier flights across the North Atlantic. Other alternatives were Blimp (shit bag) squadrons flying Anti Submarine Warfare (ACW) missions along the coast line of the North Eastern United States and the Hurricane Hunter Squadron stationed in Guam. The barrier concept was an over-ocean extension of the Distant Early Warning (DEW) line that provided radar surveillance across Canada.

Since the option of being sent to a blimp squadron was a possibility, I made the decision to spend a Saturday flying a four-hour test flight to gain familiarity with the lighter-than-air Navy. Big mistake! The flight was scheduled for four hours. About an hour into the flight, the wind really began to blow and you have never been sick, until you get sick on a blimp. That sucker was worse than attempting to ride the mechanical bull at Billy Bob's in Fort Worth. I really do not know how many directions a lighter-than-air vehicle can traverse, but believe me, that sucker tried them all. The scheduled four-hour flight actually lasted seven hours. It took three hours for the ground crew to anchor the blimp to the mast on the ground. Every time the pilot made an approach, the wind would pick up and we would have to go around and try it again. When we finally landed, I staggered out, kissed the ground, and swore that if I got orders to a blimp squadron, I would go over the hill. Frankly, I still get sick just thinking about that flight and it has been forty-seven years.

Finally, our orders came in, graduation occurred, and I was going home for two weeks of leave before reporting in to the receiving station at Treasure Island, San Francisco, California, for further transfer to Airborne Early Warning Squadron 16 (VW-16) at Naval Air Station Barbers Pt., Hawaii. (Thank God it wasn't a blimp squadron.)

The two-weeks' leave was a great time in my life. Without any plan, my best friend that I had joined the Navy with and another guy from our hometown, also in the Navy, were home on leave. Three sailors without a clue of what the Navy was really about had a great time in impressing all of the stay-at-homes with our life's experiences. I attempted to discuss the temptations available at Tijuana with some of my high school buddies, but no one believed me. In fact, some of those things I did not believe myself. During that period of leave I did meet a young lady that became my wife a few years later, but at the time, neither of us realized the attraction.

I caught a greyhound bus in Lake Charles and proceeded cross country to San Francisco. Boy, you really come to appreciate how big Texas is when you ride a bus from Orange to El Paso. I continue to believe if buses did not stop at every wide place in the road to eat, pick up or discharge passengers you could make better time on a bus than you can on an airline when crossing the country.

Once I arrived in Treasure Island, I got my first taste of what the Navy was really all about. We mustered on squares every morning and were assigned to working parties. The guy in charge of my working party was a black E-3 with a hash mark (signifying more than four years of service, which made him senior to me.) For some reason, probably my attitude, he did not like me and went out of his way to give me the short end of the stick at every opportunity. What he did not know was that I had been selected for promotion to petty officer third class (E-4.) On the 16th of the month, my promotion was finalized. Before I hit the rack on the night of the 15th, I set up in my bunk and sewed on my third-class crow. I intentionally kept this a secret until the morning muster had been completed. When the working party assignments had been made, I stepped forward and asked the first class in charge if, even in this chicken-shit outfit, did a petty officer third class outrank an E-3 with a hash mark? He said sure. I showed him my brand spanking new third-class crow and told him it was effective that date. He said congratulations; you are now in charge of this working party. Lesson learned: never screw over someone junior to you, for someday; he may be your boss. When the muster was secured, I dismissed every member of that working party except for one person and worked that bastard until midnight. (I leave it to the reader to speculate on the identity of the working party member not dismissed.) I actually was disappointed at the end of the day to find out that our flight to Hawaii was scheduled for six A.M. the next day. I really believe I would have enjoyed staying at Treasure Island for at least one more week to see if I could drive that guy over the hill.

CHAPTER IV

AIRBORNE EARLY
WARNING CONTROLLER (VW-16)

After a long and crowded flight from the San Francisco area to Barber's Point I disembarked from the aircraft and found my way to the Squadron Duty Office of my new home away from home, VW-16. After routine check-in procedures, the duty driver gave me a ride to the squadron billeting area. The barracks was an old two-story building with a tyrant serving as the Barracks MAA. He was a first class boatswain's mate with about 22 years of active duty service and ran the place with an iron fist. The structure was an open-bay building with vintage before the start of World War II. I was somewhat surprised to see that the barracks was almost empty.

The next morning I checked into the squadron working spaces and found out that I was one of only six enlisted personnel, E-6 and below, assigned to the squadron. It was in September 1957 and the Pacific Barrier was scheduled to begin operations in January of 1958. Since we had only a few personnel assigned, all of the routine clean-up details required to keep assigned spaces shipshape, became almost a full-time job. The aircraft for the three operational squadrons were all assigned to a maintenance squadron, not to the specific squadrons as is normal throughout Naval Aviation. Once a month, all of the flight crew personnel assigned to the squadron were loaded up in aircraft assigned and flew an eight-hour training flight over and around the Hawaiian Islands. We did not get much training, but the flight pay was nice.

With the passing of time came a steady but slow build up of enlisted personnel. While I cannot swear to this, I really believe the initial cadre of personnel assigned to VW 16 could have played significant roles in the movie, *McHale's Navy*. We had two full-blooded Indians, who were highly decorated Marines in the Second World War. Both of them received battlefield commissions during the war, lost a lot of men, and transferred from the Marines to the Navy after the war in return for assignment as third-class petty officers. Both of them were aviation radiomen who refused to take any rating examinations because they did not want any responsibility. Both had, even then, serious drinking problems, but were two of the best radioman in the squadron.

One of the men in the squadron, another aviation radioman, was a total nut. For some reason, he kind of adopted me by taking me under his wing, so to speak, and began to show me the ropes. About three months after checking in, we had a scheduled personnel inspection. Believe me, that was a big deal. When we fell into ranks, according to height, I found myself standing by this first class. His name was Murell, and we called him Red for obvious reasons. I noticed that instead of having dress shoes on, Murell was wearing scuffed flight boots. I knew that he would be in serious trouble once the captain observed his non-regulation attire. At that time, I had never personally laid eyes on our captain and shared this with Red. He said, "His name is Curtis, and he is a really nice guy except for this personal habit he has."

I said, "What habit is that?"

He replied, "Well, I don't know why, but the captain carries around a pet spider on the end of his nose." I found that hard to believe, but I was an eighteen-year- old kid trying to figure out what the Navy was all about. When the inspection began, while I was still concerned about Murell's shoes, I was focused on seeing the pet spider of the captain. When he approached me, I carefully searched for that pet spider while he was looking me over. The captain had about six long black hairs on the end of his nose that looked exactly like the spider that Red had described. Nervous concern about the shoes and the resemblance of those hairs to a spider combined to break me up. I was in an uncontrollable laughing period. Finally, the captain glanced over at Murell and asked him, "Red, what the fuck is wrong with this kid?" Red replied, "Captain, Calhoun is a good kid, just learning, fresh out of boot camp and really nervous. I will keep a close eye on him and make sure he gets squared away." The captain said, "Good, let me know if you have problems with him." After this conversation, the captain walked on by Murell and never noticed his shoes. Lesson learned: always have a plan.

Shortly after I checked into the squadron, I noticed that everyone not on watch disappeared at about 1630 (4:30 PM.) After a couple of days I decided to find out where they were all going, as I feared I was missing out on something good. One afternoon, I followed the crowd to the television room.

This was essentially a lounge equipped with soda and snack machines and a TV set. When I entered the room, much to my surprise it was standing room only. Almost everyone in the room from the ages of 17 to 40 were wearing Mickey Mouse ears and singing along with the Mouseketeers. These defenders of freedom were all focused on the daily showing of *the Mickey Mouse Club*. All had written in to gain membership and were avid viewers.

We continued with a lot of cleaning, polishing brass, and working in trainers, but the flow of new personnel into the squadron came to an abrupt halt. Lot's of rumors, very little information. Finally, one morning at quarters, the captain announced that the powers-that-be in Washington (always referred to as "THEY") had made a decision to decommission VW-16, transfer 50% of the squadron personnel to our sister squadrons, VW-12 and VW-14 in Hawaii and the other 50% to the squadron in Guam. The following Monday I received official notification that I had been transferred to VW-12. Since the squadron was expanding, the folks transferred to VW-12 did not even have to move to another barracks. Thankfully, most of the close friends I had made were also transferred to VW-12.

CHAPTER V

AIRBORNE EARLY
WARNING CONTROLLER (VW-12)

Concurrent with my checking into my new squadron, I discovered that I had been designated as a crew leader. This designation for a petty officer third class was somewhat surprising, and was not based on any particular talent of mine, but on the fact that I was a school graduate. Each crew was composed of seven officers and 15 enlisted personnel. The enlisted personnel were a mixed bag of technical specialist, two aviation mechanics (ADs) serving as flight engineers, three aviation electronics technicians (ATs) two aviation radiomen (ALs), one aviation electronics (AE) and seven air controller early warning (ACWs.) The officers consisted of four pilots, one of which was the pilot in command, two navigators, and one Combat Information Center officer (CICO.) The mission of the crew was to insure that the aircraft was positioned on pre-coordinated tracks to enhance the ability of the controllers to detect and report targets, surface, sub surface, and airborne of interest.

The ACWs were all junior personnel, and as such, were not only responsible for detecting, plotting, and reporting targets but also for the provisioning of the aircraft, clean up of the aircraft, both inside and outside and anything else, the more senior members determined was necessary. Since I had been appointed as the crew leader I became the focal point of all of the senior folks, both officer and enlisted, when something was not accomplished to their satisfaction. Bottom line, the ACWs were the actual slaves in the outfit, and I was the whipping boy. Lots of good experience for later years gained, which served me very well in future assignments.

The first task we had after reporting to our new squadron was to build flight crews and begin to train as a team. The aircraft we were flying was the EC-121 super constellation. This aircraft represented about a seven-million-dollar investment for the taxpayer, and at that time was considered a huge investment. Initially, the pilot in command was at least a full commander (O-5) with a minimum of 12,000 hours of flight time. The flight engineers all were E-6s or chief petty officers with a minimum of 20 years of experience. While I am sure the classifications for the various radars and similar equipment have been lifted by now, at the time they were all classified, therefore, I will not get specific, but will say we could see a long way with very precise accuracy.

The commissioning date for the barrier operation became the driving event for our training. The flights were occurring on almost a daily basis. Each flight was scheduled for eight hours, debriefs were thorough and intense. Personnel, regardless of pay grade or position who failed to meet standards were replaced. The pilot in command was the final decision maker. His decisions were made based upon personal observations augmented by input from subject-matter-expert crewmembers.

Prior to final readiness certification, each crew had to participate in what was referred to as a cross-country flight. Since we were home based in Hawaii, our cross country consisted of flying from Hawaii to San Diego, California, where we spent 36 hours renewing acquaintances in Tijuana, then to the Naval Air Station Whidbey Island, Washington. During our three day layover at Whidbey four of us, in an attempt to improve relationships with foreign countries, made a bus trip to Vancouver, BC. (More on that later.) After leaving Whidbey Island, we proceeded to King Salmon, Kodiak and Adak, Alaska, spent the night in Adak, and completed the flight back to Barber's Point via our soon-to-be-deployed home, Midway Island.

The bus ride from Whidbey Island to Vancouver proved to be uneventful. We were all excited as we had heard that the young ladies in Vancouver had a thing for young American Sailors, we were all in uniform, with some money in our pockets and viewed this as an opportunity to actually be a star in any sea story that might result from the trip. We had been told by some of our predecessors that the place to make contact was the Green Hotel. Since none of us had been to Vancouver, as soon as we arrived on the bus, we flagged down a cab and told the driver we would like to be taken to the Green Hotel. He replied, no problem, the fare will be $20.00 for the four of you. Each of us dug out a $5 dollar bill, passed it to the driver and entered the taxi. He promptly did a U-turn, stopped the cab and said, destination the Green Hotel; have a good time, mates. We were a little disturbed, but we had asked him to take us to the Hotel. He had accomplished that, and the fact that the name of the establishment in letters three feet high had been visible to us from our initial location, about 30 feet from the place was obviously not his fault but ours.

After this start, I assumed that things would go downhill from there, but I was wrong. When we entered the bar it was occupied by a bartender and nine young ladies of various descriptions. They took one look at us, broke out a deck of cards and begin cutting cards for choice of sailors. Needless to say, after a difficult time in finding a hotel that would lodge us for the night, a good time was had by all, at least, I had a good time and so did my shipmates.

Late the next morning after saying good by to our new friends, we searched for somewhere to get breakfast. As we walked down the street everyone we met, both men and women, young and old, kept saying, "Sorry about the Sputnik yanks." We had no idea what they were talking about and kept checking each out thinking that we had something called a Sputnik on our uniforms.

After a few minutes I spotted a restaurant and we crossed the street to go inside. A newspaper display stand was located adjacent to the entrance. The headlines read, "USSR launches Sputnik." With that cleared up, we went inside, ordered breakfast, and began to shop for more girls. Shopping was so good, we kept postponing our bus ride until we had to rent a cab to get back to Whidbey before our flight left. The plane commander had two engines running when we raced across the ramp to climb aboard. Going absent without official leave (AWOL) on that trip was a near thing, but looking back, the trip would have almost been worth it.

The trip to King Salmon and Kodiak were uneventful, but a couple of things happened in Adak that are worth sharing. My crew was becoming disenchanted with performing the clean-up duties in the aircraft. I became fed up with their bitching and told them that when we arrived at Adak, I would personally do all of the clean-up thus giving them a break. They asked me if that included dumping the Honey Bucket? (Toilet used to collect body waste aboard an aircraft.) I said, "Yes, I will dump the honey bucket by myself."

Needless to say, the word spread throughout the crew and I believe every liquid aboard the craft was dumped in the honey bucket before we touched down. Additionally, the plane commander, without my knowledge contacted the folks at Adak and requested that a vertical ladder rather than a platform ladder be provided on our arrival. Since we were only going to be in Adak for one night and the officers had a function they had to attend at the club that night, they had all changed into civilian clothing before we touched down.

Since I was cleaning up the aircraft, I was the last one off the plane. I did not notice the ladder when I went to the back of the aircraft to get the honey bucket. When I reached down to release the container I noticed that it was full to the brim with liquid and other material. You can appreciate how heavy this container was and how unstable it would be. Anyone with a lick of sense would have backed down and called for help. Not me, I had made my brag and now had to deliver. I struggled with the container to the after hatch of the aircraft and only then noticed the vertical ladder. The ground folks at Adak had dug this sucker out of a snow bank, and bits of ice and snow were attached. I also noted that every member of the crew, officer and enlisted were standing around the base of the ladder waiting for me to yell, "Uncle" and ask for assistance.

Again, common sense did not prevail. I struggled to get the container on the ladder and essentially walk down the ladder with the container in front of me. On the third step, my foot hit a patch of ice, and I began to fall forward. My survival instinct kicked in. I released my hold on the container with my right hand and grasped the ladder to keep from falling. The container swung upside down and essentially dumped the contents on at least 50% of my laughing crewmembers. Laughter ceased immediately, and for some reason soon after we returned to Barber's Point a squadron directive was published prohibiting anyone from attempting to dump a honey bucket without assistance.

The other significant event that occurred during our Adak trip was seeing my high school buddy who had joined the Navy with me. Jerry was assigned to Adak as a cook. He happened to be off duty during our visit and we had a grand old time. When he found out I was stationed in Hawaii and he was stuck in Adak he was extremely jealous. I asked him how he liked duty in Adak and he said, "it is okay, but you have to wear tennis shoes in the shower because the floor is so slick." I did not catch his meaning for a few minutes but the absence of women at Adak soon clarified his statement.

One other interesting thing happened while my crew was in Adak. While I was running around with my high-school friend, some members of my crew checked out a vehicle and went to explore the island. Adak can be a dangerous place for a lot of reasons; therefore, there is a strict policy of checking in and out with the officer of the day (OOD.) When the scheduled time to report in had expired with my crew being no shows, the OOD sent out a search party. The party located my crew in an abandoned village constructed during the Second World War. They had been exploring, got stuck, and were walking out of the area. The only problem was they were tromping through a mine field. The leader of the search party told them to freeze in their current positions and had to break out a demolition team to sweep a path for the crew to follow in returning to the base. (You can imagine the hell that was raised about this little incident, as the presence of mines and do not trespass signs were clearly marked.

Soon after our return from the round-robin training flight we deployed to Midway Island to formally begin the operational phase of the Pacific Barrier Operations. When we arrived at Midway, about a four and a half hour flight from Barber's Point, we were all in for a shock. The facilities at Midway were essentially the same as they were at the end of World War II. Most if not all of the buildings had bullet holes left by the Japanese, gun emplacements ringed the Islands, and most important, most of the chow was World War II vintage. The eggs (cold storage) were green in color and had to be served scrambled, as they would not hold their shape for frying. The cigarettes were Lucky Strike Green, Old Gold, or Philip Morris. They sold for ten cents a pack and were so dry that you had to be careful when lighting, as one draw and you could burn your lip.

When we left the flight line we were transported to our home away from home, the in-flight barracks. Much to our surprise, the permanent residents of the island were not happy to see a bunch of aviator types coming into their home. In fact, our crew was met by a bunch of folks that demanded that we get an officer to speak to them before they would let us in. Being outnumbered about 200 to 15, we sent someone to get our plane commander. He showed up, told the local boys that we had been ordered to occupy quarters in that barracks. They said, "Okay, we just wanted to get the word from someone with authority. (Great beginning I thought.)

We settled into the routine of flying barrier missions. The drill was that we had to have eight aircraft on the barrier at any one time. To meet that schedule, we launched every 54 hours with a five-hour pre flight, two-hour post flight, and the actual flight, which was between 14 and 24 hours depending on weather conditions. During our off time, we caught up on our sleep, were assigned to working parties (primarily unloading supply ships), and played poker. The poker game started when we arrived, and ended with the last barrier flight about seven years later.

These poker games were something else. We had a few card sharks in the squadron, a lot of folks like me that knew nothing but could afford to lose because we would be fed and have a bunk, money or not and a lot of brown baggers that could not afford to lose. "Brown baggers" was a term used to describe members of the crew that were married with a family. Since we did not make much money, most of the married folks brought their lunch in brown paper bag, thus the term brown bagger was adopted. We always wanted brown baggers in the game because they were easy to read, and more importantly, easy to bluff. I learned a lot from those games. Over the two-year period, I probably broke even, but my claim to fame was having the second best hand in a $54,000 pot one night playing High/Low split. I had four fours; the winning hands had four Jacks and four Deuces. (Really took a bath on that one.)

One other gambling story which must be told: At the end of a pay period, most of the money on the base had migrated to about four folks. The rest of us just stood by waiting for payday. On one of these occasions, a destroyer came into Midway for fuel. On the way in, a call was made from the ship wanting to know if anyone on Midway was willing to shoot dice. Obviously, the money men were all for that. The ship docked, fueling began, and a third-class petty officer came off the ship with an AWOL bag full of cash. He made contact with our folks, laid down a blanket in one of the heads and 30 minutes later went back to the ship with $76,000 of hard earned cash. Never again did we accept the invitation from a visiting ship to play games.

After a couple of deployments, we settled down into a routine. Some of the older folks liked the taste of the hard stuff. The favorite was Canadian Club. The booze was $1.80 for a quart but mix was hard to come by. The old salts solved that problem by using orange Kool-Aid as a mix. One enterprising young man decided to use some excess juice from the flights and make some home brew. He was from Kentucky, knew all of the secrets, made his mix, placed it on the roof of a barracks and let it age for 12 hours. That was some very bad stuff.

Shortly after we began the barrier flights we were informed that we would have to go through Survival Evasion Resistance Escape (SERE) school. This was a one-week effort. The way it worked is, without advanced notification, on return from a deployment the aircraft would be met on the flight line by members of the survival-school faculty. The entire crew would be loaded on a bus and taken to the area where training was to be conducted. We would be briefed and then turned loose on a very barren countryside to survive in the wilds. The last day and a half would be spent in the evasion part of the course. Some folks in the squadron took the notification as a warning and always returned after deployment with a bunch of goodies stowed in the pockets of their flight suits. Others, such as me, ignored the warning and came ill prepared for this ordeal.

Sure enough, at arrival from our third deployment, we were captured. The briefing part of the course was sufficient to scare you to death. Under normal conditions, survival in Hawaii should have been a piece of cake. It just so happened that when we were captured, it was in the midst of a historic drought. We were supposed to live off the land, but the animals were all looking for water, and the creeks were all dried up; thus both food and water were scarce.

The first scheduled event was for us to be transported to the middle of the bay adjacent to Pearl Harbor in a motor whale boat. When we arrived we all jumped in the water, and our life rafts were thrown in after us. Naturally they were not inflated. Under normal circumstances this would not have been a problem. In this case, the air bottles used to inflate the rafts were not attached. When the rafts hit the water, the bottles sank to the bottom of the bay. The water was approximately thirty feet deep with a very murky bottom. Some of us younger folks began to dive for the bottles while the other folks desperately tried to keep afloat. After what seemed to be an hour, we finally located the bottles, inflated the rafts, and climbed aboard.

The next effort was to inflate a balloon and raise a communications antenna. This step was necessary to notify the school staff that we were onboard the raft and needed to be rescued by helicopter. We finally inflated the balloon and raised the antenna. The antenna wire was 300 feet long. When we got it raised we found out that it was an obstacle in the traffic pattern into and out of Honolulu International Airport. This notification was received after being raided by a U.S. Customs Service boat. The folks aboard threatened to have us arrested for creating a danger to commercial flight activity. We tried to explain, but they were not listening. During the debate I was able to raise the school staff and requested rescue. They acknowledged the request and dispatched a helicopter.

When the helicopter arrived things began to get scary. The drill was for the helicopter crew to lower a horseshoe-shaped collar. We would get in the collar one at a time and be lifted to safety. Sounds simple, but you cannot believe the turbulence a helicopter creates when hovering over water. After what seemed two hours (actually about 15 minutes), we were all aboard and taken to the survival site.

We all debarked from the helicopter and ran around for about 15 minutes like chickens with our heads off. Finally, someone took charge and began to form working parties to explore for food, gather firewood, dig trenches for shelter and locate water. We were all given one C ration and one bag designed to distill salt water and turn it into fresh water.

It became obvious that game was scarce and water was non-existent. The plane commander collected all of the water distillation bags and C rations and established a rationing system. The next day, after a long and sleepless night, we spent in cross-country navigation, exercising our woodsman crafts (I had none), and in general, getting really tired without accomplishing much.

The food and water supply was getting serious. Finally the plane commander contacted the school headquarters and explained the situation. After some internal discussions they acknowledged our dilemma and agreed to send a rescue flight with supplies.

About an hour later we sited a C-45 (SNB) flying low over our area. We ignited a flare to locate our position. The pilot acknowledged the signal, climbed to an altitude of 1000 feet and his crewman kicked out a parachute and pallet of supplies, food and water. (There are a number of really fierce trees in Hawaii) They grow to a height of about 40 feet and are equipped with thorns about three inches long.) The loaded parachute with cargo landed directly atop one of these trees. The thorns penetrated at least 70% of the water bags. We all rushed to that tree and tried to climb, to no avail. Most of us then lay down and attempted to catch the falling water in our mouths. We finally were able to dislodge the pallet from the tree and salvage the food. Alas, the vast majority of the water was long gone.

We finally completed the survival portion of the school and prepared for the escape and evasion portion. We were briefed that at seven A.M. the next day we would depart a certain area with a goal of transiting through the training area to a safe haven. During our escape phase faculty members would be searching for us. If we were caught, we would be confined to a POW camp for interrogation. If we made it to the safe haven area we would be transported to a chow hall and fed a big breakfast, then back to our quarters for rest.

I cannot explain it but for some reason, most folks want to be a hero. I was no exception. About thirty minutes into my escape phase I spotted a 6 x 6 vehicle. On the ground, leaning against one of the rear tires was a service man dressed in the clothing of the bad guys. His rifle lay across his lap, and it was obvious that he was asleep and goofing off. I could relate to that, and saw an opportunity to be a hero. If I could sneak up on that guy and capture him, not only would I have a high degree of personal satisfaction, my feat would be talked about in the squadron for years.

Without hesitation, I seized the opportunity and began a slow crawl across the open space. I had to take a round-about route in order to circle the vehicle and approach the aggressor from his blind side. After I reached the vehicle, I paused for a few minutes to gather myself and build up my courage for the big leap. Finally I persuaded myself that the time was right and made my move. I reached down to grasp his rifle. When I made contact and began to lift the weapon I noted a string tied to the rifle leading to his right hand. As I lifted the rifle, I also lifted his hand. In his hand was a pistol pointed at me. He said, "I got you, hero; there is one like you in every class, but most of them are a lot smarter than you are."

Without alternatives I raised my hands and said, "What do you mean about being smarter?"

He said, "Take a look at the field you just crossed. I looked at the field and saw a trail about 18 inches wide that I had made on the dew-covered grass. He had me in his sights from the time I started this heroic journey. He said,"It was all I could do to keep from laughing out loud at your efforts." With that, he marched me to the holding area.

Since I was the first man captured it was a long wait for transportation to the POW camp area. After about ten hours of being verbally abused, we were released and taken to get our first hot meal in a week. The education we received was worth the effort. I learned a lot about myself and my shipmates and felt confident that should the worst happen I would be better prepared to face the consequences.

The training we received while in the POW camp was interesting. I am sure that if the bad guys really want to find out what you know, sooner or later you will tell them. I also learned that I have a long memory. The camp commandant was a guy from Georgia that liked his job too much. During his interrogation of me, he spit in my face. Now that is something no one should do to another person. I realized that if I made a stink it would result in nothing but trouble, but I did remember that individual. A number of years later while I was stationed at Ream field in Southern California, I looked out of the tower window and spotted this guy getting out of his truck in front of the operations building. I ran down the stairs, and when he opened the door, I knocked the crap out of him. My operations officer observed my actions and was going to place me on report. This guy looked up, recognized me and told the commander not to worry, my punch was long overdue. I found out later that someone had told school officials of his actions and he was relieved for cause.

In an organization such as the Navy folks at the bottom of the food chain often think that the big guys commonly referred to as "They" do not have a clue of what is going on. This perception is frequently correct; however, like a blind chicken getting a grain of corn, sometimes "They" do know what they are doing. As the barrier deployments began to become a drag, some of the controllers in the squadron got tired of the grind. In an effort to make a change, two of the controllers essentially turned in their Air Crew Wings. The folks in charge immediately recognized what was going on and promptly transferred these individuals to the Radar Picket Ships that were being used as Radar Navigation Fix's for the barrier operation. The folks on the ships immediately transferred these disgruntled controllers to the communications section of the ship. Their job was to communicate with the barrier flights as they over flew the ships positions. Needless to say, these aviators on the ships shared the pitfalls of destroyer duty with their aviation counterparts. The stories about sea sickness, cold chow, long deployments, etc, immediately terminated any thought of additional flight crew termination actions.

Despite the fact that my tour in the squadrons was the highlight of my naval career, young folks get bored easily. My friend Wayne Bates and I decided that we would put some spice in our lives by not shaving or taking a shower during the entire deployment. Midway had a shortage of fresh water so we used salt water to shower and bathe in. This did the job but the only soap we could find that would lather was Dial. This was the excuse we used. The only problem was that everyone in our crew thought this was a great idea. I can tell you that about half way through the deployment we all got together and called a truce. The air was getting a little close during a fourteen-plus hour flight, so we cleaned up our act. (It is amazing what one will do when Mom, Dad ,or significant other is not around to provide adult supervision.)

As previously mentioned, we often were assigned working parties to unload ships. On one occasion, the day I was promoted to second class petty officer, I was unloading food stuffs. One of the items was sticks of pepperoni. I pilfered one stick about two inches in diameter and two feet long and threw it into a nearby dumpster. After the working party secured, I waited around until the coast was clear, retrieved my ill-gotten gains and began the trek back to the barracks to share my treat with my shipmates. I could not walk across the base with a large stick of Pepperoni on my shoulder so I elected to stick the prize down in front of my 13-button dungaree trousers. I took a short cut through housing and about half way through, I passed a house with four wives sitting on the porch playing cards. As I approached their position one of them began to point at me. Soon all of the women were staring and making all kind of noises. I realized what they were looking at but there is no way that I was going to pull out that stick of Pepperoni. I just kept marching by, minding my own business. I have often wondered what tales were told about that adventure.

When we were back in Hawaii, we had the opportunity to play sailor. Because we were associated with Air Traffic Control, we made friends with the controllers working for the Federal Aviation Administration at Honolulu. We made a deal with them to notify us when a flight was coming in from the mainland (United States), especially flights loaded down with college girls coming over for either spring break or summer vacation. When notified, some of us would rush to clean up, change clothing and go to a lei stand. When the aircraft arrived, we would meet these girls at the gate, place lei around their necks, welcome them to the islands and introduce ourselves as the official welcoming committee. After the first introduction, it was fair game. (Lots of fun had by all.)

One of the most humorous things that occurred involved a flight engineer. He had about 16 years in the Navy, was a great story teller, and hung around the bars around Honolulu telling sea stories for drinks. Frequently he scored with the opposite sex. After one of his successes we deployed to Midway and soon thereafter he had to go to sickbay for some treatment. He was diagnosed with the clap. In those days, when such a diagnoses was made, the patient was interviewed in an attempt to identify the source.

The flight engineer responded to these questions by telling about walking through officer housing at Midway and being approached by a lady. One thing led to another and a sexual liaison followed. The results of this tall tale was that every officer on Midway Island had to report to sick bay for what was known as a "short arm" inspection. Needless to say, the inspection proved negative and our guy really had some explaining to do. (Just some sailor humor folks.)

We soon settled down to a routine. We spent 28 days deployed to Midway. While in Midway we flew, caught some Zs, played poker or softball, or performed duties associated with working party assignments. Our 14 days in Hawaii were spent either conducting training flights or chasing girls. The chasing girls were lots more fun than the training flights. I think most of us grew up during this period of our lives.

On a flight returning to Barber's Point after one of our deployments one of the turning points of my life occurred. We were about two hours from landing when we received a call diverting us to a Search and Rescue mission. A PANAM C-97 passenger aircraft was missing on a flight from San

Francisco to Japan. We were vectored to the last-reported position and began to fly a search pattern. We continued the search until we were relieved because of low fuel and returned to base. On arrival, an aircraft was ready and we just walked from one plane to another and were airborne in about 30 minutes. This went on for three days before the search was called off. Just before we landed, again we were diverted because another PANAM aircraft carrying passengers, this time a C-124, was missing. We repeated the search, return for refuel, food and search for two days. On the third day I spotted some questionable returns on my radar scope. I notified the pilot in command and gave him a vector to the target area. He approached the area and descended to approximately 100 feet above the water. We searched the area for 10 to 15 minutes without sighting anything. The pilot notified us and began to climb back to altitude. Approximately five miles from the initial contact I again noted a target. I notified the boss and he reluctantly reversed course and began descent. I left my radar station and proceed to the after hatch of the aircraft. I was able to maintain communications because of a long cord attached to my headset. Shortly after I arrived at the viewing port in the after hatch I noted floating blankets, seats, etc, and immediately contacted the pilot.

He said, "Calhoun what do you have?"

I responded, "Boss, I have a lot of derbish floating around."

He said, "What the fuck is derbish, do you mean debris?"

I said, "Yes sir, cots, blankets, seats, stuff like that."

He said, "God job, you dumb shit."

The point of this story was that I was so embarrassed by my mistake, which soon became part of the squadron lore, that I made a vow to began studying and make something of myself. (There were no survivors.)

One of life's lessons was learned the hard way. Our plane commander was really, in our view, an old man. He was overweight and embarrassed all of the crew because of his inability to march or perform the basic drill and command functions which are normal at morning muster (quarters.) The other crews in the squadron liked to make pointed comments about our boss and despite trying to defend him; we did so without much emotion because they were only saying what we all really believed. The Plan of the Day announced a personal inspection and the retirement ceremony of our plane commander. We fell into ranks front and center to the dignitary platform. Much to our surprise, we saw our fat, non-military plane commander in dress uniform for the first time. His medals and ribbons reached from the top of his shoulder almost to his waist. During the reading of his bibliography we found out why he could not perform a graceful "about face." Our commander was a veteran of the Battle of Britain. During that conflict he had been shot down three times. He had been awarded every significant award available from the United Kingdom and followed that up with heroic performances throughout the Second World War. He had been awarded three purple hearts, one of which was for the loss of his left leg below the knee. Lesson learned: never make judgments on people based on their appearance. What might look like a wimp could be a tiger in disguise. I still feel bad about misjudging my commander. He was a hero, but we never knew it until it was too late for us to express our appreciation to him.

One day we were informed that someone in the Bureau of Naval Personnel had discovered that there was no shore-duty opportunities for air controllers, early warning (ACWs—us guys), and that the air controllers, both radar (ACRs) and tower (ACTs) did not have sea-duty opportunities. Someone put two and two together and made the decision that AC Ws would be sent to AC A school and assigned to shore based controller billets while the ACRs and ACTs would go to ACW A school and be assigned to sea duty billets performing the functions of an ACW.

One of the interesting things that resulted from the decision to essentially consolidate the Air Traffic Control ratings was the addition of 30 questions on the Navy-Wide Rating Examinations that were totally focused on ACW-related information. Since all of our duties were classified, the regular ACs did not have access to that classified information for study purposes, while all of the information associated with their job performance was available to us. Many of the ACWs either took annual leave or on their off-duty time began to visit locations where regular ACs were assigned. Additionally, since the ACs were certified by the Federal Aviation Agency (Administration) (FAA), we began a ground school featuring the subjects tested by the FAA. Most of the ACWs in VW-12, not only were promoted on the next rating cycle, many of us obtained our FAA certification.

I was rapidly approaching the end of my enlistment, so I had a decision to make. Should I ship over and stay in the Navy for another four- or six-year period, or leave the service and take advantage of my recently acquired FAA certification and begin a career as a civilian air controller. After considering the pros and cons of each alternative, I made the decision to stay in the Navy. After all, I was a second class petty officer (E-5), with less than four years of service. My base pay was $160.00 per month, and if I decided to marry that girl I had met while on leave before I reported to the squadrons, I would receive an additional $77.10 per month to augment her allotment and $30.00 per month to pay for my food if I elected not to eat in the government-provided mess. To me, the decision was a slam dunk. Looking back on it all that was probably the best decision I have ever made.

Once the papers were signed, I was eligible for two weeks of re-enlistment leave. I took advantage of that leave, went home, reintroduced myself to that girl, and before the leave was completed I had purchased a used 1957 Ford and had become engaged to be married. Guess you can tell that sailors don't waste a lot of time in some areas.

When my leave was over, I caught a greyhound bus and made my way back to the receiving station in San Francisco. Since I had been through this experience before as a non-rated man, I felt confident that things would go smoothly now that I was a second class petty officer. Boy was I wrong about that. The first time through, I had a three-day delay. I expected to catch a flight the day after I checked in. Wrong again. I spent ten days at the receiving station and I can truthfully say they were the most miserable ten days of my life. Since I was returning to my squadron, I did not bother to take my pay record with me when I went on leave. I arrived at Treasure Island with ten cents in my pocket, minimal material in my shaving kit, and the only military clothing I had was my dress blues, clothing that I had worn while riding the buss across country.

Things got pretty grim. They put me to chasing prisoners, and I noted that the prisoners were able to draw $5.00 per week for health and comfort. I attempted to draw from that fund, but because I had no pay record my request was refused. At night, I would go into the showers and pick up various partial bars of soap to bathe with. I found used razor blades, and in general, made do. I refused to spend my dime. I do not know what I could buy with a dime, but as long as I had it, I was not flat broke. What made this even more difficult is the fact that I had three pay checks waiting for me back at the squadron, and my re-enlistment bonus of $1,800.00 was deposited in a bank in Hawaii, but my checks on this account were safely stowed in my locker at Barber's Point.

Finally my ordeal was over. I was assigned a flight back to Barber's Point and left Treasure Island without looking back. When I arrived at Barber's Point, some of my friends met the aircraft but I stunk so bad they made me walk to the barracks. When I opened my locker, I dug out a bar of soap and razor and proceeded to the shower. I undressed in the shower and threw my dress uniform in the trash, as the white piping was beyond help. I have never been so glad to be anywhere as I was that night in the barracks at Barber's Point.

When I went to work the next day my orders had arrived transferring me to the Air Traffic Controller Class A School located in Olathe, Kansas. I had six more weeks in the squadron before I left. This gave me time for one more deployment to good old Midway Island and a series of goodbye parties both on the Island and back in Oahu. I took maximum advantage of all of these opportunities and left the squadron a much more mature individual than I was when I reported. I had learned a lot about the operational Navy and perhaps more about leadership than any tour of duty I ever had during my career. Additionally, I had made life-long friends, many of whom I continue to communicate with today.

CHAPTER VI

AIR TRAFFIC
CONTROLLER SCHOOL (CLASS A)

When I left the squadron I caught a military flight to San Francisco and once again made that long bus ride across country to Louisiana. During that bus ride I received the worst ass-chewing that I experienced during my almost-forty-year career. I was not feeling too well, and despite the attention being placed my way by four very attractive young ladies I was not responding. After almost thirty hours of this, I was awakened from a sound sleep by a very disturbed, large, overweight man. He started by telling me that I was a disgrace to my uniform. When I asked what he was talking about he responded with, "You asshole, there are four young ladies attempting to get your attention, and you are totally ignoring them. What do you think your actions are doing to the well-deserved reputation of the American sailor?" I tried to explain but he was not listening. He said he was a retired chief cook and I was a disgrace. I apologized and immediately began to act like a sailor. (A good time was had by all.)

While I was on leave, I traded that 1957 Ford (busted block), in on a 1956 Chevy, married that girl, and went on a honeymoon to Galveston, Texas. After a short, but successful honeymoon, we returned to Louisiana and made plans to travel to Olathe, Kansas for school. The wedding is worth a short story.

We decided on a short-fused wedding. Neither of our parents had the funds to pay for a big shindig so we decided to just run off and do it. We found out that Texas did not have a three-day waiting period, so we began to hit various small towns trying to find a place to obtain a license. After three aborted tries we hit pay dirt in Jasper, Texas. It was a Saturday, so after getting the blood test, we had to wait for three hours for the results. The folks in the courthouse were nice enough to stay open late to issue the license after the test results were final. After getting the license, we began the journey to Galveston. Along the way, we passed through a small town, Hampshire Texas, with a general store and a gas station where we spotted a sign that said, "Justice of the Peace."

"This is the place," I said. I parked the car and went inside the general store and asked the fellow inside if this was the place one could get married? He said, yes if you have a girl. I told him, I had one and went back to the car to spread the news. My bride to be used the restroom in the gas station to change clothing for the ceremony.

With the primping completed we entered the store and prepared for the big event. The owner/operator of the store was also the justice of the peace. After checking out some folks with a bill of groceries, he walked over in front of the little post office and stated that the ceremony would begin. We were in front of the post office standing between a bread rack and a rack holding Twinkies, fried, and moon pies. Hanging overhead was an assortment of fan belts, radiator hoses and bicycle tubes. All in all, a very romantic setting, one we would never forget. The justice of the peace began the marriage ceremony by stating the words without pause. When he finished, I asked him to run that by me one more time and stop every once in awhile so I could catch up. This not only broke the bride up but all of the folks that were buying groceries paused to see the show. Finally, we made it through and he said, "You can now kiss the bride." I tried, but she was laughing so hard, I had to wait a few hours to get that done.

When we left home on our way to Olathe, we stopped by the Air Force Recruit Training Command to see my bride's brother. He was going through recruit training, and I was amazed that folks in Air Force Boot Camp had better quarters than chief petty officers on shore duty had in the Navy. After visiting him, we hit the road. After about four hours of driving, all of the lights on the dashboard turned red and the car coasted to a stop. I got out, opened the hood, surveyed the contents, found nothing missing and reported to my new wife, that I did not have a clue about what was wrong. (You folks must understand that I don't know anything about machinery. I can change a tire, check oil, and fill wind shield wiper fluid reservoirs. After that, I am totally lost.) We were about five miles out of Elmore, Oklahoma. Finally a kind truck driver stopped and gave us a ride into town. I located a garage and they dispatched a tow truck to the car. The driver raised the hood, checked the oil and reported that I was out of oil and the engine was frozen.

I said, "O, shit, what do I do now?" Back at the garage, the mechanic told me that he could replace the engine for $400.00 but it would be a week before he could get the engine and complete the installation. I did not have a week so I had to leave the car with him and return later.

The mechanic allowed us to go through our stuff and pick out essentials to set up housekeeping, plus some of my uniforms and my wife's clothing. We packed one pot, one skillet, two plates, two cups, two sets of flatware and a set of sheets and towels, and that was that. After the packing was completed, the mechanic took us to the bus station and we bought two tickets to Olathe, Kansas to begin our new life. (Hell of a start. I continue to be amazed that it lasted 33 years.)

We arrived in the little town of Olathe at approximately ten P.M. The bus stop was in the middle of town, so naturally, I along with five suitcases, she was carrying her makeup bag, walked three blocks in the wrong direction before finding someone to ask for directions. He told us to turn around and walk back for six blocks and we would find a low-end hotel. His directions proved to be correct, not only about the distance but the description. The room rent was $5.00. You can imagine what the room was like. After getting settled in, my wife indicated that she was hungry. The only place open in town that time of night was an ice cream stand, so after a 10-hour bus ride, my bride had a banana split for supper.

The next morning I asked my wife to stay in the hotel while I went to the base to see what I could do about housing. Naturally, to set a trend, as soon as I left to catch a ride, she began walking the streets, trying to find a place to rent. I must admit she had more luck than I. Since the base did not provide housing for students, I drew a blank. When I got back to the hotel to share the bad news, she informed me that she had found a one-bedroom apartment surrounded by churches for only $75.00 per month, and had already paid the first months rent. Naturally, I appeared to be angry, but in fact I was actually very relieved. She took me to see the place, along with the five suitcases. It was very nice, and I told her she had done good.

Next step was to buy our first bill of groceries as a married couple. I have to confess that after paying the rent, the only money we had was change we had been saving since our marriage, a period of approximately three weeks. I had no idea how much money we had. It was stowed in plastic toothbrush cases. We arrived at the store and she began to pile everything under the sun in the cart. Toilet paper, paper towels, dish soap, bath soap, a mop, broom, etc. Finally I asked if we were going to buy anything to eat. She smiled and put a couple of pounds of ground meat, some potatoes, a loaf of bread, jug of milk and a few other things in the basket. I hurried her to the check out stand

and held my breath until the clerk had finished checking the groceries. The total came to $35.75. I dumped the change and when we finished counting it out, the total was $35.79. (Guess luck was with us from the start.) We rolled the loaded cart out the door and I tried to figure out how I could carry eight bags of assorted stuff for ten blocks. As luck would have it, the guy who had rented the apartment to my wife earlier in the day was driving by, noted our situation and being a good Midwestern type of guy, stopped and gave us a lift to our new home.

We began our life with newly wedded bliss. The first meal she cooked was probably the worst meal I have ever eaten in my life, but I asked for seconds. Things went well. I started school and found out that the curriculum was extremely difficult but manageable. We had no money, no transportation, but we had each other, so things were going well. A number of the folks, many of them married, that were in the squadron with me were also students, so we had some folks to pal around with. They had transportation, but like us, very little money, so we shared scraps and really enjoyed life. About two weeks after arriving, I got a call from the garage telling me that my car was ready and the bill would be $390.00. I called my mom and asked for a $400.00 loan. She sent the money; I bought a bus ticket for $7.00 and hit the road on a Saturday. I arrived late in the afternoon, paid the man, put $3.00 worth of gas in the tank (thank God it was almost full), and began the trip back to Olathe. As I recall, it was about 400 miles, and I still don't understand how I made it, but when I rolled into the driveway at our little apartment, I ran out of gas. It was a week until payday so the car sat until I could get some money. We were out of cigarettes, so my wife had the brilliant idea of taking all of the cigarette butts out of the ash tray, breaking them down and making a large cigar out of the tobacco recycled. We did that and after one puff, you were dizzy for about two hours. Despite all of the problems, we made it until payday.

The course of instruction provided by the staff of the Air Traffic Control School Class A was very interesting, informative, and difficult. The greatest difficulty I had was the way the staff of instructors treated the students. They were accustomed to teaching students right out of Recruit Training and were not prepared for the influx of fairly seasoned petty officers transitioning from the early warning squadrons. During that period of time the Federal Aviation Act of 1958 was enacted. This action not only established the Federal Aviation Administration, it changed a lot of the contents of the lesson plans being used in the course of instruction. One example was the changing of Civil Air Regulations Part 60 (CAR 60) to Federal Air Regulations Part 91 (FAR 91).

The frustrations grew to the point where I requested to be dropped from the school. The driving issue behind my decision was my perception that while the air controllers were smart, they did not have the ability to make leadership type decisions. Additionally, while in the squadron I had been respected for the job I was performing to the best of my knowledge and ability to get a group of personnel to do a job. Finally, to be truthful, I missed the flight pay.

When I reported to the board responsible for either retaining students or dismissing them from the course, the officer in charge of the board, along with all of the members became angry when I began to explain my reasons for requesting a drop. (I left out the flight-pay reason.) The officer demanded that someone obtain my record from the school. When provided, he reviewed and really blew his top. He said, "We are dropping out 89% of the students from this course, and you have a 98% average. I just reported aboard for a two-year tour, and I am telling you that the only way you are going to get out of this school is to either graduate or apply for a drop after I have been transferred." That settled the matter and I continued to do the best I could in mastering the course of instruction. (Proved to be the best thing that could have happened to me, but at the time, I was not mature enough to appreciate the decision) Thank you, Chief Warrant Officer Cook, wherever you are.

As graduation approached we all became anxious for orders. Since all of the ACWs were coming off sea duty we expected to be sent to shore duty. None of us had any idea where a good place to go for duty was, so most of the folks asked for assignment at the nearest Naval Air Station to their home. Since Louisiana did not have any major Air Stations, I requested California. I had friends from the squadron that had been assigned to Mirimar, Alemada, North Island, and Ream Field, so I thought I could be stationed with someone I knew. As luck would have it, my orders came in to Naval Auxiliary Air Station, Ream Field, Imperial Beach, California. That was the place where I had performed temporary duty out of boot camp, so I was familiar with the area as well as the base. My wife was very excited about going to California, and I felt this would be a good place to start my career as an air controller.

CHAPTER VII

NAVAL AUXILIARY AIR STATION, REAM FIELD

After a very difficult trip from Louisiana to California (little money, lots of flea-bag motels, ran out of gas twice), we pulled into the main gate at NAAS, Ream Field, south of San Diego. My friend Wayne Bates, from the squadron, and his wife had invited us to spend our first night with them, so at least we had a place to stay for the night. All of these folks were new to my wife but in a very short time, I could see that the womenfolk had bonded.

The next day I went out to the control tower to let everyone know that I was in the area and would be checking in as soon as I found a place to live. One of the folks, actually the guy I was relieving, indicated that their house would be available as soon as he departed, about six weeks, so sight unseen I committed to moving in his place. We made the decision to live in a motel on the beach for the six-week period. That was after we were shown a rental house for $85.00 per month (a lot of money in 1959). This house was located in an alley behind a beer bar. When we were looking at the house I noticed that all of the furniture in the small living room was arranged on one side of the room. I asked the young Marine's wife why she had the house decorated that way and she replied that at high tide water came into the living room. That plus the location was the deciding factor on the motel.

Since we did not have any furniture, moving in was pretty simple. We unloaded the suitcases, took out a box of pots/pans and two plates, two glasses, two knives, forks and spoons, along with a coffee pot and two cups, and were ready to set up housekeeping. This was a nice six weeks early in our marriage. The major event was being tricked into spending the night on the beach looking for grunion. I still don't really believe that such a thing exists. I do know that on that night, despite our best efforts, the grunion were missing in action.

One other story of interest was the first time my new wife observed me watching a football game on television. I had played all sports in high school and thought I was a pretty good athlete. (I was not as good an athlete as I thought.) I never have been able to watch an athletic event in a passive mode. The game was Louisiana State University (LSU) vers the University of Mississippi. Billy Canon was the stud for LSU, and the game was a hard-fought defensive battle. With only a few minutes to go the score was 0 to 0 and Old Miss was forced to punt. Cannon received the punt deep in LSU territory and ran the kick back at least 175 yards for the winning score. During that runback, I believe I blocked everyone on the Old Miss team at least three times. When Cannon crossed the goal line I attempted to find my wife. She had locked herself in the bathroom for self protection. The room was a total wreck. I had overturned all the chairs, knocked all the lamps over, and overturned the sofa. After that she always attempted to find somewhere else to be when I was watching a football game.

I checked in for duty and found out that I was a section leader in the control tower. Since I was a second-class petty officer I was not shocked at the assignment, that is, until I went to the tower for my first watch, and saw that the other two men in my section had graduated from the basic Air Traffic Controller school two weeks before I had. Since emergency procedures were stressed so strongly in school, I was somewhat concerned about how things would go. The guy I relieved, my friend Wayne Bates, told me not to worry about it, as he had been there for two months and had not seen an emergency. I relieved the watch, and the first seven transmissions I worked included five emergencies. I forget to mention that Ream Field was a helicopter base, and helicopters create a lot of background noise with the rotors. Although I could only understand about half of what was being said, we worked the emergencies to everyone's satisfaction, despite not having a clue of what was going on. After it was over, I made the statement that despite not knowing what to do or even understanding what was going on we had done a pretty good job, so this Air Controller stuff must be a snap.

After the six weeks passed in the motel, we moved into our first home. It was a small, furnished one-bedroom house, painted red and white, located on Palm Avenue in Imperial Beach. It was actually a dream home for newlyweds. Between car payments and rent we had very little money. My total salary including allotment and commuted rations was $267.10 per month. With a car payment of $85.00 and rent of $85.00 plus utilities, there was not much left for food, entertainment, or for that matter, anything else.

We were young, in love, and someway we managed to entertain ourselves. We visited other married folks in the division, played a lot of cards, and shared food at the end of the pay period.

One story bears repeating. Our commanding officer was a young captain who had some unique ideas. One of these ideas was to announce personnel inspections in the Plan of the Day the day before the inspection. Short notice and little money often created problems that no one should have to overcome. I had the eve watch on a Thursday, and when I checked in for my watch and read the Plan of the Day, I noticed that we had an inspection the next day at 0800. I had two problems, one no money, and two, I needed a haircut. When I got off watch at midnight and hurried home I had to wake up my wife and ask her to give me a haircut. We did not even have a pair of scissors. Bless her heart; she did the best she could with one of my disposal razors. Actually, she did all right on the top and sides but gapped it pretty bad in the back. I got dressed the next morning (thank God my service dress blues were clean) and with great reservation fell in to muster for inspection. My shipmates had a great time discussing my haircut, and we made tentative plans for me to pass out and the guy on each side of me; drag me away before the captain approached our ranks. The captain screwed up the plan by choosing to inspect our division first. The captain was one of those guys that inspected each individual by facing them and going over them from head to toe before performing a right face and going to the next man. He looked me over really thoroughly and complemented me on my appearance. The problem was after he finished a rank of personnel; he would march behind that rank and take a good look from the rear. I knew when he saw those gaps there would be hell to pay. In an attempt to mask the haircut, I rolled my shoulders forward thus causing the flap on my jumper to ride up on the hairline. The captain was disturbed about my posture and pulled each of my arms down. When he did that, those gaps stood out like a sore thumb. He said, "Sailor, where in the hell did you get that haircut?" My pride would not allow me to tell the boss that I did not have any money and my poor little wife had to cut it with a razor so I said, "Captain, I worked late last night and when I got off all of the barber shops were closed so I went down to Tijuana for this haircut."

He said, "It will take at least two weeks before you look presentable."

When the inspection was over the captain addressed the troops. He said, overall everyone looked good and he was pleased. He also said, "I saw two or three Tijuana-type haircuts, and they were horrible. If you get short on time because of your work schedule I recommend you let me chew your ass rather than going down there to get butchered. I swear one of you folks will not look decent for at least a month." Now I know that I was the only one with a Tijuana haircut and he made up the other folks to make me feel better. Lesson learned: never be so broke that you cannot get a haircut on a short-fused notification.

With the passing of time and my increase in experience I became very comfortable with performing the duties associated with an Air Traffic Controller. The vast majority of our traffic was helicopters. Other than the background noise, the complexity of the various traffic patterns made controlling helos a unique experience. The Navy finally made the investment to instrument the helicopters. This turned a Visual Flight Rules (VFR) weapon system platform into an all-weather asset. Navigational aids were installed and we developed instrument approach procedures for flight with this newfangled capability.

The change from a VFR operation into an all weather operation required selected controllers to obtain certification as a fully rated controller. I was one of the chosen few, and believe me, the book work was not only time consuming, it was difficult. Finally the day came for our examination. A chief petty officer from Naval Air Station Mirimar, was the local examiner. He came down and administered the book-test portion of the examination. At the conclusion of the book portion of the examination, those of us who were successful (I made the cut), were required to go to the control tower and demonstrate our proficiency in the actual control of traffic.

The traffic load was heavy, and we were going at it hot and heavy. I overheard the chief from Mirimar saying to my boss, a lieutenant commander, "That young man can control the crap out of helicopters."

My boss said, "That young man can control the crap out of anything." Since I was on the controller position at the time, I felt really good about that. After successfully gaining my designation as a senior controller, the chief asked me if I would be willing to come to Mirimar and demonstrate my ability to control fixed-wing jet traffic.

Naturally, I said, "Yes, any time any place." Little did I know that he was serious.

One week later, the chief called from Mirimar and asked me if I could be there to assist in the recovery of an Air Wing that afternoon that was returning from a six month deployment. I told him that I would be there and asked my boss for permission to go to Mirimar and show the big boys how Air Traffic Control was done. He allowed me to leave. When I arrived at Mirimar I asked for directions to the control tower and proceeded down to the area of Base Operations. The chief did not know that I had a number of friends stationed at Mirimar and had spent countless hours in the evening shooting the breeze with those folks in the tower. When I arrived, I was escorted to the tower. The chief met me in the tower and told me that the aircraft should be arriving in about fifteen minutes. I replied, "Tell me the duty runway and the pattern altitude, and get out of my way."

When the air wing began to arrive I assumed the local controller position and began to work all of the aircraft. The chief was shocked by my performance and what he thought was my natural ability to control traffic. Again, I had spent many hours in that tower and was very familiar with the procedures, but he was not aware that I had ever been in that tower. At the conclusion of the recovery, he congratulated me and asked me if I would be interested in transferring to Mirimar. I told him that I appreciated his confidence but I was comfortable in my position at Ream Field. He said he would put in a good word for me, and I believe he did that, as I received a lot of complements from a lot of folks about my no-notice performance. Lesson learned: sometimes it is better to be prepared than to be good.

I returned to Ream Field and assumed my duties as a section leader in the division. A couple of months later I made one of the big mistakes of my career. We were planning a recovery of a helicopter squadron that was returning after a six-month deployment. One of the pilots in that squadron was a good friend. When he established radio contact and recognized my voice, he asked me if I would call his wife and children and notify them that he would be landing in about thirty minutes. I not only contacted his wife, I invited them into the tower to view the arrival of the squadron. About the time they arrived in the tower, the pilot called and declared an emergency, rough running engine and violent vibrations in the helo. Naturally they recognized his voice and began to panic. Just as they crossed the beach, about ¾ mile from the runway, the tail rotor of the helo became detached and flew off. This resulted in a total loss of control, and the helo nosed over and drove itself about 18 feet into the wetlands between the beach and the runway. There was no doubt that all personnel on board had perished. Not only did I know that, so did the wife and children of the pilot. I cannot explain how difficult that afternoon was for all concerned, but I did learn a really tuff lesson.

One afternoon we were monitoring an emergency on the guard emergency frequency. The aircraft in difficulty was planning an approach into Mirimar. I noticed a parachute just west of the airfield along the beach front, and immediately assumed that the condition of the aircraft we were monitoring had deteriorated to the point where the pilot had bailed out of the aircraft. I immediately hit the crash phone and declared an emergency. The crash truck was located near the control tower. When informed of the position of the parachute, rather than going the long way around through the main gate, he crashed through a gate adjacent to the tower and proceeded rapidly to the scene. About the time he crashed through the gate, I noticed that the parachutist was now rising from the ground to an ultimate altitude of 250 feet. Now I was really confused, as that was not the way it was supposed to work. I called Mirimar and inquired about the emergency aircraft. The told me he had made a safe landing. Now I had a problem. I had alerted the entire base to an accident, allowed a crash truck to break down a gate, and now I was observing a parachute rising instead of falling.

My operations officer was in his pick up driving hell bent for leather to the scene. He asked me what was the situation, and I told him I did not have a clue. The emergency I thought we were responding to had landed safely 30 miles from our location, I had a crash truck failing around, followed by an ambulance, and my boss driving like a bandit through wetlands looking for wreckage. When the investigation was over it was determined that two parachute riggers from one of the squadrons had borrowed a parachute and 250 feet of line, tied the line to the bumper of their old car and took turns in testing out the parachutes by driving as fast as possible, thus jerking the guy into the air up to an altitude of 250 feet before slowing down to a stop and allowing the gentle glide to a safe landing. After a massive ass-chewing of all concerned by the operations officer, everyone returned to work. I guess that was parasailing at an early stage of development. Lesson learned: never assume you know what the hell is going on because there is a good chance you don't.

I cannot overstate how financially difficult it was to make ends meet. We almost went down the tubes over a water bill. Our little house was really nice, but the yard needed a lot of work. My wife and I raked the yard and planted flowers. Naturally that resulted in a great deal of watering. Being natives of Louisiana, we never thought about the price of water. When our first water bill came in it amounted to $62.00. That was about the amount of money we had each month to buy groceries to live on. We struggled through that period of time, but needless to say, the yard became neglected.

Our first Christmas was pretty grim also. I wanted to do something special for her and she wanted to do the same for me. What we actually did was, she bought me a double pack of razor blades and I bought her a two-liter bottle of Pepsi. Both gifts were wrapped in Christmas paper and displayed prominently under a dying bush in the yard that we had designated as our Christmas tree. (Looking back, it may have been my best Christmas.)

Because of continuing financial difficulties, my wife and I decided that she had to go to work. She obtained a position as a telephone operator in an office located in down town San Diego. After a month of commuting, we made a decision to rent an apartment located about one block from where she worked. The apartment was in an older building located on 9th Avenue. Shortly after moving in, I persuaded the apartment manager to allow me to refurbish our apartment if the owner would agree to pay for any material I used. This deal was struck, and I began. When completed, if I do say so, the place looked really nice. Shortly after I was finished the manager and his wife accepted a position managing a sixty-eight apartment complex. (Where we lived there were a total of seven apartments located in two buildings separated by one city block.) Because of the work I had accomplished on our apartment the outgoing manager recommended me to the owner as his replacement. The owner, a man about sixty-five years of age, came down and interviewed me and my wife and offered us the job. The salary would be $10.00 per month for each apartment rented plus $3.00 per hour for each hour I worked in performing maintenance to the complex. The only catch was we had to move from our recently redecorated apartment to the one directly below, since this was the apartment being vacated by the outgoing manager. With great reluctance, we agreed to move, and my career as an apartment manager as a part-time job began.

The first challenge was to locate tenants for our old apartment. We placed an advertisement in the San Diego Union and began to interview prospective tenants. Since they would be living directly above us, we wanted folks that would be well behaved. We felt that we had hit pay dirt with our first interview. The apartment was a two-bedroom apartment, and the applicants were a brother and sister and one of the sister's female friends. The interview was going well until the sister began to thrash around, and finally fell on the dining room floor of our apartment. I sensed that she was having an elliptic fit. I had read somewhere that the danger of such a seizure was that the individual would swallow her tongue and choke to death. I took action by jamming a pencil in her mouth and attempted to call a doctor. Before I could make a connection, the seizure passed and she appeared to be unharmed. Despite this event, we decided to rent the apartment to them, as it did mean

$10.00 per month to us and relieved us from the burden of prospective tenant interviews.

These folks moved in and everything was normal for about three weeks. One night about eleven P.M., my wife and I were in bed when all hell broke loose upstairs. First I hit the ceiling with a broom but nothing happened. I got dressed and walked up the stairs to their apartment door and began to knock loudly. I assumed that another seizure was taking place. After about the third knock, the door swung open, and instead of seeing a young lady laying on the floor in distress I observed three young ladies, one of which I had thought was a young man, in positions on the floor that my rural south Louisiana background had not prepared me to view. They immediately got off the floor and attempted to pull themselves together, an act very difficult to do when all concerned were buck naked, thus they failed miserably. I began to ask questions but did not understand the answers. Finally I called the police. The arrived, viewed the tenants and informed me that they were well-known lesbians. I had heard the word but really did not understand what I had seen. I asked the officer in charge if I could evict them because of other tenants with young children. Again, this was in 1960, so I was within my rights to ask them to leave. Lesson learned: times have really changed.

I replaced these tenants with a young married couple that also had an unmarried sister of the wife living with them. My wife worked with the married woman, and her sister was a student at San Diego State. The husband was a young sailor stationed on the USS *Bennington,* home ported in San Diego. We all became fast friends, a fact that becomes important later on in this story.

My next adventure as an apartment manager concerned one of my tenants that lived in the building up the street. He was a really nice guy with a wife and five children. He had been living in his apartment for five years and always paid his rent on time. One Saturday night about midnight he called me and said, "Mr. Calhoun, I hate to bother you, but things are going on in the apartment on the first floor that my wife and I cannot put up with any longer." I asked him what the problem was and he said, "Rather than me telling you, why don't you come up and see for yourself." I agreed and immediately got dressed.

When I arrived at the apartment building (it was equipped with a small pool), I saw a lot of young men in various states of sobriety. I immediately assumed they were either sailors or marines on liberty and obviously they were having a good time. The tenants were four young women that had resided in the apartment for approximately one year. I waded through the young men and finally worked my way to the front door of the apartment. Along the way I passed a fairly long line of young men awaiting a turn. When I finally got to the door and knocked, one of the young ladies shouted out that I should calm down and wait my turn. I responded with another knock which resulted in a rapid opening of the door. Again the sight was something a poor boy from Louisiana was not familiar with, but with keen insight, I recognized what was happening. It seems as if the young ladies had decided to go into freelance business for themselves, and I had interrupted the grand opening. Needless to say, the cops were called, and I was acknowledged by all as a party pooper. Lesson learned: apartment management is a tuff way to make a living.

I finally cleared the apartment building of hookers and lesbians, and things settled down. The young sailor on the Bennington that I mentioned earlier was approaching the end of his enlistment. He and his wife had decided to remain in San Diego after his discharge, so he had to find a job. He took the test to become a member of the San Diego police department and passed with flying colors. The only problem was he could not go to work for the police department for six weeks after his discharge. He approached me for help. He needed a job but could not think of anyone that would hire him for a six-week period. We broke out the advertisement section of the San Diego Union and I noted an advertisement that guaranteed a salary of $125.00 per week and that training would be provided. Again, this was 1961, $125.00 was pretty good money, and it was obviously some type of sales position. I suggested that he respond to the advertisement. When he made the call he was informed that the position was selling Fuller Brush in the Pt. Loma area of San Diego. He asked me what I thought, and I told him that they would pay him $125.00 for the first week while he was training and he was guaranteed another $125.00 for the second week, even if he did not sell a thing. He agreed and took the job.

On Wednesday of the second week my friend Garry came to me and told me that he was not cut out for sales. Orders had to be turned in each Friday. He had to have orders of approximately $250.00 or he would lose his job. At the end of the day on Wednesday he had sold a total of $49.00 worth of merchandise. I asked him if he had a catalog and order book along with a few samples of the type of product that sailors would use. He said yes, gave me the material and the next day when I went to work During slow time in the tower and around the operations building I sold approximately $135.00 worth of merchandise. His sales complemented with mine put him over the top for his first week. In the middle of the second week he again informed me that he would not make his quota and would resign the following Friday night. I asked him to allow me to accompany him to the meeting with his boss, and he agreed to do so. That Friday night we went to his boss's house and he tendered his resignation. The man he worked for told him to try to stick it out for at least one more week, as his first two weeks' sales were really close to quota, and the extra week would allow him to train a replacement. Garry told him that I had been selling the majority of the material he had been placing on order and he was not cut out for sales. About that time, I asked for Garry's job on a part-time basis. He said that the quota for a part timer was $125.00 per week and did I believe I could meet it. I assured him that I could, and he hired me on the spot.

I worked in the tower over the weekend, which gave me Monday and Tuesday off. I hit the streets in the Pt. Loma area about eight A.M. and ceased making sales calls about 8:30 P.M. Monday evening. I followed the same work schedule on Tuesday, and at the end of those two days I had placed orders for $330.00. As time permitted during the remainder of the week I continued to take orders and turned in orders in the amount of $570.00 for my first week. My commission on that volume of sales amounted to $290.70. This salary for one week was slightly more than I made for a month's work with the Navy including benefits. I was hooked and continued to work for Fuller Brush until my transfer about one year later. I loved the interaction with the customers, and the product was the best of its kind. I cannot overstate how my confidence grew from being a successful door-to-door salesman, for I believe if you can make a living doing that, you can do anything.

Shortly after my part-time career as a Fuller Brush salesman began, after three years of trying, my wife reported that she was pregnant. Since this would be the first grandchild for either set of parents, it was obvious that either her mom would come to San Diego or she would go to Louisiana. The choice was easy to make, and I put her on a plane for Louisiana. (I could afford a plane ticket because of the Fuller-Brush money.) My Navy responsibilities, along with the increased demand placed on my time by Fuller Brush, limited my time to do a good job as an apartment manager. With regret, I notified the owner that I would terminate my responsibilities at the end of the month and move to a small apartment on Pt. Loma to be closer to my Fuller Brush route. He accepted with regret and told me that if I ever need a job to give him a call. I learned a lot during my employment as an apartment manager and am forever grateful to him, not only for the experience, but for the little money that proved to be so important to us during hard times.

I continued to have a great deal of success as a Fuller Brush salesman and according to all reports was doing an excellent job for the Navy as a controller. The organization at Ream Field was small in number, approximately 25 controllers, and after a controller had about six-months' experience the routine nature of the job became fairly simple. One day, as a part of my Tower Supervisor duties during a routine inspection I noted that we were in short supply of Verry pistol flares. The Verry pistol was used to signal a pilot to land, not land, or use caution when either the tower or the aircraft experienced a radio failure. We also had a light gun for this purpose, but the Verry pistol was a good back up. I called down to the Weapons division and requested that the petty officer in charge draw a box of flares from the magazine and let me know when they were available for issue.

Being a sharp sailor, the ordnance man went to the weapons storage magazine, drew a case of flares, and proceeded back to the operations building. When he arrived, he called the tower and notified me that the flares were in the ordnance office waiting for me. I was busy at the time and did not get down to his office for about 30 minutes. At that time I smoked, still do in fact. The difference being that this was before political correctness, and most sailors did smoke. The bottom line was I was smoking when I entered the Ordnance office. Before assuming responsibility for the case of flares, I reached over to a large ashtray fabricated out of a used shell casing and began to put out the cigarette. When the hot ash hit the bottom of the ash tray, all hell broke loose. A puff of smoke followed by a small noise left the room full of smoke and me with an arm that had turned black from my wrist to where the sleeve of my short sleeve dungaree shirt began. I had some pain and frankly was scared to death. Folks began to run around in a panic, and the dispensary was called to dispatch an ambulance. When they arrived the corpsman began to clean my arm with some type of alcohol. As my arm began to be visible through the residue from the smoke it became obvious that I had two very small burn marks. After being cleaned up, I along with my supervisors began to investigate what happened. The answer was that the Ordnance man had found an extra flare and decided to investigate its contents. He had cut off the top of the flare and poured the powder in the ashtray. Lesson learned: don't smoke around ordnance men. You never know what they have been up to.

Shortly after my near disaster with the Verry pistol flare I received a phone call from my father-in-law notifying me that my wife had been taken to the hospital to deliver our first child. I already had blanket leave orders approved so I contacted my boss to let him know that I was on the way, made arrangements to have my Fuller Brush Products delivered, and hit the road for Louisiana. Think I broke a cross-country speed record. I only stopped for gas and bathroom breaks. Thirty-one hours after leaving San Diego, I pulled in to my father-in-law's drive way in Sulphur, Louisiana. When I entered the house, I was directed to one of the bedrooms. Lying in the bed was my wife and a beautiful daughter. I had secretly wanted a son, but when I laid eyes on her I immediately fell in love. My wife's first words were, "This is your T-Bird." (I had won a 1957 Thunderbird in a poker game while deployed to Midway Island and sold it when I was transferred from the squadron. I assume that I had talked about wanting another one quite a bit.) I told my wife that our daughter was a perfect substitute for a T-Bird, and the nickname stuck.

After ten days' leave spent getting reacquainted with my wife, her family, my family, and my new daughter, I hit the road to return to San Diego. I planned to come back for them as soon as wife and baby were able to travel. When I got back to San Diego, with great reluctance I resigned from my position with Fuller Brush and moved out of my little house on Pt. Loma back to a small, two-bedroom home on Evergreen Avenue in Imperial Beach.

Three months later I received a call from my wife informing me that she and my daughter were ready to travel. I put in for leave and immediately hit the road again. Since I had very little time, as soon as I arrived and loaded up the car my little family again hit the road back to San Diego. My car was a small, English Ford Capri. It had a small bench back seat and two bucket seats up front, no air conditioner, and an AM radio. Having a newborn baby also translated into having to load a lot of stuff that I had not had to bother with before. In addition to babyfood, diapers, blankets, etc. we had a baby bed. I laid all of the small stuff on the bench seat and made a bed for the baby. I tied the baby bed to the top of the car, frame, mattress and all, and began the trip.

The first 1200 miles went pretty well. Like the slobs we were and since we had no refrigeration, when the baby finished eating all or part of a jar of baby food we threw it out the passenger window. Since we had no way to dispose of dirty diapers and there were a lot of them, we just flung them out the passenger window. After 1200 miles, the baby flat got tired of traveling. Every time the engine started she would begin to scream. At first, I would stick my hand back to the seat where she lay and she would suck on my finger. About the time we reached Yuma Arizona she got tired of that and just screamed. As I approached Yuma the bed on top of the car had slipped forward to the point where I could hardly see out of the windshield to drive. I pulled into a gas station to get gas and attempt to address the slipped bed. While I was working on the bed I walked to the passenger side of the car and about fainted. The passenger side of the car and the box containing the bed was covered with dried baby food, baby shit and diapers stuck to the car and the bed container. I cannot explain the stench of this combination. I told the man running the station that I had seen the movie *The Grapes of Wrath*, and the Okies had nothing on us. He laughed, noted the haggard condition of my wife, the new baby, and the military sticker on my windshield. Without saying a word he brought us some cold drinks, prepared sandwiches, and would not accept payment for the gas. Lesson learned: despite the difficulties you encounter, this country has some really good folks.

When I checked in for duty after we arrived in San Diego, I found out that my orders were in. I was to leave in six weeks to report for duty in the Advanced Air Traffic Controller School located at Naval Air Station Glynco, Brunswick, Georgia. As you recall, that was where I had gone to the initial Air Traffic Control Early Warning School, so I was at least familiar with the area. This set of orders meant that we would have to drive across country once again. Since the school was only scheduled to last twelve weeks, and I had no idea where I would be stationed after school, we had decided that my wife and baby would stay with her parents while I was in school. (In the Navy you get a lot of family separation.)

CHAPTER VIII

AIR TRAFFIC
CONTROL SCHOOL CLASS B

When I checked into Glynco to begin the advanced course of instruction, I was informed that they had a backlog of students for that course, and I would not start school for three weeks. To justify my paycheck and in recognition of my status as a second-class petty officer, they placed me in charge of cleaning one of the main barracks on the base. I was assigned nine personnel to keep a three-story building housing three hundred and twenty personnel in inspection-ready condition. Initially this appeared to be a good deal, but I found out that seven of the nine personnel were lazy trouble makers and that at the end of the third week we were having an admiral's inspection of the barracks. In addition, I was informed that the barracks I had been assigned had not successfully passed an admiral's inspection for the last three years, and the captain of the base had a special interest in making sure the barracks passed the scheduled inspection.

This command interest placed a considerable amount of pressure on me and my working party. Since I had basically a bunch of screw-offs working as compartment cleaners if we were going to succeed I had to develop a strategy. You must understand that all of the men assigned to me, with one exception, were young, non-rated men from the south. You must also understand that this was 1963, and folks, especially young men from the south, were not accustomed to taking orders from young black men. I had one young black man in my working party. He was bright and had a desire to please. I put him in charge and in front of all of the members of the working party I stressed that he spoke for me, and if anyone gave him any trouble, they would have to answer to me. I also told them that if we successfully passed this inspection I would make sure they got a full week off, as we were going to have to work long hours to pull off a successful inspection.

The strategy worked to perfection. That young man proved to be an excellent leader. He led by example and worked harder than anyone in the group, including me. Once we had the barracks looking shipshape, I had to develop a strategy on how we would get an outstanding inspection report. I will now interrupt the sequential nature of this story to share with you a lesson I learned while planning this strategy. This was used very successfully for the barracks inspection, and in later years I used a similar strategy to succeed in negotiations with senior officials in the FAA and the U.S. Air Force.

Basically when personnel are assigned a job, they want to impact the results. If they do not place their mark on the final product, they feel and more importantly, their seniors feel that they did not do their jobs. That is why when you work for someone in an administrative position they are compelled to make some changes to your draft work, even if the changes lessen the impact of the message being sent. When working with the Air Force all you have to do to drive the result is to draft documentation that reaches the conclusion you desire. The trick is to misspell a word in the middle of the second paragraph. Air Force reviewers and also FAA personnel will identify the misspelled word, make a correction, and approve the document as written. In the barracks inspection, if you have a spotless building the inspection party will stay around for at least two hours and tear the place up trying to find a major discrepancy. I decided that we would leave one sheet of toilet paper lying on the floor of the head (bathroom) on the first floor of the barracks. This was a very minor infraction and would not impact the final grade given. It worked like a charm. The chief inspector focused in like a hawk on the gear adrift, tasked his writer to enter the discrepancy and breezed through the entire barracks in less than fifteen minutes. When he had finished the inspection, he called me and my working party to attention and said that was the best-appearing barracks he had ever seen. When he left, I immediately secured all of the working party and told them not come to work for the next week. I had a bunch of happy campers. Now I had to figure out how to cover my six after giving my working party a week off when no one could grant more than forty-eight hours of liberty.

When the captain found out about the outstanding grade we had received he called me into his office and expressed his gratitude for the excellent work I had done. I told him that all of the credit belonged to my non-rated working party, and in recognition of their contributions I had granted them a week of special liberty. The executive officer about had a fit, but the captain said, "Excellent." Once again I had applied some of the leadership skills that I had observed during the *Mr. Roberts* movie.

The following Monday I started my course of instruction in the Advanced Air Traffic Control School. The wash-out rate was extremely high. As I recall it was somewhere around 90%. As we began the course of instruction it became apparent that if we were going to succeed it would be by hard work. The first week one of our instructors gave us a pop test. This little exercise of his almost resulted in my flunking out of the course. All of the questions were multiple choice. He arranged the order of the options in such a fashion that the most correct answer was always alternative four. This was true on each of the twenty questions. I had a very good knowledge of the material being tested and when I saw a distracter that matched this knowledge, that was the distracter I selected. When I completed the examination, I was sure that I had aced the test. Much to my surprise when the grades were posted, I had missed every single question. This test did not count toward a final grade point average, but it did shake my confidence to the point where I questioned every answer I chose throughout the entire course. I barely struggled through until we got to the laboratory portion of the course. This was practical application of lessons learned, and I breezed through that portion of the course.

This was the most difficult course I took during my forty-year Navy career. Not only was the volume of information staggering, the complexities of the application of that information were awesome. I do not believe I would have succeeded if it had not been for the dedication and ability of my instructors. This dedication and the effect it had, not only on me but on all of my classmates, persuaded me to strive for a billet in that school as a future career assignment.

Eight weeks into the school we were tasked to fill out a dream sheet. This document was a listing of our preferred duty station for our next assignment. I assumed that I would be going to sea and requested three aircraft carriers home ported in Norfolk Virginia. I also had to make one choice for overseas assignment. My friend Wayne Bates from the squadron and Ream Field in Imperial Beach had received orders to Naval Station, Rota, Spain. For that reason I also selected Rota as a duty choice. Much to my surprise, when the orders came in about two weeks later, every man in my class was assigned to an Aircraft Carrier except for me. I received orders to Rota, Spain. Rota was considered sea duty because of the limitations on dependent travel and because of the limitations placed on assigned personnel, because of the Status of Forces agreements between the U.S. Government and the Spanish Government headed by Francisco Franco.

At that stage of my life I was a pretty good athlete. The instructors from my school had placed a sizeable wager with the Marine Instructors in other schools. The price was the base championship. Winner collected all of the bets. Since I was a pretty good catcher in fast-pitch softball, the staff of B school someway pulled some strings and kept me as an assistant instructor in the laboratory phase of the school for an additional month. During that month the playoffs and championship game would be played. Since I was now a certified member of the staff, I was allowed to play on the instructor's team.

During that month the Junior Chamber of Commerce had their National Convention at Jekyll Island located close to the base. One of the instructors had membership in the organization and was tasked to round up some extra ladies for the attendees. The idea was to extend invitations to these folks and allow them to attend the banquet free of charge and essentially serve as hostesses for the shindig. For some reason this staff member assumed that I knew a lot of young unattached ladies that would be receptive to such an invitation. I satisfactorily accomplished this task by cruising the parking lot of local establishments and handing out invitations. On the night of the banquet with a covey of vehicles, we all met the ladies at the parking lot of the local Bob's Big Boy restaurant and provided transportation to the site of the banquet on Jekyll Island. Needless to say, a good time was had by all.

We successfully completed our run through the softball competition and met the Marines in the championship game. It was a hell of a game: lasted sixteen innings. We won by a score of one to zero, and my friends enjoyed the benefits of their labor. The next day I executed my transfer orders.

CHAPTER IX

NAVAL STATION, ROTA, SPAIN

The travel ban on dependents forced me to leave my wife and new baby with her parents in Louisiana. At the time of my transfer the advertised delay in dependent travel was six months. Considering that I could have been assigned to a carrier for a three-year period with cruses every six months, a trip to Spain after only a wait of six-months did not sound like such a bad deal. I spent my two weeks home with my family and caught a bus for the receiving station in Norfolk, Virginia. After spending only three days awaiting transportation in Norfolk, I was assigned a flight to my new home in Spain. Naturally being a country boy from Louisiana, I thought that everyone in Spain was a Mexican and their favorite meal was refried beans, rice, and tacos. Boy, was I in for a surprise.

When I arrived at Rota I immediately went to the operations duty officer's desk in an attempt to find out where I checked into the Air Traffic Control Division. The chief on watch was an air traffic controller. In fact, he was the division leading chief. When he saw my second-class-rating badge, he asked me what my name was and where I was going. I told him my name and indicated that I was reporting for duty in Rota. He said, "I am not expecting anyone to check in other than a black second class, and I have already transferred him to the Aircraft Maintenance Division, because no black man is going to work for me." I showed him my orders, and he became angry. It seems that my buddy from the squadron that had preceded me at Rota had told everyone that he knew me and that I was black. (At that time I believe the total number of black service men in the Air Controller Rating in the Navy was four.) Most of the personnel in the rating were from the Deep South and at that time, I am sure some sort of unofficial selection for the technical specialty was being applied.

Once we got my race squared away, the chief made a call and I was transferred back to the ATC Division. I was immediately assigned as a section leader in the control tower. We had a lot of good personnel, but they had little experience. At that time the Air Controller rating was accepting transfers from over-manned ratings throughout the Navy, so we had a lot of senior folks with minimal actual experience as controllers.

Initially there was little challenge to being a controller at Rota. It was a laid-back base that primarily supported a squadron of A-3 aircraft and a detachment of Anti Submarine Warfare (ASW) P-3 aircraft. Traffic was very light, and obtaining qualification took about 30 minutes for a previously experienced controller. The vast majority of the personnel in the division that I had previously known were assigned to the Ground Controller Approach (GCA) unit. As I recall, there were five personnel assigned to the GCA unit that had served with me in the squadron. This made off-duty socializing a little difficult, since the historic relationship between the control tower and the GCA unit was, at best, strained.

About six months after I reported for duty we had an accident off the coast of Spain. This accident resulted in the loss of an atomic weapon in the water off the coast of Spain. The timing of this accident was critical, as I had been to Madrid to brief the Spanish air minister on the need for an Approach Control at Rota rather than retaining the status of a VFR Tower with a GCA unit. The briefing was turned down with the statement of "All of that Airspace and those few aircraft, you will never have an accident." Disappointed, I caught a plane back to Rota to spread the bad news. While I was airborne, the accident occurred. When I landed, I was informed to get back on the next airplane to Madrid. The Spanish had changed their minds and were willing to grant Approach Control jurisdiction to Rota.

Because I was the only advanced air traffic controller graduate assigned to the tower division, in addition to my duties as a section leader, I also became responsible for developing and administering a training program designed to train our controllers to become approach controllers. This was an exceptional challenge, but one that I could accomplish. Since my family was not at Rota, I had a lot of time to devote to this task. Ultimately, we had a training program that turned out qualified approach controllers despite the lack of hands-on experience.

One of the more memorable experiences of my tour of duty at Rota was a joke played on me by one of my best friends. Since my family was not in Rota at that time, in addition to studying for advancement and participating in all of the available sports programs, I spent a considerable amount of time in downtown Rota. Since it was a small farming community there wasn't much to do other than kill time in the various bars and bodegas in town. My running mate was an Electronic Technician assigned to the GCA unity. His name was Bob Caton, and he was a lot of laughs. He and I had found a bar, I believe it was named the American Bar, where we hung out, saw the floor shows, and got outside a considerable amount of cheep booze.

I was always talking about how much I liked Tequila. They did not sell Tequila in Rota, so I thought that would be a safe subject. One night, Bob asked me if I had ever tasted Ouzo. I told him that I had not. He said that it tasted a lot like Tequila (it did not), and would I like to give it a try. I told him yes, and he signaled the bartender and asked for a glass of Ouzo for me. He gave me eight ounces of the stuff, and I drank it down. Frankly, it was horrible. When I finished, Bob asked me if I liked it, and I replied ,yes, so he ordered me another glass. I finished the second glass and was ready to party.

Bob said, "Jim, I am not feeling too good. Let us go back to the barracks." I told him to go ahead, as I was going to stay on liberty and see if something interesting could develop. He said, "I am not going to leave without you, but I really feel bad." Bob was my friend, so I agreed to go back to the base. When we got back to the parking lot, he went to his barracks and I proceeded to mine. When I opened the door to my barracks, I spotted a vending machine with ice cream sandwiches inside. I realized that I had a horrible thirst and was extremely hungry. I remember selecting two sandwiches and making my way to the main entrance to the barracks area. After that, I can only relate what was told to me by my friends.

Essentially I was told that I ate those sandwiches, paper and all, fell to the floor, and pulled myself to my bunk area by grabbing the baseboards of the building. I took off my boots, threw up in one of them and horsed myself into my rack. For the next two days, I lay flat of my back. I was essentially paralyzed. I knew what was going on but could not speak. My eyes were wide open. Every once in a while a friend would poke my eyeball with a pencil eraser to see if I was still alive. They had cleared my absence from work with my chief, so I was not in trouble.

When I regained my senses, they had a great time describing my actions. I did not know that you were supposed to mix Ouzo with water on a four to one ratio, and it is a miracle that I did not die from this experience. The moral of this story is when you are young and in the military some strange things happen. I have never tasted Ouzo since that time and have no desire to do so.

The date for my family's arrival was approaching, and there were no houses on the base to be had. I began to look for a place to live and found a new apartment on the sixth floor of a new building build in downtown Rota on the beach. The ground floor was occupied by a bar, but the apartment was nice. I rented this place for $60.00 per month and began to scrounge around for some furniture. It took a bit of doing, but finally I had a couple of beds, some kerosene space heaters, a two-burner stove, and a refrigerator I had rented from Special Services on the base. Now all I needed was my wife and daughter.

The word soon spread around the little town about this nice apartment. Many of the *working girls* decided to make this their home away from home. Needless to say this was an ideal situation at the time but would be difficult to explain after my wife arrived.

The big day arrived, and my wife and daughter, along with a number of other dependents flew into the base on a charter flight. I met them at the airplane and took them out to their new home. My wife was shocked at what we saw on the way to the apartment. My friends had arranged for a baby sitter and were hosting a welcome party for my wife at the ACEY DUCY club. (Enlisted club for E-5 and E-6 petty officers.) What I did not know was that my friend, Bob Caton has also invited all of the girls from town that had used our apartment as their private social club. Needless to say, this was a long night. Some way I survived it, but it was really close. Everyone in the club except for my wife knew what was going on, but to their credit, no one spilled the beans. Thank God, Caton got transferred two weeks later, or neither I nor my marriage would have survived.

One of the good things about being stationed overseas is the comradery that is established between all of the personnel and their families. Because you all are Americans living in a foreign country, circumstances force everyone to essentially band together. At that time, the pay for enlisted personnel was extremely low. All of us were living from payday to payday. Frequently, just before payday, the wives would compare notes to determine what each family had in their pantry that could be contributed to a neighborhood-prepared dinner. I can remember many times that one family would contribute hamburger, another vegetables, while the third would have hot sauce and tortillas. Combined, this set the stage for a Mexican dinner.

Nothing fosters this building of relationships better than intramural sports. I had become heavily involved in the various sports programs before my family arrived in Spain. After their arrival this involvement presented an opportunity for my wife to become acquainted with the wives of personnel assigned to our division. These activities included fast-pitch softball, flag football, basketball and baseball. Controllers were normally pretty good athletes. In fact, in my opinion, the only difference between a controller and a pilot at that time was a college degree. We had excellent reflexes, were very competitive, and had comparable IQs. Our department won all of the available honors, and I was selected as the Athlete of the Year.

One of the big events in Rota was the annual open house. This was celebrated in conjunction with the Thanksgiving holiday. In fact, the flag football championship was played as part of the celebration. We called it the Turkey Bowl. During this celebration the gates were open, and all of the Spanish Citizens were invited aboard. In an attempt to repay the base for its generosity, local Spanish officials proposed that after the Turkey Bowl game, the soccer team from one of the local bodegas would challenge an all-star team from the base. We thought that was an excellent idea, and after a one-hour break from the football game, the soccer game began. At the end of the first period the Spanish team was ahead seventeen to zero. We found out pretty quick that while they could not play with us in our sports, we had no chance in competing with them in theirs.

Things were going well. I had been selected and promoted to first class petty officer, my family had finally arrived, and shortly after their arrival, my wife became pregnant with our second child. My experience suggest that when things are going well, stand by for a ram. The ram came when the Navy decided to conduct the (at that time), largest peace-time exercise on record. The exercise was named Operation Steel Pike. Essentially four squadrons of Marine fighter aircraft accompanied by support aircraft flew from bases on the East Coast to Rota. This transatlantic flight resulted in en-route refueling a number of times, and we had a bunch of weary aviators when they arrived at Rota. The concept of operations for this exercise was for Rota to serve as an aircraft carrier and work very similar to a carrier, conducting round-the-clock operations. The only problem was that Rota was not equipped to handle that number of aircraft. We had a single runway with chain-type arresting gear, minimal ground-handling equipment for jet aircraft, and a crew of relatively inexperienced controllers. Needless to say, I earned my spurs during this exercise. The operation lasted thirteen days, round the clock. I never left the tower during that time, and seldom laid down the microphone. We had Marine ground troops sleeping on the ground adjacent to the runways and taxiways; a detachment of Navy Seals were also camped out in that area. Bottom line, we supported 186,000 flight operations in that thirteen days and when it was successfully completed, our green crew of controllers had grown up.

One of the interesting things about being stationed in Rota was the requirement to speak Spanish before you could leave the base and go on liberty in the town. After sunset all Americans had to wear either a sports coat and dress trousers or a suit and tie. We felt that this was a bit stupid, since most of the buildings were made of adobe and the vast majority of citizens were dressed like farmers or fishermen. The language requirement was addressed by a base-sponsored course of instruction in Spanish. You have not been entertained until you hear a senior petty officer from Louisiana and a senior chief from Oklahoma attempting to converse in Spanish. Castilian Spanish is spoken in northern Spain. Castilian Spanish was taught in the base-sponsored course of instruction. Andalusian Spanish is spoken in Southern Spain. Rota is in Southern Spain. When we graduated from this class, we could converse on a limited basis with other graduates and folks from Northern Spain but since we could converse with school graduates in English and no one outside the gate understood what we were saying, we all felt that we had wasted two weeks of time.

In an attempt to perform as I felt *Mr. Roberts* would, I damn near destroyed my career. When I was a youngster, my dad was away fighting the war, and when he returned his health was bad, so his employment options were limited. He always worked, and finally he and my mom started their own business, but there was never very much money. Christmas time was pretty grim. We really did not realize we were poor, as everyone we knew was in about the same financial condition. Presents were few and far between. My wife knew this, and after we got married, she attempted to buy me at least one toy each year for Christmas. One year at Rota, she bought me a *Have Gun, Will Travel* set. The set consisted of a cap pistol, belt, holster, and a canteen. The gift was a marketing initiative of the television series by the same name. When I woke up on Christmas day, after the girls (I now had two) opened their presents, I opened mine. As soon as breakfast was over I went out in the neighborhood and played cowboy and Indians with all of the children in the neighborhood. About one P.M. I began to think about my sailors on watch on Christmas Day, and went down to the tower to wish them a Merry Christmas. When I got there the three folks on watch were fighting to stay awake. There was absolutely no air traffic, and there was no scheduled inbounds or out bounds. After spending a few minutes with them, I went back home, and while making the four-mile drive had a great idea. When I arrived at my house, I went in the kitchen and filled my canteen with bourbon. I went back to the tower and poured about two ounces of bourbon in each of their coffee cups. We had a holiday drink and I returned home very satisfied with myself.

About two hours later the phone rang. The caller was the section leader in the tower. He said, "Jim you have to come in. After you left, we received an inbound for a flight of six Air Force aircraft. The hot sun complemented by that bourbon has all of us about half in the bag." I about crapped my pants. I jumped in the car, broke all speed records getting back to the tower, and assumed the watch. About thirty minutes before the aircraft were scheduled to land, we received a call from the Air Route Traffic Control Center in Madrid informing us that the flight had cancelled and landed in Madrid. The moral of this story is, "Take care of your troops," but do it in a legal manner.

After that narrow escape, things went well. On a personal note, my wife had a miscarriage and soon thereafter became pregnant again. Three months into the pregnancy she was admitted to the hospital for another miscarriage, but she did not lose the baby. When she was released from the hospital, she was allowed to come home with the understanding that she would have to stay in bed or risk losing the baby. I was working every day and had two small daughters to take care of. I don't know how we would have made it except we were in Spain and could afford to hire a full-time housekeeper. The cost was $10.00 per week, and this young lady was in our home from six A.M. to six P.M., Monday through Friday. She not only took care of my wife and the children, she also cooked, cleaned, and washed our clothing. We are forever in her debt. I was awaiting orders and became very concerned about being transferred before the baby was born. We went to the hospital, and the doctor indicated that if we could arrange a flight with minimum stops, my wife should be able to make the journey without unacceptable risk to the unborn child. I was able to arrange the flight and my family left Spain for her home three months before my transfer date.

One of the significant events that occurred during my tour at Rota was that my division officer made a decision that I was qualified to compete for selection and promotion to warrant officer. I frankly had not thought much about attempting to get a commission. I was often frustrated about decisions that were made concerning Air Traffic Control without any controllers being involved in making those decisions. My boss persuaded me that if I wanted to have input on decisions like that I must strive for a commission. He wrote an excellent letter for me, and I did well on the local interviews. Sad to say, when the selection decisions were promulgated my name was not on the selection list. This attempt, although not successful, did "light my fire." After all, *Mr. Roberts* was an officer, he was my hero, so it was imperative that I gain a commission.

I had been lobbying for duty as an instructor. I wanted to return to NAS Glynco and teach in the advanced school. My chief petty officer was a good friend with the detailer, and he intervened in my behalf. The orders came in transferring me to Glynco to instructor duty. The school assignment for me was not specified.

I had bought an automobile through the credit union. The car was to be picked up in New Jersey. When I left Rota, we flew into McGuire AFB in New Jersey and I obtained transportation to the location specified to pick up the automobile. I had not driven in traffic at speeds in excess of twenty-five miles per hour for better than three years. You can imagine the shock of driving in New York traffic. Somehow I made it to Louisiana. Don't remember much of that trip. I knew that the delivery date for our baby was close, and I was really pulling for a boy. When I arrived in my wife's home town I stopped in a drug store and asked the clerk if she knew my wife. She said that she did. I asked her to call her home for me and see if she was there. She did and did not receive an answer. (This was before answering machines.) I then asked her to call the hospital and see if my wife was a patient. She did and told me that my wife had given birth to a healthy baby boy the day before. Man was I happy. I ran around the store buying candy, cap pistols, baseball gloves, and a football. I thanked the young lady and went directly to the hospital. When I drove into the parking lot, my wife's twin sisters were standing outside smoking. When they saw me they ran over to give me the news. I told them I had found out, asked where my wife and son were, and got their assistance in carrying all of that stuff inside. When I walked into the room, they were both lying there. My wife looked proud as a peacock, and my son was beautiful. Think that might have been the happiest moment of my life. I had a great wife, two beautiful, healthy daughters, a son, and orders to instructor duty. Life was good.

CHAPTER X

INSTRUCTOR DUTY NATTC GLYNCO, BRUNSWICK, GEORGIA

After two weeks leave it was time for me to hit the road and check into my new duty station. The baby was too young to travel, so once again I left my family with my wife's family and left for Brunswick, Georgia. I had an uneventful trip, checked into the base, obtained quarters in the barracks and reported to the school building for duty.

Much to my surprise the powers-that-be had me scheduled to be an instructor in the basic Air Traffic Control School. I had my heart set on being an instructor in the advanced school, as I felt I owed the instructors of that course a tremendous debt for the education they had provided me when I went through the course. Being very dissatisfied with this decision, I went down to the Advanced School spaces to see if I could lobby for a job. When I went into the office, the chief setting at the desk acting as a telephone watch was a good friend who had been in the advanced school with me three years earlier. I told him I was reporting for duty, and the front office had me assigned to be attached to the basic school staff. He said he would put in a good word for me and get back to me. That was about the best I could hope for, so I thanked him, exchanged a few sea stories, and went back to the basic-school ready room.

About an hour later the leading chief of the advanced school called me and asked me to come over for a chat. When I arrived, the senior chief in charge and the Advanced School officer in charge introduced themselves and indicated that my friend, Chief Cochran, had indicated that I would be a good member of their staff. I told them that I had studied very hard and felt that I could do a good job. The officer, Lieutenant Dave Radford said, "Are you willing to take a test?"

I said yes.

He said, "We have three final comps that we rotate administering to the students prior to their graduation. If you will take one of those tests and make better than 70% I will go to the front office and ask that you be assigned to me."

I said, "Well, Lieutenant, let's do better than that. I will take all three of your tests, and if I do not make at least 80% on each of those tests, I will forget about being an instructor in your school and go back and do the best I can working in the basic school."

He was somewhat shocked but agreed.

I took those three tests, 150 questions each, and completed them in about four hours. The leading chief stayed with me after hours while I finished the test. When I turned them in, he immediately went down to the testing center and had the test graded. I had made 97 on one test, 94 on another and the third test I scored a perfect 99. He congratulated me, said the average score by students was 73 and assured me that I had a job in his course beginning the next day.

I went back to the barracks that night and was extremely proud of myself. Some of the guys asked me how my first day went and I told them that I had been competing for a job in the advanced school all day. They asked me how I had done and I responded, "Pretty well, but we will find out tomorrow if I have a job or not." They all wished me well, and we all went over to the enlisted men's club for a drink. After one drink I went back to the barracks, took a shower, and went to bed, for I was totally exhausted. I had a lot riding on the day's events and had done my very best. The rest was up to the powers-that-be, and I was totally confident that the Navy had always treated me very fairly, and I saw no reason to expect anything else.

The next day, I arrived early at the school. When I walked into the office, the lieutenant and senior chief were already at their desk. The lieutenant looked up at me and said, "Welcome aboard. You did a hell of a job on that series of tests yesterday. Frankly, I did not believe anyone, even members of my staff, could have made those scores." I told him I appreciate his remarks. He said, "Now that you are one of us, I have an instructor that has been trying to go on annual leave for the last six months. I cannot allow him to go on leave, as he is the only qualified instructor I have in the Procedures for Controlling Instrument Traffic (PCIT.) This is the most difficult course of instruction in our curriculum. I have reviewed your test scores and in the area of PCIT you did not miss a single question. I appreciate that I am giving you a sticky wicket, but if you could pull it off, you will really help us out, and it will be an excellent start for you on your tour of duty here with us." I told him that I would be more than glad to give it a try.

After meeting with the current PCIT instructor and receiving a copy of his lesson guides, I went to the classroom and after introductions began to teach. I was not aware that my classroom was located adjacent to the front office. There was a one way mirror in that office, and the instructor, officer in charge, and leading chief were monitoring my work for the first two hours of instruction.

When the class came back into session after a break, those three individuals came into the class unannounced. I immediately thought that I had screwed the pooch some way, but Lt. Radford, came to the front of the room and said, "Petty Officer Calhoun, congratulations. You are now qualified to be an advanced Air Traffic Control (Class B) Instructor. Petty Officer Hussey, your predecessor is now checking out on a well-earned leave." I was overwhelmed not only by their confidence but at the reception of the class to this announcement. This was the start of a marvelous tour of duty. I don't know if it was a better deal for me or for the students. I know it served as a jumpstart to my career, and I am confident that my efforts made a positive difference in the lives of my students.

I stayed with my original class until they finished the first phase of the advanced school and then had to check out and go to the Naval Air Technical Training Center in Memphis Tennessee for three weeks of instructor training. I thought it was a waste of time, since I had already taught a difficult subject to a class, and by all accounts had performed at an acceptable level. That story did not carry much weight, so off to Memphis I went.

When I checked in I was billeted with all of the folks that would make up my class. All of us were pretty excited about instructor duty. As you can imagine, we had a diverse list of characters in that class. Looking back, the time spent in this course of instruction was a good investment not only for me but for the Navy. We all learned how to develop a lesson plan, points to consider when instructing, and most of all, the folks were given the opportunity to speak on various subjects to a mixed audience.

Two particular events that occurred during the three weeks of instructor training are worth sharing. The first concerns a rash of fires we had on the base. The local area around Memphis was celebrating fire prevention week. We had an unexplained fire break out in the stable area and another in one of the barracks area. This put the command on high alert. One Friday on the noon break all of my class except me went over to the Navy exchange to cash a check for weekend-liberty money. I was busy developing a lesson plan. They all returned in time for the class to start. About an hour later the fire alarm went off. We vacated the classroom and observed the Navy Exchange burn to the ground. Since the exchange had not had time to make a bank run, all of my classmates' checks were burned; thus they had liberty money without penalty. That night I went into town for liberty, and when I returned to park my car in the lot between the Navy Exchange and the chief petty Officers Club I noticed a lot of smoke in the air. Thinking it was a flashback from the fire that had occurred earlier in the day; I parked my car and started to walk to the barracks. I then noticed that the Chief Petty Officers' Club was a smoking ruin. The place looked like a war zone after an aerial attack. I was transferred back to Glynco before anyone was ever caught for lighting the fires, but you can bet that we did not sleep well for the remainder of the time I was stationed at Memphis.

The other event that occurred during instructor training that bears repeating concerns an Amish member of our class. He was soft spoken and had a very difficult time in speaking before a class. The instructor was constantly on his case. He became extremely nervous and was very close to flunking out. I had a long talk with him and he indicated that he had no difficulty in speaking about things he was familiar with, but when attempting to explain things he did not understand he could not maintain focus, nor could he speak in an authoritative voice. I shared these discussions with the instructor. He decided to allow this young man to deviate from the scripted lesson and develop a lesson based on a subject he was familiar with. He brought some props, which consisted of a stick, a flat piece of wood, and a piece of string with a loop. He called this device an Ojibway bird trap, named after the Indian tribe of the same name. The way it was used was to plant the stick in the middle of tall grass with the point sticking above the surrounding grass. Since the tip of the stick was sharpened the bird would land on the flat piece of wood. The wood was set to drop when the weight of the bird settled on the slab of wood. The piece of string with a rock on one end and the loop laid over the flat piece of wood would fall down, drawing the string tight around the leg of the bird. His emotions were so strong and his delivery so sharp, that the grade he made on this presentation carried him to a successful grade for the course. I ran into him about 15 years later and he said, "I would never have made it if you had not helped me out." Again that *Mr. Roberts* trait persuaded me to do the right thing.

During our off time during the week most of the class spent our time in the Fleet Reserve Club off base. This was in every respect "a watering hole." Watering holes tend to attract lots of characters, some of whom are women.

The day of our graduation a decision was made to hold our graduation party at the Fleet Reserve. Unknown to most of us, one member of the class had smuggled in a 100-pound bag of dried corn on the cob. After a brief discussion a decision was made for all of the class members to grab an ear of corn and on the last break before club closure we would all stand up, turn around and begin shelling corn while yelling out, "PIG, PIG, PIG." The plan went off as scheduled, a riot broke out, and every member of my class was banned from the Fleet Reserve for one year. (We did not care, as we all left for our permanent duty stations the next day.)

One example of the crazy things sailors do is evidenced by the alligator episode. The Naval Air Station Glynco, Georgia, was located close to the Georgia/Florida state line. The state of Florida had a money-making scheme centered on Alligators. The idea is to either display alligators in their natural habitat and or selling baby gators to tourist. One of the individuals living in the barracks procured two of the baby gators on one of his liberty trips to Florida.

We would take the small gators into the gang showers and allow them to enjoy the ambiance of their surroundings. Everyone enjoyed watching these critters roam around this big room. We received notice that our barracks had been selected as an inspection destination for the forthcoming Admiral's Inspection. Essentially, the admiral accompanied by his party would enter the barracks and he would randomly select lockers for inspection. The guy that owned the gators was in a quandary. He was concerned that his locker would be selected, and he would be unable to explain the presence of gators, but he also did not want to just turn the critters loose. After a great deal of discussion we persuaded him that the odds of his locker being selected for inspection were very small, and he had nothing to worry about.

The day of inspection arrived. The inspection party entered the barracks and the first locker selected for inspection was that of the owner of the gators. He had the little critters stowed in a shoe box in the bottom of his locker. Air holes were punched in the box to assure fresh air. The admiral gave the locker a courtesy review and spotted the box. He asked the owner of the locker the obvious question, "What do you have in the box, sailor?"

The individual, after a pause responded, "I have a couple of baby gators in the box, Admiral."

The admiral replied, "Don't give me any shit, sailor; what is in the box?"

The sailor replied, "Admiral, you have my permission to open the box and see for yourself; however, I must warn you that those little suckers are prepared to jump when they are exposed to light."

Without delay the admiral reached down and opened the box. The gators jumped out of the box, and the admiral set a world record for the standing vertical leap. After the gators were corralled and placed back in the box, the admiral said, "Well, I asked for that, didn't I? I don't want to know what you are doing with gators in the barracks, but I assume that it is a Georgia-type thing."

With that, he and his party left the area, and we never heard a word about his gator discovery. The admiral's name was Jumping Joe Clifton. Based on his reaction to the gators, I could understand the origin of his name.

After successfully completing this course of instruction, I returned to Glynco to take up duties as an instructor. Approximately four weeks after I returned my name came up on the top of the base housing list, so I was able to send for my family. I now had two daughters and a son; we were all together, and life was good. I really enjoyed my job and became quite good at it. I was working really hard, and in my off-duty time was studying very hard in an attempt to be eligible for selection for chief petty officer. At that time advancement in the Air Controller rating was very difficult. A scoring system referred to as "The Multiple System" was used. This consisted of giving points for time in service, time in rate, medals, and your score on the Navy-Wide Service Examination. The examination consisted of 150 questions, 30 of which were relating to military subjects, and the remaining 120 questions were technical questions on the rating. I remember the first time I took this examination. In order to reach the cut score for promotion I would have to correctly answer 190 questions on this 150-question exam to be promoted.

While I understood and appreciated the advantage provided to the more senior personnel based on time in service in the promotion system I felt the system was unfair to the more junior personnel. Not only would a selection-cut score be beyond their reach, they received no credit for an exceptional test score. I felt this would dissuade such junior personnel from studying for rating exams, thus decreasing their technical knowledge. Based upon the example set for me while I was stationed at Naval Station, Rota, Spain by Chief Sam (Bud) Goble, I drafted a letter to the chief of Naval Personnel. In this letter I proposed that some multiple points be awarded to individuals who passed the rating examination but because of cut-score limitations were not promoted. Approximately six months after I submitted the letter a directive was promulgated giving either 1 ½ or two points multiple to personnel who successfully passed the exam but were not promoted because of quota limitations.

In addition to working hard and studying, I also began to teach gouge at night to senior petty officers preparing for the rating exams. Looking back, this was a bit dumb on my part, since I was sharing my technical knowledge with my competition for advancement. I enjoyed doing this, made a lot of friends, and as any instructor will tell you, you learn as much as you teach when you are teaching. This effort did do my reputation in the community a lot of good, made me look good in the eyes of my bosses, and later in my career, really benefitted me in my relationships with all of the senior enlisted men in the rating. (No regrets, even if it did delay my promotion to chief petty officer by two years.)

Enlisted personnel are always searching out ways to make additional money. This was before the days of child-care centers, and, for the most part, working wives. I felt that being a full-time mother was the most important job a married woman could have, and this decision was a joint decision between my wife and me. Since I had realized some success in selling Fuller Brush in San Diego I was looking for something that I could do in my off-duty hours. One of the instructors in another school was making a fair amount of money selling stainless-steel, waterless cookware. He invited me to one of their cooking parties one night, and I was very impressed. After the dinner I asked him how I could get involved. He indicated that all I had to do was buy a set of cookware and he would train me, not only on how to use the equipment but how to present it, set up parties, and close sales. While the price was high for the minimum-sized set I could buy and be capable of demonstrating all of the features of the system, I was confident that the investment would be worth the cost.

After buying the set of cookware, I attended a couple of parties and felt confident to go out on my own. My experience as a door-to-door salesman in San Diego proved to be very valuable. I concentrated on selling cookware to single, working girls. There were a lot of them in the local area, and I felt that if they were home at night instead of out on a date, they would be receptive to inviting in a male to have at least some conversation. Since most of those young women lived with female roommates, this gave me the opportunity to maximize sales with minimum outlay for food. I also used the pricing of the merchandise to a good advantage by putting together packages of cookware, crystal, cutlery and china. I called this the Single Working Girls Special, and sold a lot of sets. I promised if they would buy a set of my merchandise and did not snag a husband I would do everything in my power to set them up. Believe it or not, not only did I sell a lot of cookware, I teamed up some young teachers with young Naval Aviators, and most of them ended up being married. I really enjoyed the face-to-face dialog and made some pretty good money while doing it.

One of the most unforgettable experiences I had while selling cookware was making back calls one night after a dinner party the previous evening. I had appointments from residents of two small towns located approximately fifteen miles apart. I made my first appointment in one town and then traveled to the other town for two appointments. When I arrived I had a two-hour wait before the scheduled appointment. Rather than waste that time, I decided I would just walk the streets with my sales kit and see if I could make some cold call sales.

I approached this old southern mansion with a wrap-around porch. Sitting on the porch were four young ladies. That was a target no salesman worth his salt would pass up. I walked up the drive and introduced myself. The young ladies were obviously bored and invited me in for conversation. After a very short time of introduction and idle chit chat, I was in the living room sitting on the floor with dishes, crystal, cutlery and cookware strewn all over the room, with all four of the young ladies actively discussing the various characteristics of my merchandise. Right in the middle of this discussion an older lady came in the room. She paused for a moment and then asked in a loud and demanding voice, "What in the hell are you doing?"

I told her that I was doing my very best to entertain these young ladies, and if I were really lucky, perhaps I would sell them something.

She snorted and said, "Well at least we are in the same profession. I am trying to sell pussy and you are trying to sell cookware." I looked puzzled, I suspect, as she also said," Can you imagine how my clients will feel when they come in to get serviced and see all of these girls preparing for homemaking?" The light finally dawned on me that I had set up my display on the floor of the living room in a whorehouse. I attempted to make a graceful exit. The madam left the room and three of the four girls placed an order for the single-working-girl set. The fourth girl already had china and crystal, so she settled for just a set of cookware. Needless to say, it was a successful night, but I never told my wife where those sales were made.

I was working full time as an instructor, studying as much as possible, and peddling cookware with every spare minute. After about a year of that I began to feel burnout. Despite my success in the cookware business, I really loved my job and wanted to make chief petty officer very badly. I decided that I could not do all to a level that I expected of myself, so with great reluctance,

I gave up the cookware business and worked to be the best instructor I could be.

I guess something worked, as I was selected and promoted to chief petty officer off the next rating exam. In addition I was also selected as the Instructor of the Year for the command. I cannot explain the joy I felt when notified that I had been selected for chief. I think I can speak for all former naval personnel who come into the service as enlisted men that chief is the goal that we all strive to achieve. Despite all of the promotions that I received during my naval career and the successes I enjoyed, the greatest achievement I attained during my career was being selected for chief petty officer.

No one who serves in the Navy and is fortunate enough to be selected for chief petty officer can ever forget their initiation into the ranks of chief. While I personally thought that a lot of the events associated with the initiation were demeaning and childish, and I made my feelings known, I was determined to go through the ceremony no matter what the cost. Since I was well known throughout the community, a lot of out-of-town visitors came from the ships and air stations located within a reasonable distance of NATTC, Glynco. I was honored by their presence. Since my feelings about the initiation were well known, the folks in charge of the initiation made the decision that I would be the first and last new chief to be initiated. I can say, to the best of my memory, that they did a bang-up job. I am sure most of the attendees were entertained. My memory of the later portion of the events is somewhat fuzzy. I remember the oath, a ceremony I will never forget. I do not remember leaving the club and going home. I do remember waking up to a houseful of visitors enjoying themselves at my expense. Bottom line, I would go through both of those initiations again on a weekly basis, as the honor of being a chief was worth it all.

Unless you have been in the Navy I could never explain to you the difference between a senior first class petty officer and a chief petty officer. Before my selection for chief, I had been highly respected by all of my peers and seniors. My council was sought on most of the issues associated with our training curriculum. I was a valued member of the boards convened to pass judgment on student performance, conduct, etc. After being promoted to chief, my suggestions became policy and my wild-ass ideas became goals to achieve, not only for the students but for the staff as well. With one exception, the staff of the advanced school was the best group of men I was privileged to work with during my entire career. They were smart, dedicated, and totally committed to sharing their knowledge with all of their students. We had one staff member who was, in a word, a prick. He was only in the instructor business for the perceived prestige. He was arrogant to a fault, did not respect the students, and in general violated the tenants of *Mr. Roberts*. He and I had a consistent conflict. We were both phase supervisors, but he was one year senior to me as a chief petty officer. He did everything in his power to make my life miserable, and for a period of time, he succeeded.

One of the opportunities available to chief petty officers assigned to a training command staff was the opportunity to attend the Chief Petty Officers' Academy. This was not only an opportunity, it was mandatory. I know of no one that viewed this opportunity as a positive event. The course of instruction was for five weeks and was held at the Naval Air Station located in Pensacola Florida. The curriculum was loaded with drill and command, speech making, bunk and uniform inspections, with a heavy dose of Naval History, English, and World Affairs. In other words, most of the fresh-caught chief petty officers viewed this opportunity as five weeks of unadulterated horse shit. I was no exception.

My name came up to be the next guy to be assigned to the chief Academy. I gave it my best shot to snivel from the assignment, but better men than I had tried to avoid this assignment and like them, my plea fell on deaf ears. With great reluctance I accepted my orders and hit the road for Pensacola. When I checked in I found that each class was composed of sixty chiefs. The class was divided into three different platoons, and the competition between these platoons was furious. At the beginning of each week class standings based on the performance from the previous week were posted. These standings not only impacted the liberty hours available, they also determined the order of going to chow. The folks running the school, as an enticement to excel, only cooked sufficient food to feed the first two platoons. The platoon in third place was forced to eat C-rations for a week. In our case, since we finished third for the first three weeks, we really got tired of C-rations until we finally received the message that team work was much more important than individual achievement. Once that was understood, we finished first for the rest of the course, and did, in fact, win the designation as honor platoon.

One of the things that all military readers of this diatribe (even members of the Air Force) understand is that when you get a bunch of military folks together, sooner or later, the stern attention to detail and blind acceptance of strict military standards gives away to foolishness and horse play.

For some reason that I cannot recall, I had been selected by members of my platoon to be the guy in charge of marching the platoon from place to place around the base. I had no difficulty in executing routine drill and command instructions but I was not capable of nor did I believe that members of my platoon were capable of executing the fancy moves frequently displayed by military members in parades, air shows, or even open house ceremonies. We found out that as a part of graduation, we were required to drill in front of the reviewing authority, in this case, the flag officer in charge of the training command at Pensacola. Since this event would be a part of our final grade, we had to do something other than marching in a straight line in three columns. In addressing this issue, we had a number of meetings and finally decided on a strategy that would either win the competition or have us disgraced in front of the entire school.

At that time there was a popular television show on. It was named *F Troop*. We had a chief in my platoon that was stationed at the Naval Air Station Whiting Field. Whiting Field was located approximately twenty miles from Pensacola, so this guy could go home on weekends. He was a parachute rigger. This combination of events led to us having him make a flag. The flag was Navy blue with gold writing. The writing was *69 F* since we were the F platoon in a company going through the school in 1969. The plan was for us to sew this flag inside the shirt of one of the guys in the center of the first squad. When we centered on the reviewing stand, I would give the commands for left step, right step march, members would separate and the individual on the left of the chosen one would reach across his body and grab the end of flag. On command, the platoon members would take additional steps to gain separation, thus allowing the flag to be displayed. In the dead of the night, we practiced this maneuver until we had it down pat. On the day of graduation, this scheme came off perfectly. Not only did we bring down the house, we won the drill and command competition. This win allowed us to be the honor platoon of our graduation ceremony.

I learned a lot during that course of instruction and look back on it as being one of the highlights of my Naval Career. I finished third in leadership, first academically and first in speech. I continue to believe that my class standing in this course was instrumental in the success I enjoyed later in my career. I was sad to see that this course was cancelled about three years after I had graduated. I believe that the lessons learned were valuable not only to me but to every student, and I am sure that all of us were better sailors after being exposed to this course. (As a matter of interest, we started with sixty personnel. We graduated twenty-nine.)

After graduation from the CPO academy I returned to Glynco and resumed my duties as an instructor. Two weeks after my return, I received a phone call from my mom suggesting that I come home, as my dad was not doing well. Since my family was not in the habit of making calls of this nature without justification, I knew that this was bad. I contacted my boss and arranged for leave. Prior to our departure, we got the news that Hurricane Aubrey was approaching the Gulf Coast. Since my route of travel was Highway 10, which runs from Jacksonville Florida, to Los Angeles, California, I was very concerned. I had an old Volkswagen bus that leaked through the windows. The heater did not work, and the transmission had a tendency to slip out of fourth gear. Despite these problems, mom had called, so we hit the road. It must have been a sight to see. My children were wrapped in blankets, my wife was wiping the windshield so I could see to drive, and my right knee was wrapped around the gear shift to keep the vehicle in gear.

When we approached the Pensacola area, we were informed that all traffic along Highway 10 was being rerouted north to Highway 20, because everything in the Gulfport area was under water. This delayed our arrival about 20 hours. My father was in a coma and never recovered consciousness. Deep down, I believe he knew that I was there, but one of the big regrets of my life was that I did not get there in time.

After the funeral I did my best to take care of his affairs. Considering his reluctance to write things down, I think I did a fair job. When we were leaving, my mom tried to have me take either her car or my dad's pickup, as she knew the shape of my Volkswagen. I told her not to worry and hit the road. This worked well until we arrived in Slidell, Louisiana. As we reached the outskirts of town, red lights came on the dash of the old car, and power began to fail. I was adjacent to an old motel, so I made a sharp turn and pulled into the drive way. The engine died, and there I sat with a wife, three children, six hundred miles from my destination with a broken-down car.

The first thing I did was to see if the motel had a vacancy. They did. I rented a room and called my mom, told her where I was, what had happened, and that I needed a vehicle. We decided that my sister would drive the pick up to Slidell, turn it over to me and return home on the bus. I knew it would take approximately seven hours for her to get to me, so we settled down for a long wait. This motel did not have a restaurant, and my children were hungry. I asked the motel owner where the closest place to eat was, and he said about five miles. My mom had given us two paper bags of Bartlett pears before we left, so we ate pears for supper.

I had a decision to make about what to do with my Volkswagen bus. It was not running, I did not have a clue of what the problem was, and did not want to come back from Georgia to pick it up. I approached the owner of the motel and offered to give the bus to him. He thought I was nuts and was somewhat suspicious about the whole deal. Finally he called an attorney and asked him to come over and check this deal out. He came over, reviewed the title and told the motel owner that everything was legal. I signed over the bus to him and returned to my room. The motel owner saw my children sitting outside eating green pears. He felt sorry for us, returned my room rent, and gave us $3.00 in change to use in the vending machine for soft drinks. (I have often thought about returning to that motel, sighting that old Volkswagen and asking him how he obtained the vehicle. I think his version of this story would be much more interesting than mine.)

My sister arrived about 1:00 A.M.. I took her to the bus station, bought a ticket, and returned to the motel, picked up my family, and once more hit the road. We arrived at our home about 3:00 P.M., and I had time to buy some groceries before I had to go to work the next day. (This story is an example of another benefit enjoyed by a career military man that the recruiters do not explain.)

When I returned to work, I became concerned that my tour was rapidly approaching its end, and in my view some of the governing instructions associated with Air Traffic Control in the Navy were less that desired. I called our man in Washington to express this concern. He told me that he had too much to do to worry about that administrative crap, and if I wanted some instructions written I should do so. Being the type of person I am, I took this as an open invitation to actually do something. I began to write. When I finished I turned in the draft document to the officers in charge of the school. They spent about three days reviewing the document and called me in to discuss its contents. Commander Kirby was the officer in charge of the schools. He started off the debriefing by complementing me on the outstanding job I had done in putting the information together. He ended the discussion by saying, "Chief, you must understand a basic fact of military life, when you have officers and enlisted personnel in an organization the officers are always in charge. The way you have drafted this document, chiefs make all of the decisions, formulate policy, and essentially eliminate the need for officers. I understand that you have applied for warrant officer. If your document is approved as written, not only will you never be selected for a commission, there will never be a commissioned Air Traffic Controller." Obviously, I had written the document from my point of view, that of a chief petty officer. I took the document back to my office and revised the chain of command, thus placing officers in charge. After some reworking, and a couple of meetings to discuss the contents, that document became the bible for the provision of ATC services in the Naval Service.

Remember the prick member of the faculty I mentioned earlier? One morning he and I were the only two members of the staff in the instructor workroom. I was working on a lesson plan, and he was reading the morning paper. The phone rang at his desk but you have to understand that if anyone junior to him was in the room, they had to answer the phone regardless of circumstances. I crawled over three desks and picked up the phone and answered, "AC B School ready room, Chief Calhoun speaking, May I help you, sir?"

The caller replied, "Chief, this is Commander Kirby. How would you like to be a warrant officer?"

I responded that I think I would love for that to happen.

He replied, "Well congratulations, I have a friend in Washington. He just called me and told me you were on the list. The list will be published this afternoon." I thanked him for the call and hung up the phone. As was his custom, as soon as I hung up the phone, the prick chief demanded to be debriefed. I told him that the caller was Commander Kirby. He asked me what the fuck that asshole wanted. I told him that he had called to notify me that I had been selected for warrant officer and when promoted, I was going to have his ass. He got very pale, rushed to the bathroom (head), and asked for the rest of the day off. As for me, I could have had a fatal heart attack immediately after notifying him of the promotion and died very happy. If I had died on the spot it would have taken an undertaker two days to erase the smile from my face. Once again the lesson here is, do not screw over folks, for in the future they may become your boss.

I cannot express the joy I felt by being selected for warrant officer. In my mind I was selected to represent all of the excellent people in the enlisted ranks of our community. I knew that they had a lot of great ideas and felt that I might be able to be their spokesman to get those ideas to the attention of the decision makers in the community. From the time of notification to selection was approximately three months. In that time I continued to perform my duties as an instructor in the school. The major difference was that I did not have to be intimidated by my adversary, the prick chief . One of the most gratifying things that I observed was that all of my peers not only on our staff but the members of the staffs in the other schools seemed to be pleased with my selection.

The officer in charge (OIC) of our school was under orders, so a decision was made that I would become the OIC when promoted. This would be for a short period of time (three months), as a relief had been ordered in and I would be transferred as soon as he arrived. The promotion was a private affair. Actually, I went over to the commanding officer's office, he congratulated me, swore me in, and told me to get to work. I returned to the school and asked the leading chief to come into my office. We discussed the fact that the vast majority of the staff of the school would soon be leaving, with the exception of the prick chief. We also agreed that his projected demeanor was not what we wanted to leave in the school we had both worked so hard to build. With that in mind, I contacted the OIC of all of the schools and suggested that we work out an internal transfer of the troubled chief. The relationship between him and me was well known, and he agreed that such a transfer would be in the best interest of all concerned. That afternoon I called him into the office and informed that effective immediately he was being transferred to become an instructor in the officers course. He stormed out of the office, but I suspect that even he agreed that this was in the best interest of not only the school but for him.

In addition to being the OIC of the advanced school I was assigned the collateral duty of inventorying and inspecting all of the equipment that had arrived for the new school building. This was a big job. I was assigned a seventeen-man working party to assist me in this effort. The gods smiled on me, as the senior member of the working party was a first class petty officer who had served with me in the squadron. He was a trouble maker in the squadron but had the reputation of being an excellent motivator of men. I called him aside, explained the scope of work to him and asked him to do a good job for me. He did just that. In addition to a complete inventory we were able to identify approximately $37,000 in defective equipment. These deficiencies were replaced at no cost to the government. I was able to obtain a Special Evaluation for him for his good work. He ultimately retired as a master chief petty officer. I am sure this evaluation played a role in his success.

I had no idea how to ask for or lobby for orders as an officer. In the past I had always gone where the Navy sent me. I felt it was a fair organization and the system would identify my skills and send me where they could best be utilized. Initially I had tentative orders to become the radar officer at Quonset Point, Rhode Island. Before those orders could be finalized, we were notified that the base would be closed, and I received tentative orders to become the radar officer at Oceana, Virginia. Before those orders were finalized, someone realized that one of the individuals selected for warrant with me was the son of the leading chief of the facility at NAS Norfolk. Someone thought it would be nice for the father and son to be senior officials at two of the major naval facilities in the Norfolk area, so my orders were changed to become the OIC of the Ground Controlled Approach (GCA) unit at Naval Air Station Atlanta, Georgia. I was somewhat disappointed because I was looking forward to having a supervisory position at a major facility, but looking back, this was the best thing that could have happened to me.

Prior to checking into my new duty station I had to go to the five-week Officers Indoctrination School. This course was held in Pensacola Florida, and was commonly referred to as the "Knife and Fork" school. The purpose of the course was to familiarize recently selected officers to the mysterious world of officers. You must understand that the separation between officers and enlisted personnel at that time was significant. The course consisted of Basic English, History, International Affairs, and Drill and Command. Since I was a recent graduate of the Chiefs' Academy, most of this information was a review of what I had learned in that course so essentially the course was a breeze.

One story worth repeating was the celebration we had as a part of the graduation from the Officer Indoctrination School. The night before graduation, the personnel detailers responsible for detailing warrant officers and limited duty officers came down to address the class and participate in the pre-graduation party held out in town. We had an excellent dinner and all tried to impress those folks who would, in some way, be responsible for our future for the next few years. We all went out to a country and western bar for a few drinks. They had a special on "Purple Jesus" that night. I do not recall what the contents of this witch's brew were, but it was really potent. I think the major ingredients were grape juice and gin.

I stayed with the folks from the detailing office after most of the other folks went back to their barracks. I arrived back to our quarters about three A.M.. I knew my roommate was already asleep so I entered into the common space rather than the jointly shared bedroom. I took off my clothing, turned out the lights and opened the door to the bedroom with the intent of silently getting into my rack and catching a couple hours of sleep. When I entered the bedroom my feet slipped out from under me and I fell flat on the floor. I struggled to my feet, turned on the lights and viewed the biggest mess I have ever seen. My roommate had a little too much Purple Jesus and deposited the excess on the floor. Realizing he had made mess and remembering the etiquette lessons we had been exposed to in our classes he attempted to clean up that mess. He did so by stripping my bed and using the sheets as cleaning devices. Obviously I could not get any sleep in that environment so I decided that he should not sleep either. I turned on the shower to cold, pulled him out of his bunk, and set him in the shower. He needed a bath, but I almost froze his butt off. After the dust settled, and even to this day, we still get a chuckle out of the events of that night, but as I recall, nothing was really humorous to either of us that night.

Another story I must share occurred during the admiral's social secretary's briefing to us on manners and etiquette. Most of this lecture was so basic that we all took exception to it. After all, we had mothers that had taught us how to behave in public, but the tone of the presentation made one think that we had all recently evolved from caves.

One section in particular chapped my butt. The lady was totally serious about leaving your spoon in the ice tea glass. She also was anti-toothpick. We had a break for lunch midway through her presentation. During the lunch hour I went to the Navy exchange and procured an eye patch. I also went to the gedunk and lifted a knife. When we returned from lunch (naturally I was seated in the front row of the classroom, as all troublemakers are) it took a very short while for her to notice me setting in my chair with an eye patch over one eye digging in my mouth with the knife. She said, "Mr. Calhoun what happened to you?"

I said, "Well, mum, I am the type of guy that likes to practice new knowledge immediately after be exposed to foreign material. I had grave reservations about the spoon in the tea glass but based on your instruction, I tried it out. As you can see, my fears were justified as the doctors are concerned about my sight. As far as the knife is concerned, while I have always believed in toothpicks, you told us to remove the obstacle hung in our teeth with the instrument we placed the food in our mouth with. Since we had peas for lunch and some honey on the table to make them stick, I used a knife to place the food in my mouth. I am now trying to dislodge some of the food particles from my back teeth." She became very frustrated and left the room. We never did receive the remainder of her lecture, but I don't think it hurt us very much.

CHAPTER XI

NAVAL AIR STATION
ATLANTA, GEORGIA

After graduating from the Officers Indoctrination Course I returned to my wife's home for a couple of weeks' leave. She was well along in another pregnancy, so we decided once again to leave her and the children there until I could check in, find out about housing and my duties, and then if time permitted relocate them to Georgia before the baby came. This was a non-starter from the beginning as my mother-in-law was not about to let her daughter give birth to one of her grandchildren without her being there.

I drove to Atlanta and was somewhat intimidated about what I was getting into. Again, I was very comfortable as an enlisted man but that world of officers was totally foreign to me. I checked into the bachelor officers quarters (BOQ) and was assigned a really nice room. I had begun to unpack my clothing, uniforms, etc., when I heard a knock on the door of my room. I was not aware that I knew anyone there, so I opened the door to find out what I had done wrong. Standing in the door was a lieutenant commander. He took one look at me and said, "Well, Calhoun, if you remember me, do you still think I am queer? I about crapped my pants. This guy had been a first-class petty officer the last time I had seen him. He was a member of the board of the basic ATC School when I had requested to be dropped from the course. One of the reasons I had used was that in my opinion the lack of decision making on the part of controllers I had observed while going to that school made me question their manhood to the point where I was not looking forward to standing a mid-watch with any of them. I must have looked pitiful standing there. He laughed, shook my hand, congratulated me on my promotion, and directed me to join him in the bar for a drink. Being new to the officer corps, I knew that this was not the time to start disobeying orders, so I shut the door and followed him down to the bar.

After ordering drinks, we retired to a table and he informed me that I was going to be his relief. He had just been promoted to lieutenant commander and was under orders to transfer to be the Air Traffic Control Facility officer at Naval Air Station Cecil Field, Florida. I asked him how the job was and he said, "All you have is a GCA unit and a flight clearance office. This is an Air Force Base with a civilian contractor (Lockheed) as the prime tenant. The only Navy here is a couple of reserve fighter squadrons and a couple of logistic support aircraft. The only officers on the base that are regular Navy are you, me, and the commanding officer, and I am leaving in about three weeks." I sat there is somewhat of a daze, as I was not prepared to be in charge, had no experience with reserves, and immediately felt that I had made a big mistake. He said, "Don't worry about a thing, the CO is a really good guy, and I am sure you will do well."

One thing led to another, and one drink led to several. About 11:00 P.M. he had the bright idea that he should introduce me to the commanding officer. I attempted to explain to him that both of us were somewhat under the weather, and I felt that I was not really ready to make my first impression with the big boss. He said, "I told you he was a good guy; let us go wake him up and make him give us some whiskey." Despite my protest, and in my view a logical reason not to go to the Skippers house, we left the club and walked about one hundred yards to "meet the man."

When we arrived at the house all of the lights were off. I again attempted to dissuade him from this visit. He assured me that it was okay, and proceeded to throw gravel against a window. Soon the lights came on, and a tall, distinguished man wearing a robe came to the front door, and without looking out, opened the door and said, "Edwards, get your ass in here and tell me what you want at this time of night."

I immediately recognized that this was not the first time this had happened and followed him into the captain's quarters. When we got inside, Lieutenant Commander Edwards introduced me to the captain as his relief. He told him that I had called him a queer in a formal board meeting approximately ten years ago and wanted me to tell the captain that my judgment had improved considerably since then.

The captain acknowledged me, and said, "Welcome aboard. Your judgment in companions is suspect. I believe your original impressions of this man may have been correct. Both of you get your asses out of my house. I will see you in my office at 0800 in the morning. Good night."

I turned to leave, and Lieutenant Commander Edwards said, "Captain, I am really disappointed in your lack of hospitality."

The captain said, "Bill you are a dumb ass, but since we are all awake, I think a welcome aboard drink is in order." He also said, "Mr. Calhoun, you and I both know that Edwards will not be able to be in my office by 0800 tomorrow, but I do expect for you to be there." I replied, "Aye, Aye, sir, I will be there." Really did not have a lot of options. After a short drink, we left the captain's home and staggered back toward the club.

My new-found friend stopped two doors down and said, "This is where I live, will see you tomorrow night, good luck with the old man in the morning." With that, he wished me good night and disappeared into his home. I continued down to the BOQ fully aware that my career as an officer was over before it started.

The next day I reported to the captain's office, fully expecting to get my butt chewed for visiting his home late at night and at least half drunk. He never said a word about that. He indicated that he had reviewed my record and was very pleased to have me aboard. He also said that he, I, and LCDR Edwards, along with about sixty percent of the enlisted men assigned to my division were the only regular Navy personnel assigned to his command. He knew that I would probably have some difficulty in fitting in, as the reserves are somewhat different from regular Navy. Little did I know how much difficulty that fitting in would be.

I left the captain's office and went down to the Operations Office to check in. When I got to the office, Mr. Edwards was already there. He began to introduce me to all of the personnel standing around. In the middle of this, a short, heavy-set commander came into the room and asked where his air traffic control expert was. Since Mr. Edwards was an air controller I assumed that was who he was looking for, but this was the commander's way of welcoming me aboard. After introductions, he asked me a very simple technical question, which I answered. He said, "It is about time we had someone that knew what he was doing around here. Welcome aboard. I want you and LCDR Edwards to go with me for lunch in down town Atlanta today." Obviously, I could not say no. He said be ready to leave about 11:30. I told him I would be there.

I arrived back at the office in time to join the operations officer for lunch. We got into his car and proceeded to Atlanta, a trip of approximately twenty-five miles. I was totally unfamiliar with Atlanta and was somewhat amazed at the sights. We were in the Peachtree area. We parked the car in not the best part of town and proceeded to walk down an alley. As we approached a doorway about two hundred feet from the entrance to that alley, I observed a long line of people. I had no idea why they were standing in line. I assumed this was a really nice place to get some lunch. As we approached the front of the line, I saw what the attraction was. You must remember that I was originally from a small town in South Louisiana. I was not prepared for what I saw. It was a topless shoe shine stand. They had three well-endowed ladies busy working on shoes. They really had the art down pat and did a vigorous job in working the shine rag, spitting on shoes, and getting a lot of body movement into their work. I was impressed. My new boss thought that would be the best way to welcome me aboard, and hindsight suggests that it did make a lasting impression on me.

We got back to work in the early afternoon, and I went out to my GCA unit. The unit was located on the other side of the runway environment on what was referred to as the Air Force side of the base. When I arrived, the folks on duty all mustered to meet the new boss. All of the folks in this case consisted of four personnel. They were the duty crew and the duty technician. I asked where everyone was, and the section leader said, "What you see is what you get." I was somewhat shocked but that was just the first of many shocks. I asked where the chiefs were, and they told me they were all at their part-time jobs working for the in-service food provider at Atlanta International Airport. I told the section leader to contact every person in the division and have them at muster at 0800 the next day. The section leader said, "Okay, boss, but some of them will not like it." That ended my first day as an officer at my first duty station.

The next morning I met my crew. Frankly it was a mixed bag of folks. Some of the people were surface radar men that had been assigned as an experiment to see if surface radar operators could transition to controlling airborne traffic. It was obvious that senior leadership was sadly lacking. In fact, I fired both of the chief petty officers that were supposed to be running things, as they were focused on their part-time jobs in the food service area. I questioned the qualification level of the crew and was informed that the bare minimum of personnel required to be qualified were in fact qualified. One of the first classes in the crew was a former student of mine. I knew he was sharp, so I tasked him to work with me and get me qualified as soon as possible. We spent the rest of the day making radar approaches and reviewing the book work associated with local area qualification. At approximately 5:00 P.M. he said, "Boss, I don't have anything else to teach you. You have accomplished everything necessary to gain qualification here, so I am prepared to certify you as qualified." With that, I felt that I could actually take over running the organization.

The first Friday that I spent in Atlanta started off with a personnel inspection. I was assigned a platoon of reserves. I believe my platoon had forty-two members. Being a recent graduate of the Chief Petty Officers Academy, and a person who took a lot of pride in military appearance, I was shocked at the appearance of the personnel that I observed while performing a pre-inspection. When my pre-inspection had been completed, I had three personnel remaining in the ranks. I had dismissed the remainder of the men and told them to wait for me in the hangar out of sight. When the captain approached my platoon the first thing he said after receiving my report was, "Mr. Calhoun, where are your personnel?"

I told them that I refused to present such a bunch of dirt bags to my commanding officer.

He said, "Jim we must be nice to them. They are reserves and will not come back next month if we are not nice to them."

I replied to the captain, "I don't give a damn if they come back or not. They looked like crap."

The captain turned to the executive officer and directed him to make sure that I was assigned to present the folks that worked for me at future inspections. I don't know if that did my career much good at the time, but I did get the command's attention.

After this start, things began to work smoothly. At the time when a GCA approach was conducted in Instrument Weather the officer in charge had to either make or monitor that approach. Since I was the only officer assigned, that translated to the fact that I had duty every day. The reserve officers soon found out that I had the duty every day, so they persuaded the senior watch officer to assign me command duty officer and operations duty officer duty every Monday and Tuesday. (Monday's and Tuesdays are the weekends at Reserve air stations.)

A number of interesting things occurred during my tour at Atlanta. First was my struggle to understand how the Air Force worked. While the Air Force does a great job in what they do, their commitment to getting the job done in comparison to that commitment of the Navy is not the same. I could not believe that they would close up operations at the end of published operating hours even if you had aircraft in the landing pattern. I had a difficult time in understanding the Air Force Controllers' reluctance to provide specific directions to pilots rather than the general advisory nature of their control instructions. Needless to say, we had a lot of run-ins.

Shortly after I arrived at Atlanta for duty we received word that the chief of Naval Operations, Admiral Zumwalt, was coming aboard for a visit. Admiral

Zumwalt had recently sent a number of directives to the fleet relaxing historic standards. He identified these directives as "Z Grams." Many of the senior personnel in the Navy took exception not only to the content of these Z Grams but the method he used to promulgate his views. I was one of those folks. The admiral's visit was one of a series of similar visits throughout the fleet. I assumed the purpose of these visits were to personally address the opposition in the fleet to his messages and his method of dissemination. I was fairly vocal in my opposition to some of his ideas. The captain made an excellent decision by directing me not to attend this meeting, as he was concerned that my vocal opposition would bring discredit to the command.

The admiral arrived at NAS Atlanta flying as a passenger in an Air Force B-66. This pissed me off. If the head man in the Navy flew around in an Air Force Aircraft, what kind of a message did that send? His aircraft was parked directly outside the Operations Department spaces. My office was in that building. I stayed out of sight until the party left the flight line area and proceed to the location where the meeting was held. After they left, I proceeded to the aircraft, climbed the boarding ladder, and affixed a "Fly Navy" sticker to the fuselage. After CNO completed his meeting, he and his party proceeded directly back to the aircraft. After a brief grips and grins with the reception party he climbed the aircraft ladder, noted the sticker, paused and then proceeded to board. He gave no sign that he had noted the silent protest, but I am sure he took note. (Sometimes a man just has to do what a man has to do.)

One of the more memorable instances that are worth sharing is the weekend when some visitors from the Playboy Club in Atlanta came to visit. Since the reserve weekend is Monday and Tuesday, most of the personnel on the base were not available when the visiting party showed up. The public affairs officer contacted me and asked me if I would allow this visiting party to tour my spaces including the GCA unity. When I asked him who was in the party, and he replied a mother bunny and four bunnies from the Playboy Club, I could not turn him down. I contacted my crew in the GCA unit and informed them that we would be having five female visitors to the unit and asked them to make sure everything was shipshape.

When we pulled up into the parking lot, and the well dressed mother bunny and four bunnies all decked out in costume got out of the van, you should have seen the expression on my personnel's faces. I have never seen a bunch of sailors on such good behavior. Finally, I herded the entire gang out to the GCA unit. While we were in the trailer, we received a call from the tower notifying us that a transient Marine Corps aircraft was requesting a practice approach. The weather was extremely good, so when we approved the practice approach I told the bunnies to gather around and observe. I also made arrangements for the door from the trailer to the runway to be opened when I gave the signal. I asked the mother bunny to instruct the bunnies to depart the trailer on command, line up, and on command render a salute. During the approach, one of the bunnies was standing very close to the final controller. When he assumed control, his mind was not necessarily on his business. Needless to say, he struggled, but because the weather was good no harm was done. As the aircraft flared over the runway end on his approach, I opened the door and directed the bunnies into position. When the aircraft approached a position abeam the GCA unit, I instructed the bunnies to salute. Simultaneously the controller instructed the pilot to conduct an eye's left. When he gazed in our direction and saw four beautiful girls outfitted in traditional bunny uniforms rendering him a salute he damn near ran off the runway. His final comment was that if he knew the Navy recruited controllers like that, he would have never joined the Marines.

One story worth repeating and may get me in trouble had to do with the fly-in of most of the members of congress to attend the funeral of the Honorable Richard Russell, senior Senator from the State of Georgia. The day of the funeral arrangements had been made for all of the attending members of congress to fly into the base at Atlanta. The weather was very bad, low ceiling and visibility. The aircraft carrying the congressional delegation were two C-141 aircraft. Those aircraft were being built at the base. I was in the GCA unit for the approaches, and both aircraft missed approach because the runway was not in sight at landing minimums. (My outside observer could see the landing aircraft over touchdown, but the pilots could not acquire the runway visually.) I knew that the turmoil would be unmanageable if these aircraft had to divert to another airport. The logistics of relocating all of the ground transportation to a new site and the delay involved would be unacceptable.

Since the aircraft in question were being built at our base, the Air Force was testing out a landing system. Since this was a test operation, all of these approaches were monitored by my GCA controllers. We had monitored hundreds of these approaches, and when the aircraft were lined up on glide path with the experimental landing system, they were flying my lower safe-limit cursor perfectly. The lower safe-limit cursor was one degree below my published glide path, but I knew if I brought these aircraft in by directing them to fly my lower safe-limit cursor rather than the published glide path, the operation would be safe. With that in mind, I cleared the GCA trailer of all personnel (I did not want my controllers to observe an unsafe operation) and made the approaches using the lower safe-limits cursor rather than the published glide path. Both aircraft flew perfect approaches, landed safely, and the party proceeded to the site of the funeral without incident. (My controllers were impressed that I could recover those aircraft in that weather and I never revealed my secret until now.) Sometimes you just have to do what you have to do to get the job done.

I received a call that my wife had given birth to a baby girl. As I made preparations to leave for home, I received another call that the baby had passed away. Needless to say, I broke all land speed records getting home. When I got to the hospital, I noted that my wife was in pretty bad shape mentally. I was able to persuade her that our kids and I needed her and she had to snap out of it. Being a strong woman, she made a full recovery. I, with a lot of help from my family, handled the burial details. Once that was accomplished, I returned to Atlanta for duty. Soon thereafter, I returned to Louisiana and picked up my family and took them to our first duty station as a commissioned family.

My billet as the Air Traffic Control officer forced me to occupy one of the five houses on the base reserved for officers. We moved into the house next to the executive officer and one house from the commanding officer. My wife was very apprehensive about our new station in life, but as we found, out the more senior the officer is, the nicer folks they and their families are. My wife's best friend soon became the executive officer's wife. I cannot overstate how welcome her kindness was in helping her in this transition.

Since I now had my family on board I could begin to concentrate on some of the things that I felt I needed to do. I could not understand why the Navy was making the investment in funds and personnel to provide a GCA unit that was supporting a traffic load of 70 % civilian traffic, 27 % Air Force traffic and only 3 % Navy traffic. When I asked the captain, he said, "Good question." I asked him if I could write a letter to the chief of Naval Operations asking the chain of command that same question. He agreed. I wrote the letter, and about three weeks later we received a response stating that my letter had been reviewed by the responsible officials, liaison had been established with the Air Force, and the Air Force had agreed to assume the responsibility for GCA service provision within three months. While Atlanta was a good deal for the folks stationed there, there was no justification for the Navy to expend scarce resources for such a minimal return.

World events initiated my next urge to change the system. The news was dominated by campus unrest as the result of student dissatisfaction with our involvement in the Viet Nam War, in particular a report of a Navy Seal taking on all comers in Berkley as they were making a run on our nation's colors. Apparently this individual, a former second class petty officer, took a stand against a group of students determined to desecrate our colors. This hit close to home for me, as I wondered if I would have had the personal courage to stand up as he did.

Based on this idea and realizing that most veterans enrolled in college were probably attending on the GI Bill and were not particularly interested in participating in this type of turmoil, I drafted a letter to the Veterans Administration. This letter essentially pointed out the dilemma veterans faced and suggested that many veterans would not take advantage of their educational benefits in order to avoid such incidents. I recommended that such benefits be awarded to a blood relative selected by the requesting veteran. I felt the benefits had been earned, and if they were not used, would be wasted. I also felt the nation would benefit if we had a more educated population. The Veterans administration replied that the education benefit earned by the Veteran must be used by that individual. They did praise my initiative for submitting the suggestion. Approximately ten years later I have been told this idea was considered by the committee that drafted the Sonny Montgomery GI Bill education policy. (Nothing ventured, nothing gained.)

About two months after receiving this letter announcing Air Force assumption of GCA responsibilities at Atlanta, the Navy had a terrible accident in Kodiak, Alaska. This accident resulted in the death of four of the most senior controllers assigned to the base. Because of my reputation and the fact that I had become available with the transfer of the GCA unit to the Air Force, I was nominated to assume the duties as the officer in charge of the ATC facility in Kodiak. Not only did we have to continue to provide services to the civilian and military users of the airport at Kodiak with a reduced number of personnel, we had to rebuild the expertise we had lost as the result of this accident.

I received orders to report to Kodiak, so we packed up and began the long, cross country trip to Seattle, Washington, where we would catch a flight to our new duty station in Kodiak Alaska. I had visited Kodiak a number of times while I was in the squadron, so I was really looking forward to this tour.

CHAPTER XII

NAVAL STATION, KODIAK, ALASKA

I planned on making our trip cross country to Seattle on the way to Kodiak as a kind of vacation, since we had really never had one. I had a really nice traveling car and intended to make the trip in style, stopping along the way to see the sights. Thought it would be good for the family, especially the children. As with all plans, about the time we got to Oklahoma City my plans went to hell. My mechanical ability is non-existent. As we made our way across country the car ran really well when I was traversing flat terrain, but it began to slow down if we climbed even a small hill. While the first part of the trip was over flat land, I knew that we had high ground ahead. As always, money was short, and I did not have any credit cards, so I was actually afraid to stop and have someone check out the car.

We made our way to Cody Wyoming, where we spent the night. When I got up the next morning it was snowing. The month was September, and we were all dressed in Atlanta-type clothing. Needless to say, everyone was cold. When we left Cody heading west, we approached a huge mountain range. Initially I was going down hill, so the travel was a bit easy even though the snow was falling pretty fast. When we got to the bottom of this mountain and begin to climb I knew we were in deep shit. The further we traveled the slower we got. About 100 yards from the crest of the mountain the car flat-out stopped. I pondered on this for a while. I knew the mountain we had just come down was actually taller than the one I was trying to climb, so turning around and attempting to go back and find a different route was not an option. Finally I decided to back down the hill and ask my wife and children to get out of the car and walk up the mountain while I attempted to climb without their weight. Since they were in shorts, and my son was pretty small, my wife did not think too much of that idea, but I explained that there were no other options. Frankly I did not think about me getting out and walking with the children

97

while she drove the car. That is my story and I am sticking to it. They got out of the car and I hit the gas. With a little rocking on my part, I finally made it up the hill. After about a 30 minute wait, the family joined me, and we proceeded on our journey. Needless to say, the mood in the car was less than friendly.

We struggled through the mountains to Idaho. We stopped at a shopping center in Boise where we bought some cold weather clothing for the family. We arrived at some small town where I had to stop for gas. I asked the attendant (a young man about nineteen years old) if there was a place to eat in town that was reasonable. He indicated that the place across the street served good food at reasonable prices so I sent wife and children across the street while I filled up on gas. After they left, I asked him if he knew anything about cars.

He said, "Yes, what is your problem?"

I told him that the car ran very well on flat terrain but actually bogged down when we were trying to climb a mountain.

He said, "Have you checked the gas filter?"

I asked him what that was.

He raised the hood and pointed out the in line filter.

I said, "I don't even know what that is."

He said, "I expect that is your problem."

I asked him how much it cost to fix it, and he said, "Including parts and labor, seventy-five cents."

I said, "Well, what are you waiting for?"

He walked into the station, returned with a filter, unsnapped the device, replaced it, and five minutes later I was joining the family for lunch. Bottom line, for the cost of seventy five cents I essentially screwed up any vacation plans we had, and made my family climb a mountain in a snow storm, wearing shorts, and freezing. O, well, that was not the only time I screwed things up, but it was one of the most memorable. At least that is the one I caught hell about for the next ten years.

We arrived in Seattle; spent a few days with one of my wife's aunts, and caught a plane to Anchorage with the ultimate destination, Naval Station, Kodiak, Alaska.

We arrived at Kodiak around one P.M. in the afternoon on Wein Aleutian Airlines. It is customary for all personnel not actually on duty to meet the arrivals. This is especially true when the incoming individual is going to be the boss. Since I was traveling with the family, we waited until everyone else on the aircraft departed the airplane before we attempted to unload with children and associated baggage. When I got to the head of the boarding ladder and gazed down I recognized a large number of the personnel, as they had been my students while I was an instructor. I knew the leading chief petty officer was an old friend, but I never expected to see the chief I have previously identified as a prick greeting me on our arrival at Kodiak. While everyone in the division knew I was coming, no one told this chief, as they were aware of the conflict between us when we were both instructors. When he saw who the new boss would be he became ill and had to take the next three days off to recover. I felt a bit sick myself, but since I was senior, I knew that things would work out okay.

As soon as I arrived I met the man I was going to relieve, Lieutenant Commander Clyncke. He welcomed me aboard and informed me that the Navy had decided to close the base. The date of closure was six months from that date, and that I had orders to become the radar officer at the Air Traffic Control Facility in Beeville, Texas. I was somewhat shocked about the news, but we go where we are ordered in the Navy, and I knew my wife would be pleased, as Beeville was not very far from her home in Louisiana.

My new boss and his wife accompanied us to our quarters. They were located directly across the street from his, a fact that proved to be very valuable as he could give me a ride back and forth to work until my automobile arrived from Seattle.

Our household effects had already arrived, so I spent the next day getting our personal effects in order and checked in the next day. After doing the normal administrative check-in procedure, LCD Clyncke took me in to meet the commanding and executive officer. Once I was welcomed aboard, we traveled to the Operations Department, where I was introduced to all of the departmental officers, then out to the GCA unit to meet my tower and radar crew. In many ways, it was old home week, as I was acquainted with approximately eighty percent of the personnel assigned.

In the next couple of days I became familiar with the qualifications of the personnel assigned, the material condition of our equipment ,and essentially became acquainted with the environment I was soon to be responsible for. In fact, on third day LCD Clyncke said, "You have the con; I am going to relax, enjoy the countryside, and take it easy for the next two weeks prior to my transfer."

The next day, LCD Clyncke officially turned over the division to me, and we began to rebuild the approach control capability of the division. I had to travel to Anchorage to meet with the FAA to draft letters of agreement, memorandums of understanding, and meet the folks I would be coordinating with for the next six months.

We completed all of the revised documentation and I returned to Kodiak. On my arrival I was informed that the governor of Alaska was making a request from the chief of Naval Operations to retain the Ground Controlled Approach function of the division after the Navy left, since during the winter months the citizens of Kodiak were totally dependent on reliable access of aircraft for quality-of-life items, as well as transportation and emergency medical evacuation. A decision had been made for the FAA to assume ATC responsibilities for the tower, but the FAA did not have any GCA operators. The Coast Guard was going to assume responsibility for some portions of the command, but the vast majority of the facilities would be closed and demolished. CNO responded to the request from the governor that the Navy was not in the rent-a-controller business, but he agreed to train some Coast Guard personnel to perform the GCA function, and in recognition of the unique situation, would leave the Navy controllers in place for an additional six months if the Coast Guard would assume the cost.

The Coast Guard agreed to assume the cost but refused to provide personnel for GCA training since that was not the Coast Guard mission, and it would be a one-of-a-kind assignment for Coast Guard personnel. When all of this information became public, a delegation from Anchorage came to my little GCA unit. The delegation consisted of the governor of Alaska, one of the senators, Senator Ted Stevens, and a representative. They met with me, and after an hour of discussion, they asked me for a recommendation. I replied that the Federal Aviation Administration was responsible for providing ATC services in the United States. Alaska was a state and if it were my problem, I would contact the secretary of transportation, state the issues, and request that he direct the FAA to do their job. Senator Stevens asked me if he could use my phone, retreated to my office, placed the call, and indicated that he would have an answer within forty-eight hours.

The next day I received a call from Senator Stevens indicating that the FAA was searching their manpower files to locate employees assigned to Alaska that had previous GCA experience. When experienced people were located, I would be tasked to train those folks, and they would assume GCA responsibility until the FAA could fund and install an Instrument Landing System (ILS) to replace the service being provided by GCA.

Before LCD Clyncke officially left, I drafted a memorandum for the commanding officer that laid out deficiencies I had noted on my initial inspection of the control tower. Two of the tower windows had been broken and replaced with plywood. All of the windows were smeared with grime making visibility extremely limited. When I quizzed the watch supervisor he informed me that work request had been submitted to have water piped to the tower for washing purposes, and replacement of the broken windows had also been requested. He showed me the request. The response was that the expense of replacing the windows was too great and the elevation of the tower was prohibitive to having a water source.

I noted the presence of a water fountain in the tower, so the water argument was bogus. The expense excuse did not wash, as safety is paramount. With that information in hand, I drafted the memo from myself to the commanding officer via Mr. Clyncke. Essentially I pointed out the presence of a water fountain, and tongue in cheek, expressed my opinion that the Navy was not recruiting personnel with the ability to see through wood; therefore aircraft on final approach were invisible from the tower. Clyncke said, "Take my name off that and submit it if you feel it is necessary."

I said okay, and revised the memorandum, and forwarded for action. The next day I received a call from the commanding officer's secretary to report to his office at two P.M. When I arrived for the meeting the commanding officer, executive officer, public works officer, supply officer, and operations officer were in the room. Each of these senior officers had been provided with a copy of my memo. After a brief uncomfortable silence, the skipper said, "Are the contents of this memorandum valid?" While some of the folks attempted to snivel out, it became apparent that each of these responsible officials were aware of the deficiencies I had reported. The captain chewed ass and gave directions. The next day water was delivered to the tower, and three days later a crew arrived to replace the broken windows. Since all of these folks were leaving soon, I did not suffer recriminations. I am pretty sure my career would have gone in the toilet had they been there for a fitness reporting period.

After we solved all of the political issues we began the task of performing our service to the aviation users while simultaneously attempting to close down the portions of the base that the Coast Guard would not assume. Everyone except me and fifty-six sailors had departed. Since I was a warrant officer, I was identified as the officer in charge of the Kodiak Detachment with oversight being provided from Whidbey Island, Washington. My tour in Kodiak eventually lasted sixteen months. The last thirteen months I served as the officer in charge. While I frequently reported various events to Whidbey, no one from the command ever visited, so we were essentially on our own. It was a hoot. I had all of the equipment that a full-fledged Naval Station had, vehicles, barracks, mess hall, hospital, etc., and only fifty-six sailors and their dependents to occupy the space. Gradually the Coast Guard moved in, and after six months, the FAA personnel came to Kodiak to assume control tower responsibilities but, for the most part we had our own version of *McHale's Navy.*

The FAA finally located a few controllers assigned within the Alaskan Region that had GCA experience. They began the task of relocating these folks to Kodiak, but senior management was not in love with the idea of FAA personnel providing GCA approaches to military and civilian aircraft in a location that was at least one of the five most difficult and unsafe locations in the world to provide Air Traffic Control services in adverse weather conditions.

The runway configuration driven by local terrain resulted in the instrument runway being located in what was actually a box canyon. There was a 1700-foot mountain on the left side of the runway, a 1300-foot mountain on the right side, and a 2505-foot mountain at the end of the runway. These heights were not a real problem for high performance jet aircraft but for the low-performing transports that made up the majority of traffic in Kodiak, they were a death trap if not handled very carefully. Over the years a number of aircraft had crashed while trying to make a missed approach after losing sight of the runway. In fact, we had totally different phraseology when working aircraft in Kodiak. Normally, when the aircraft departed either the course line or glide path, the controller would indicate this unsafe deviation by stating, "If runway not in sight, execute missed approach," with the reason either below glide path, left or right of course, etc. In Kodiak, the phraseology transmitted to the pilot to the pilot was, "No missed approach will be given inside of one mile." Instead the transmission would be, "Exceeding safe limits."

For this reason as well as others, FAA senior management was not in favor of assuming GCA responsibilities at Kodiak. Despite identifying controllers and making arrangements for them to be transferred to Kodiak, they continued to pursue the installation of an ILS system at Kodiak to satisfy the Instrument Approach requirement. I tried to inform them that installation of an ILS at Kodiak was not an easy thing, as the beam of an ILS system is susceptible to tide action, and the tide at Kodiak was extremely high. Despite my advice, they installed an ILS. In addition to the high tide problem, they installed the system at a location that blocked signal transmission when a large truck passed by. About thirty months after I transferred, the FAA finally commissioned an ILS, but for that thirty month period they used the Navy GCA unit we left them to support Instrument traffic into and out of Kodiak.

There were a number of interesting things that occurred during my tour at Kodiak. Some of these events are included for your entertainment, amazement, and interest.

The first of these events was the day I arrived at the GCA unit to find all of the duty crew gathered around the Dempsey Dumpster (Trash Bin.) I parked my car and walked over to see what was going on. One of the guys indicated that we had two grizzly bear cubs in the dumpster, and they were trying to figure out how to get them out. My first thought was, *Boy, this is really neat.* My second thought was, *These cubs have a mother and she is probably on the lookout for her kids and there will be hell to pay when she finds them.* I immediately told everyone to get inside and we called the game warden. About five minutes before he showed up, mother bear did. She attempted to tear that steel bin apart to get her children out. Finally, she attempted to crawl in with them. The problem was that there was more bear than door. She got stuck in the door and really began to raise hell. When the game warden arrived, he evaluated the situation, called for help, and then shot a tranquilizer into the mom's rear end. When his assistants arrived, they worked to free the mother from the bin, and then tranquilized the cubs. When they were all under control, they loaded the bears in a trailer and took them back up into the mountains. Seems that this was a normal event for the Fish and Game folks, but it was the makings of a sea story for the rest of us.

You must understand that fresh vegetables were difficult to find in Kodiak and extremely expensive when you did locate some. We were supporting a detachment of Anti-Submarine Warfare squadrons stationed at Moffett Field California. It did not take very long for a bunch of enterprising sailors to identify this problem and find a solution. The squadron personnel rotated deployment to Kodiak. Our guys found out when the next aircraft would be leaving Moffett for Kodiak and contacted the squadron duty officer to make a deal. Essentially the deal was that we would trade smoked salmon for fresh vegetables. Our folks would indicate what we were interested in, i.e., fresh tomatoes, lettuce, onions, egg plant, carrots, cabbage, bread, milk, and eggs. The relieving crew would go shopping and procure the items. When they arrived at Kodiak, we would meet the aircraft, load up the produce and take it to the ready room co-located with the GCA unit. Representatives from the squadron would come down to the ready room and spread their merchandise on one side of the pool table and we would spread smoked salmon on the other. They would push a case of tomatoes to the middle of the table and we would push sufficient salmon to the case of tomatoes until all were persuaded that a fair deal had been struck. This process continued until we had all of their produce and they had all of our salmon. Once the trading was completed, we all traveled back to the aircraft leaving Kodiak for Moffett, load up their salmon and sent them on their way. We would then go back to the GCA unit and divide up the spoils between all participants. Guess this was a primitive way to do business, but our version of the barter system was a good deal for all concerned.

With the passing of time, I received official orders to transfer one GCA unit complete to the FAA, and that I, along with three of my controllers and two technicians, would be transferred to the Naval Air Station in Fallon, Nevada, to commission a GCA unit.

The GCA unit at Kodiak had been in place since the early 1940s. It was now 1972. During that period of time a lot of excess equipment had been accumulated. I knew that I could use all of that equipment at my new duty station and also knew if I did not take it, this material would disappear from Navy inventory upon its transfer to the FAA. Since my orders clearly stated "Transfer one GCA Unit Complete" to the FAA, I interpreted that to be strict compliance with the packing list of the equipment. We reviewed the packing list and followed its contents religiously. All of the equipment in excess of this control document, we packed and marked, "Ship to the ATC Division in Fallon, Nevada. After that chore was completed, I began negotiations with CNO to obtain shipping authorization. I ran into a brick wall. I could not persuade those folks of the value of the equipment and the need to have it retained in Navy inventory. Because I was a warrant officer I could pretend to be dumber than I actually was and get away with it. I would not take no for an answer and continued to bug them on a daily basis. Finally, in exasperation, they told me that I could do anything I was willing to take responsibility for. For me that was a license to steal. Remember, I was a former enlisted man, and relocating resources to a place other than that assigned is a common practice in getting the job done. I called upon Air Force contacts to provide me a logistic flight from Kodiak to Fallon. After a lot of wheeling and dealing, along with about 100 pounds of smoked salmon, I was able to obtain that flight. We packed the gear in that aircraft, and I wrote a message to the commanding officer of Fallon informing him that a high-value cargo was coming his way, that I would provide him with a certified inventory, and requested that he make arrangements to store this equipment is a safe location until I could arrive and conduct an on site inventory. We sent it on its way and began the task of training the FAA controllers to assume the responsibility for the GCA system. Once they were qualified I informed the commanding officer at Whidbey that our services were no longer required after 31 December 1972. He authorized our departure as of that date, so we made travel arrangements and left that island paradise on the last day of 1972. Looking back, the tour in Kodiak was a great experience. We were able to do the job, received countless letters of commendation from all of the users, while having a 100% availability rate and zero accidents in one of the most difficult locations in the world to conduct flight operations. Next stop, Fallon, Nevada.

CHAPTER XIII

NAVAL AIR STATION
FALLON, NEVADA

I had no idea what I was getting into when I received orders to Fallon. After taking my family back to my wife's home in Louisiana, I left and proceeded to Fallon. It was a three-day trip, and after entering the state of Nevada, I was somewhat in shock as I traveled up highway 95 from Las Vegas to Fallon. I have never seen such terrain in my life. The contrast between Kodiak Island and the State of Nevada was impossible to initially absorb.

I arrived at the base after working hours on a Wednesday. After checking into the bachelor officers quarters (BOQ) and unpacking, I decided that I would visit the control tower as flight operations were being conducted.

When I arrived at the Operations Duty Office, I introduced myself to the duty officer and asked permission to visit the tower. He gave permission, and I climbed the three flights of stairs to the tower cab. When I arrived, I knew I was in deep trouble. There were three controllers on duty, four aircraft in the pattern and no one was watching the traffic pattern. They were all scrambling around on the floor attempting to locate flight strips. (Flight strips are a written record that identifies required flight information on every aircraft either in the air or planning to launch in the immediate future.) It seems as if one of the chiefs in the division had a bias for flight strip holders and had banned them from the tower. Instead of flight strip holders the chief had sprayed some type of substance on the tower console that was designed to hold the strips. Obviously the sticky stuff had worn off, and as a result the floor was covered with paper. Not one controller on duty had the slightest idea of who was what. Thank God the hour was late, and flight operations were secured approximately fifteen minutes after I arrived in the tower.

I introduced myself to the controllers on watch and informed them to contact everyone in the division and alert them to an all-hands meeting for

106

0800 the next day. The section leader asked me if that included the folks that were going to be coming off the mid watch.

I said, "All hands means all hands."

That concluded my first day at Fallon, and I hadn't even checked in yet. Looked like this will be a place that *Mr. Roberts* would love to be stationed.

The next morning I arrived at the Operations building at approximately six A.M. I was somewhat amazed that except for the duty officer and the duty section, no one was at work. I should have gone to the Administration building and begun to check in to the command, but I had scheduled a meeting for 0800, so I stayed around the Operations building and met the folks as they straggled into work. At about 7:45 A.M. the Air Traffic Control officer finally showed up. He was a LTJG and while technically senior to me, as a CWO-2, I wasted no time in informing him that I was sent there to commission a GCA unit and was more than willing to assume the responsibilities of division officer. He said, "I don't know anything about Air Traffic Control, and really don't care. If the skipper will buy it, you got it."

I said, "Okay, we have an all-hands meeting in about five minutes. I would appreciate it if you would disappear so I can address the troops and introduce myself."

He said, "I am out of here," and departed the area. I freshened up my cup of coffee and proceeded to the conference room to meet my troops.

I began the meeting by introducing myself and providing a brief background on where I had been, what my qualifications were, and I asked for the same information from all of the personnel present. I had taught a small number of the personnel while I was an instructor and obviously I knew the folks that had accompanied me from Kodiak to Fallon. When the introductions were completed I asked the question, "Who is responsible for the lack of flight-following strip holders in the tower?" One of the chiefs acknowledged responsibility. I told him he had until 12 A.M. to get the strips back into the tower.

After that business was completed I briefed the personnel on the plans to install a GCA unit in Fallon, that I would be busy reviewing all of the documents germane to providing ATC services at Fallon, and assessing the course rules, watch bills, qualifications of personnel assigned, etc. I terminated the meeting by scheduling a follow-on meeting with the senior personnel in the division for one P.M. that afternoon, and dismissed the men so I could go check in to the base and meet the commanding officer.

The check in was routine, but meeting the commanding officer was an event that still stands out as the most impressive event of my almost-forty-year Navy career. Fallon had a fleet reputation as a laid-back assignment. The base population of active duty personnel was approximately five hundred. The reputation of the base was that everyone assigned was retired on active duty. The primary mission of the base was to support deployed air wings as they gained proficiency in air-to-air combat and weapons delivery prior to deploying for a six-month cruise on one of the carriers. The commanding officer had reported aboard about one year before my arrival, and he had a different idea for the base. His name was Boyd Muncie, and as I found out, he was a warrior who had been there, done that, and had a good idea of the type of training and support air wing personnel needed before they deployed. He was a recently divorced man whose entire life was devoted to the Navy in general and NAS Fallon Nevada in particular. He was a strict disciplinarian and had some unique ideas on how to get things done. He led by fear and intimidation, shaved his head, and thought that any hair longer than ¼ of an inch was not military. He had a massive clean up campaign on the base; demanded physical fitness from all personnel assigned, and conducted the most thorough personnel inspections I experienced during my career.

When I was taken into his office, his first comment was, "You did a hell of a job in relocating all of that equipment from Kodiak to our command in Fallon. The ATC division is all screwed up. I expect you to fix it. Our only role in life is to make sure the air wings get the support they need in attaining an acceptable state of readiness. I hold you personally responsible for the performance and conduct of personnel in your division. Glad to have you aboard. Get out of my office and on your way back to work. Stop by the barber shop and get a haircut."

Somewhat shocked by this reception, I went to the barber shop and asked the barber what was with the skipper. He said, "You must have really made a good impression on him, as normally he fines each newly reporting officer $50.00 before he sends them to me. The secretary called and told me that you had not been fined." Somehow this old country boy figured out that things would be different during this tour.

Needless to say, the tour was interesting. We had some very good personnel assigned to the division and a lot of the other kind. The proximity of legalized gambling and prostitution resulted in a number of family problems for the personnel in the division. The outdated nature of the operating procedures, and an ineffective training program were issues I had to tackle immediately after reporting aboard. The saving grace of the division was the predominant presence of excellent weather conditions. It was obvious that the division as currently structured and trained would not be capable of supporting the volume of traffic in a safe and orderly manner during adverse weather conditions. This would be especially true with the commissioning of a radar capability at Fallon.

I began the process of selectively weeding out the non-performers and elevating top performers to positions of authority regardless of seniority. This was not welcomed by everyone, especially those who were somewhat senior but incapable of performing to the level that was necessary to get the job done.

My relationships with the officers within the Operations Department were excellent. This was made possible by the presence of the assistant operations officer, a man who had been stationed with me in Kodiak before the downsizing of that command. My relationships with the commanding officer were formed when he essentially gave me an illegal order and I refused to obey. Once I explained the potential outcome should I comply, he appreciated my input and frankly admired that I, while respectful, was not intimidated by his demeanor. (If he had only known how scared I was, perhaps our relationship would have been different, but he did not know, and I was not going to tell.)

Fallon was the most demanding operational tour of my career. Because of circumstances, world events, and timing we were able to lay the ground work for what is now the Naval Strike Warfare Center. The equipment we were able to obtain, the airspace structure we were able to develop, and the procedures implemented were necessary prior to having an infrastructure that could support not only the Topgun function of Naval Aviation but the resources necessary to provide planners with the tools to develop tactical exercises, use technology to its utmost, and most important, prepare Naval Aviation to implement National Command Authority directives.

At this stage of my career I was increasingly frustrated by the lack of solid information available for review when relieving an incumbent at a new duty station. In addition to meeting the personnel and establishing broad policy guidance it took a considerable amount of time to get up to speed. One night I was babysitting for a couple that had been stationed with me in Kodiak. The children went to bed on time, TV was not inspiring, so once again I put pen to paper. The idea was to recommend to CNO the adoption of a quality assurance checklist for inclusion in the ATC NATOPS manual. This document would address major issues that exist at every command that should be evaluated at each inspection. Additionally I felt such a checklist would be beneficial for anyone relieving an incumbent.

I put together a fairly inclusive list of issues, drafted a cover letter, and submitted the idea through the chain of command. Much to my surprise my immediate senior in the chain of command at NAS Lemoore returned the correspondence to Fallon with a fairly terse endorsement, which essentially said, they had a number of ATC experts available to them, me being one of them, and did not support such an idea. I licked my wounds and kept the correspondence in my personal "Things to Do" file. One of the first acts I took at my next duty station was to resubmit. This was a different chain of command and the concept was endorsed and finally accepted as policy by CNO. In later years my original list was expended significantly, but the concept is an annex to the ATC NATOPS manual today. (When you run into a brick wall you just need to find another place to hit it harder.)

One of the most important things I learned while at Fallon was by accident. One afternoon after working hours a group of the officers assigned to the Operations Department were having a bullshitting session. Included in this group were a number of limited duty officers and chief warrant officers. Each of us was assigned to billets related to our enlisted specialty. All of the former enlisted personnel were actually the favorites of the skipper. He felt that we brought value to his organization, and most importantly the leadership we provided relieved him from some of the distasteful aspects of command. One of these personnel was a CWO-3 whose assignment was as the range division officer. This division was populated with approximately eighty junior personnel and was ripe for disciplinary problems. He and I were discussing various leadership traits that could be applied. In the middle of this discussion he said, "Calhoun, I am going to share with you the secret of my success. This secret is not only applicable to a Navy career, it will work in your personal life or for that matter in any circumstance you might encounter."

Naturally such a profound statement captured my attention. I said, "Please go on, Henry."

He said, "I will use round numbers for simplicity purposes. We will use a base number of one hundred."

I said, "Okay."

He said, "Out of one hundred issues, seventy percent of the time, it doesn't mean shit. What I mean is that most issues are not important enough to fight. Examples include; what do you want for dinner? What kind of curtains do you like? Do you like this color of paint or wall paper? The next break point is twenty percent. On twenty-percent issues, you give your opinion and then gracefully support the initiative. If you do this, you are a team player. You do not roll over, but after considering the issue, you join in and support the concept even if initially you disagreed. If you do that, your boss, wife, mother, girlfriend, everyone will love you. You are not an obstacle to logical thinking. That leaves ten percent. The ten percent issues are not to be comprised. There is no need to debate. They are important in getting your job done, your personal relationships on an even keel, etc.; the advantage is that you determine the ten percent category." I firmly believe if one follows this concept he will have a successful career, successful personal life, and most important, will be able to accomplish his life's goals with minimal turmoil. I took this advice aboard and made it the guiding rule in my life. I believe it is responsible for any success I have achieved during my career.

About six months after I had reported to Fallon for duty I received a visit from a civilian employee. He introduced himself as an employee of the Government Accounting Office and was there to have a discussion with Warrant Officer Calhoun or Chief Warrant Officer Calhoun. I asked him what this was about. He said, "I have supply documentation associated with the transfer of $3 million dollars of equipment from Kodiak, Alaska to Fallon, Nevada."

I told him that I was the guy he was looking for.

He said, "Do you mean that you, without written authorization, transferred all of this equipment from one location to another?"

I said, "Yes, sir," and explained the reasoning behind my actions.

He said, "Well, you can thank your lucky stars all of the transfer and receipt documentation is in order. You dodged a bullet here; well done." With that, he departed the area, and I realized that my luck was still holding.

We did an awful lot of good things during my tour of duty in Fallon. The course rules were updated, training program revitalized, and the petty officers began to be leaders rather than followers. I do not mean to imply that we did everything by the book, because that was not the case. Sometimes the book is written as a cover-your-ass document rather than as something that outlines a step by step process to success. One of the things I have always believed and still believe is the major difference between the Air Force and the Navy is the Air Force is trained to do nothing without written guidance, while the Navy is trained to do anything that is not prohibited in writing. We did a lot of things "the Navy way" in Fallon.

Shortly after reporting aboard I became convinced that commissioning a GCA unit at Fallon Nevada did not satisfy the requirements for radar coverage required by the command to satisfy the assigned mission. To rectify this deficiency I called the program office in Washington charged with equipping commands to satisfy their assigned mission. I was informed that resources, both financial and equipage, were in short supply, and the weather in the Fallon area did not justify the commissioning of a full-blown Radar Air Traffic Control Facility (RATCF.)

Not to be deterred, I began generating individual letters requesting specific components of a RATCC. Each of these individual requests was approved through the chain of command. When approval of the final element for a RATCC was received, I placed another call to ask when work would begin on the facility at Fallon. I was informed that there was no way I would get a RATCC in Fallon for the reasons stated previously. When I pointed out that they had already favorably endorsed every piece of equipment that makes up a RATCC and quoted the endorsement along with the date of approval, I was met with a long silence. Finally they said they would send out a senior representative to assess the situation. He arrived on 23 December, and during his four-hour visit, we had a thunderstorm, blowing sand, snow that reduced visibility to less than ¼ mile, winds that exceeded sixty miles per hour, and a Louisiana-type frog strangler rain. When he left I asked him what his recommendation was going to be. He said, "I don't know how you did this, but I have never seen such weather in my life. I have no alternative but to recommend the installation of a RATCF at this location." (Sometimes things just work out.)

I would be remiss if I did not share a few Muncie stories with you. Captain Muncie demanded perfection, not only from every individual, active duty or civil service, employed on the base, but also from himself. He was extremely concerned about the physical fitness of everyone on the base. To emphasis his concern he called me into his office one day and declared that he was implementing a program he referred to as the "Fat Boys" club. In executing this program he appointed me as the athletic officer. My duties were to accompany him on personnel inspection and identify every member of the command that appeared to exceed the weight standards promulgated by the Navy. I attempted to talk him out of this, to no avail.

The next inspection I identified 79 personnel who appeared to be overweight. Their names were taken, and after inspection, they were directed to the hospital where their official weights were taken. Of the 79 potential members, 75 actually were qualified for the program.

This program consisted of two hours of exercise, led by me, three times per week. All members were required to weigh in on Friday. The directed goal was to lose two pounds per week. Failure to meet these standards would result in a Captain's Mast. (Administrative Punishment referred to in some services as an Article Fifteen.) No one was exempt from this program, officers or enlisted, male or female. I was required to make an official report to the captain each Monday at eight A.M.. After the first couple of weeks, and ten Captain's Masts held for failure to comply, the word spread and the folks really buckled down and accepted the program. The word around the base was that if you wanted to screw around with someone on the base, best not pick on a fat man, for he would kick your ass.

The great development that occurred as the result of this program was that the captain got married. Shortly after the wedding I began to notice that he had slacked off on his personal fitness program and was beginning to get a little puffy around the waist. After a Monday morning briefing on the program I said, "Captain, I believe that you are slightly in excess of the authorized weight standard."

He said, "That is a bunch of crap."

I said, "Well I just happen to have a set of scales outside that have been checked for accuracy by the medical personnel. Why don't you step on the scales and see if I am correct."

Being the type of man he was, he stepped on the scale and was found to be five pounds over authorized weight. He said, "All right, I have to travel to San Diego for a series of meetings the rest of this week, but will be there for the exercise program on Monday of next week."

At the conclusion of the normal exercise program on Friday, I informed all of the members that they could not miss the meeting on the following Monday. I told them that I had enrolled the captain in the program and he had promised to join them for exercise. One of the members was a seriously overweight senior chief petty officer who hated to be enrolled in that program. After my announcement he raised his hand and requested permission to speak. I acknowledged the senior chief and he said, "All of you know how much I hate this program, especially the sit ups. Mr. Calhoun, if you will start off the program with sit ups I will continue until the captain quits or I die." That got a laugh but set the stage.

The following Monday, the captain showed up on time dressed out for a work-out. His only problem was that he had worn a pair of shorts made out of some type of silky material. After the normal stretching portion of the program, we began a series of sit ups. We were in a gymnasium and the friction between the hardwood floor and the seat of the captain's pants began to take a toll. To his everlasting credit, he continued his sit ups until the count reached 83. After completing the 83rd set up, he raised his hand and indicated that because he was injured he would have to terminate the exercise program and seek medical attention. When he left the gymnasium I went over to his exercise area and noted two tracks of blood. The friction between his silky pants and the hardwood floor had worn two distinct blisters on his behind. I had nothing but admiration for him, but the troops celebrated as if they had won a major victory. On Wednesday the captain came to the exercise session with a pair of scales and a certification of their accuracy. He stepped on the scales and made allowable weight standards by a margin of one pound. He asked me if that satisfied his enrollment in the program. I replied, "Yes, sir, it does." With that, he gathered up his scales and departed the area.

On the following Monday after I completed debriefing him on the status of the last week's exercise program he said, "Everyone has done extremely well with this program." The captain indicated that he was totally satisfied with the results, and therefore was canceling the program effective that day. (When the news spread, I believe I could have run for mayor and would have been unopposed for election.)

Captain Muncie wanted to build the best deployment base in the world at Fallon to support the air wings. He had ideas of what was needed and cut a lot of bureaucratic corners, some of them, not necessarily legal, to achieve the desired results. One of the issues was the construction of an outdoor swimming pool. He wanted a pool Olympic in size with a retractable roof. The funds provided were insufficient to meet his goals. One of the problems was the high water table at Fallon. The Fallon area is essentially a dried-up lake bed. To achieve the desired depth a build up of the foundation was necessary. There were insufficient funds to accomplish this effort. Not to be deterred, Captain Muncie formed a fifty-man working party. He made arrangements with the owner of a rock quarry to obtain the necessary building materials from that site to achieve the desired foundation. The only stipulation the owner placed on this initiative was that he did not want any blasting in the area which would, in his opinion, disturb his cattle. Captain Muncie addressed this issue by procuring a number of sledge hammers, picks and shovels. He divided the working party into two twenty-five man groups. One group would travel to the quarry; bust rocks, load them on trucks, and take them to the site. The other men would, under the supervision of a civil engineer, place these rocks in such a way to construct the desired foundation

114

for the pool. When the word spread through the fleet about the chain gang that Captain Muncie had established in Fallon, no one bothered to explain that at the end of each working day, the captain would muster the working party at the pool and pass out four cases of beer and two cases of soda pop that he had procured with his private funds. Bottom line, Captain Muncie worked us like dogs, but we all understood that everything he was doing was for the best interest of the Navy. Additionally, while he could be unreasonable and in some instances downright cruel with his personnel, no one, from the chief of Naval Operations to the President of the United States, could mistreat his people. He proved this on any number of occasions, and in hindsight I can attest that he was universally respected and in some instances loved by the personnel delegated to his charge.

One of the things that concerned Captain Muncie was the lack of leadership he observed in the daily conduct of duty by senior petty officers. He was aware that I had had a tour of instructor duty, so he tasked me to develop a forty-hour course of instruction on leadership. He gave me thirty days to accomplish this assignment. The task was assigned on 1 December, so that took care of the Christmas season that year. I finished the final draft and turned it in to the captain on 23 December. He blessed the draft and scheduled the first class to begin on 1 January the following year. I taught the first three classes with all of the officers, including the captain in attendance. After the first three classes were completed, I identified three qualified instructors to take my place, but continued to monitor the course until my transfer from the command. He was a slave driver but had the best interest of the command and her personnel in mind at all times.

We received official approval for a RATCF but we still had to commission a GCA unit. That proved to be an interesting challenge. The supply system had located a GCA unit in excess of requirements and was putting it through a complete overhaul prior to shipment. We had the challenge of constructing the site for the system. The problem was the site plans for the unit did not satisfy my vision of what we needed. I wanted something that not only would do the job but would also be a facility that provided creature comforts to the assigned personnel and give them something to be proud of. My electronics personnel and I spent countless hours planning. I wanted extra structures to house maintenance personnel and their equipment as well as a ready room structure to serve as a home away from home for the personnel when they were on watch but not engaged in the control of traffic.

The first step was to persuade local public works personnel to deviate from the standard plans in constructing a concrete pad to house the facility. Each time they staked the area, I would send personnel out to relocate the stakes to depict what we actually wanted. Finally the public works officer, another old friend from Kodiak, told me he would have my ass if those stakes were moved again. To address this issue, I had one of my newly reporting electronic maintenance personnel dress in a civilian suit and represent himself as an employee from the Naval Electronic Systems Command in Vallejo, California, the organization responsible for installing ATC Systems. I provided him a copy of the modified plans we had developed, and sent him down to the base chief engineer with instructions to present these plans as the modification to the standard, designed specifically for sites such as the one at Fallon. Equipped with plans approved by higher authority, the local public works personnel followed those plans (the ones we developed) and constructed an ideal foundation for our unit.

The next challenge was to locate portable buildings that would support the extra capability we desired. The Air Force was decommissioning a radar site on the base and had some excess house trailers that were available. The only problem was that it would cost $1000.00 to move the trailer from its site in a civilian trailer park to the desired location on the base. We did not have a $1000.00 but we did have access to a pickup with a heavy-duty tow package. In the dark of the night, I and one of my technicians (the owner of the truck), proceeded to the trailer park, hooked up that trailer, and without thinking about disconnecting water and electrical hookups, pulled that sucker out of the park and onto the base. I had a first class petty officer in the division that was, in his spare time, an excellent auto body repair man. He had the tools and skills, and before daylight, that three-bed room, two-bath house trailer, with expanding sides in the living room area, was painted a bright yellow and was in position on the GCA pad. This served as the living quarters for personnel in the duty section.

I discovered that the Ordnance Division had requisitioned two portable buildings from a site in Southern Nevada. I found out when they would arrive, met the trailers at the main gate, inspected the buildings, selected the best one, conned the driver into changing the requisition from two buildings to one, and relocated one of the buildings to my GCA site. Again, before daybreak that building (the maintenance structure), was painted bright yellow. (The ordnance folks were so delighted to get one building that they never questioned the whereabouts of the other structure.)

I had one chief petty officer that worked in his off-duty hours as a plumber. We found an excess 1000 gallon water tank that he was able to modify to be a fresh-water holding tank for the facility. He was also capable of performing the required plumbing connections to provide fresh, potable water for the site. Another member of the division was a former heavy-equipment operator in a construction battalion. We were able to hotwire heavy equipment after hours, and he performed all of the landscaping work necessary to prepare the site.

Finally the day arrived when the unit was delivered to the base. We positioned the unit on the site, and the chief engineer that had accompanied the unit informed me that if he could get some help from the sailors, we would be able to commission the unit in about three months. I told him that was a bunch of crap, and we all began crawling over the unit, removing packing material and getting this sucker ready to run.

He said, "You will never beat three months, as we have to run power to this site, which means pulling cable, getting electricians to hook up knife switches, etc." I told him not to worry. We could get it done.

I have never seen anything like the effort I observed for the next seven weeks. Everyone in the division not on watch was at the site, digging ditches, pulling cable, unpacking crates, setting up test equipment. The base civilian electronic technicians and electricians came in on their off time to perform their technical magic. This was an all-hands effort from dawn to dusk, seven days per week. I had promised the folks that we could have the commissioning approach performed by a member of the Blue Angels. I did not have a clue of how this would be done, but things began to fall into place, and it looked like it would happen.

I ran into a snag that neither I nor any member of my crew could overcome. I could not get the local telephone company to make my drop-dead date of hooking up communications between the control tower and the GCA unit. Despite my best efforts, they would not accelerate the date to accommodate the availability date of the Blue Angels.

I had shot my wad. Despite my best effort and heroic contributions from every man and woman in the division, I was going to have to call the FAA and cancel their scheduled flight check. This cancellation would result in a rescheduling which would push back commissioning date to after the Blue Angels had left the Fallon area. The flight check was scheduled for two P.M. the next day. In recognition of the inevitable I called a meeting of all personnel and announced that I was forced to cancel the commissioning flight check because of our inability to establish two-way communications between the unit and the control tower. My announcement was met with shouts, screams and tears. Finally, my senior technician said, "Boss, you cannot do that. We, you included, have worked ourselves into the ground to make this happen. I am sure that some of us will get divorces over this. Please delay the call until tomorrow, and let us try to find a solution." I owed this group of men and women everything, so without much hope, I agreed to delay the call until eight A.M. the next day knowing I would be in for a serious ass-chewing from the FAA for the short-fused notification, but frankly I did not have the guts to disappoint such a loyal and committed group.

After the meeting was over I sent everyone not on duty home and went home to sit and ponder. I must admit, I was not good company, but my wife and children knew the hit we had taken and were very understanding. I finally went to bed about 11 P.M. and tossed and turned for at least an hour before falling off in a fitful sleep. At two A.M. the phone rang. It was my senior technician, Electronic Technician First Class Frank Mason. He said, "I got it figured out, boss; go to sleep. We will be ready for the FAA at two P.M. tomorrow." I could not sleep, as I thought we had exhausted every avenue.

When I got to work at six A.M. the next day, Petty Officer Mason was in the office. I said, "Okay, Frank, how did you do it?" He said, "I called one of my friends at the shipyard in San Francisco. He is on the road as we speak with sound-powered phones salvaged from a ship being decommissioned. We will hook those suckers up, test them, and communicate." He arrived at approximately nine A.M. The installation was completed and tested, and a successful pre-commissioning flight check was performed that afternoon.

The next morning at nine A.M. Blue Angel seven, with the public affairs officer of the base in the back seat, conducted the first operational GCA approach into NAS Fallon, Nevada. The controller on duty was one of my Kodiak Guys, Petty Officer First Class Glenn Moffett. The weather was clear with unlimited visibility. When the aircraft reached four miles, the power supply failed. The unit was filled with distinguished visitors. When Petty Officer Moffett keyed the mike to direct the aircraft to execute a missed approach because of loss of radar, I said, "On glide path, on course, four miles from touchdown." He repeated that transmission and kept up the cadence until the aircraft was over touchdown. (I knew that the aircraft was set up for a normal rate of descent, had the runway in sight and would continue to descend in a normal manner, because the weather was not a factor. I was confident that he would never notice he was not being given course corrections, thus the first approach into Fallon was essentially a phony, but the only folks who knew that were me and Petty Officer Moffett. If we had terminated that flight we could have never made the first approach with a Blue Angel, as I had zero spare parts to repair the power supply.) As soon as the approach was terminated, I called the tower and directed them to send a notice to Airmen advertising that the GCA unit was down for maintenance. Once that was accomplished, the party began.

One story with a *Mr. Roberts* theme demands sharing. I had a young controller from Mississippi who began to demonstrate low morale. I brought him into the office and asked him what was going on. He said, "Mr. Calhoun, my dad has a small construction company and times are hard. He wrote me a letter and stated that since the country was not at war, he felt that my presence assisting him in the construction business was much more important than anything I was doing out here in Nevada. Now my dad is a prideful man and would have never written that unless times were desperate. I don't know how to answer him, as I cannot just leave."

I said, "Dan, would you mind if I wrote your dad a letter?"

He said, "I would appreciate it."

With that I sat down and wrote a letter to his father explaining the role his son was playing in bringing deployed Air Wings up to speed before their deployment. I also indicated that while I understood his difficulty, I knew that he would not want to damage his son's career while he was learning a trade that could very well prepare him for a high-paying job when he got out of the Navy. I sent the letter off with my fingers crossed. In about a week I received a heartfelt response thanking me for my letter and stating that he understood my position and would write his son a letter to fix things. Another week passed and my controller came in with a totally different attitude. His dad had written, apologized for his previous letter, and told him to work his butt off for the guy who had taken time to address his concerns. Dan became an excellent controller and I felt really good about the way things were handled.

Every command in the Navy annually conducts a Navy Relief drive. The purpose of this event is to collect money to assist active duty personnel during periods of need. Captain Muncie appointed me as the chairman of this event and directed me to have the most successful Navy relief drive in history. I went to work. I started an aluminum can drive, set up an open house event featuring dunking booths, basketball accuracy shoots, solicited contributions from the local merchants to serve as raffle drawing prizes, and held various events requiring sponsorship in exchange for accomplishing certain tasks.

The Navy Relief drive was a huge success. My son and I climbed into and out of trash dumpsters gathering cans. I even persuaded the members of the defunct Fat Boys club to participate by soliciting sponsorship for the number of sit ups they could do. I persuaded the captain to participate in the dunking booth, and almost everyone on the base bought a chance to dump his butt in the water tank. He stayed in the booth for approximately two hours, and was dunked at least one hundred times. I persuaded seven personnel to solicit sponsorship for walking from Lovelock to the main gate in Fallon. I believe this is approximately forty miles. The walk was accomplished on a Saturday with a temperature of at least ninety degrees. Two personnel completed the walk. I still cannot believe I was able to talk them into it.

The grand prize was a motorcycle donated by the local Honda dealer. Believe it or not the winner of that prize was the wife of the Honda dealer. The best prize was a small boat. One of the chiefs in the Operations Department had a small boat he was willing to sell for $40.00. I told him if he would donate the boat to Navy relief as a prize I would give him $50.00 if I sold one hundred tickets. After selling ninety-five tickets I procured the remaining five tickets for the ATC Division. Since I was drawing for the winning ticket, I continued to draw numbers until one of the division tickets showed. Results were, we had the greatest Relief drive in history, the captain was dunked a number of times to the delight of all, a good time was had by all, the chief realized a better price for his boat than he had originally asked, and the division had their own boat.

After commissioning the GCA unit, I began to solicit my next duty station. The foundation at Fallon had been laid for continued success, controllers and maintenance personnel were trained, all of the publications were up to date, and the training program was turning out top-notch products. We had a new commanding officer, one who was very capable of keeping the course that his predecessor had laid. In short, it was time for me to go. I found out that the ATC Division in Adak, Alaska, was in a bit of trouble, and asked the placement officer if he would cut me orders to that facility. He thought I was crazy but agreed to assign me as soon as a qualified relief could be detailed to Fallon.

Looking back on the Fallon tour, a lot of good things were accomplished. Some of those accomplishments are listed herein. Other accomplishments including building a cadre of top notch controllers and technicians who enjoyed exceptional careers in follow-on tours. Additionally, we developed the concept of Fallon being a Carrier in the Desert by providing realistic training to all of the air wings in the Navy and Marine Corps. We took steps to ensure that Navy jurisdiction of the airspace delegated to the command by the FAA to support training and weapons system development was permanent, and laid the foundation for what is now the Naval Strike Warfare Center. On a personal note, I was privileged to work with some of the most talented and dedicated officers and enlisted personnel in the Navy and was honored to work for the toughest and most committed and feared commanding officer in the Navy.

CHAPTER XIV

NAVAL STATION, ADAK, ALASKA

Upon receipt of official orders to Adak, my family and I made the long trip back to Louisiana. While I could have accepted an accompanied tour at Adak for a three-year period, I had three children; two of them young daughters that I felt would not be comfortable with the isolation of Adak. Additionally, the education opportunities available at Adak would not, in my opinion, be sufficient to provide them the education I felt they would need. With this in mind, my wife and I decided to take her back to her home town with the children, rent a place for them to live, and I would take a one-year unaccompanied tour of duty in Adak.

After getting the family settled in a nice house about two blocks from her mother's home, I caught a flight from Lake Charles, Louisiana, to Adak with stops in Seattle, Washington, and Anchorage, Alaska. If I had known what I was to face in Adak, I may have missed the plane.

When I arrived at Adak I was met by Chief Petty Officer Bill Fisher. Chief Fisher was the best chief I had had working for me in Fallon, and I was very glad to find out he was stationed there. On the way down to the division spaces he gave me an overview of the operational readiness and material condition of what I was now responsible for. The news was not very encouraging. Some of the good news was that Second Class Petty Officer Mike Sanders was also assigned to Adak. Sanders had been the best controller I had assigned to Fallon. In fact he was the best natural controller I was ever privileged to serve with.

When we arrived at the GCA unit all personnel not on watch were mustered to meet the new division officer. I had now been promoted to LTJG, and a number of personnel assigned had been stationed with me at other commands. After a brief introduction I was introduced to a team from the Naval Electronic Systems Command out of Vallejo, California. They were there to conduct an Electronic Field Maintenance (EFM) pre-inspection of the GCA equipment. The purpose of this inspection was to identify deficiencies in the equipment that would be repaired when a full team came to Adak to conduct a total maintenance effort on the equipment. I asked how they planned to support flight operations during the time the equipment was down for maintenance. They said they had made arrangements to have a tactical Marine Corps system deploy to Adak for the six week period we were off line. I asked how much that would cost. They said $18,000 plus the cost of transporting the equipment and payment of the personnel involved.

I said, "I believe we can do this another way," and sat down to write a message to the chief of Naval Operations (CNO) with my suggested solution.

I drafted the message and released it. The message began with the phase, "Unless Otherwise Directed (UOD.)" This is a term that really pisses off some folks in the intermediate levels of the chain of command. This is especially true when one releases a message without authorization before one has even met his seniors, including the commanding officer.

The next morning when I arrived at work I had a message to report to the commanding officer. I was expecting this, so I had dressed up in full "Dress Canvas." When I arrived, I was escorted into the commanding officer's office. The skipper as well as the executive officer introduced themselves and asked me what in the fuck I was doing. The skipper said that he had received a call from his immediate senior at home the previous evening, wanting to know what he was doing by sending an UOD message essentially changing plans for maintenance of a system that he had already approved. Naturally the captain did not have a clue what the admiral was talking about. He told the admiral he would check and get back with him. Once he located the message, he called the admiral back and was instructed to cancel the message immediately. I apologized to the captain, but I really did not care, since CNO had a copy of the message, and my plan would be either approved or disapproved based on merit, not bureaucratic bullshit.

After getting a justified ass-chewing I completed my check in, and was informed that I was being placed on the command duty officer (CDO) Watch Bill. That was odd, since the CDO watch was normally stood by lieutenant commanders and above. I was told that since I was a previous chief warrant officer, my experience justified my assignment. Since I had nothing else to do with my time, and my family was in Louisiana I did not mind.

When I returned to the division I had a message to call CNO's office. When I completed the call, I was informed that a message was being drafted approving my plan for the maintenance of the GCA system and the tactical Marine Corps system scheduled for Adak was being cancelled.

The following day an inspection team from San Diego reported unannounced and conducted a Nuclear Training Program (NTP) inspection. At the time Nuclear Weapons were stored at Adak, and the inspection program addressed the compliance with directives from higher authority associated with the storage and security of these weapons systems. The command failed this inspection. Every officer in the Operations Department except me and the operations officer were relieved for cause. We escaped because I had been aboard two days, and the operations officer had been aboard for five days.

When the results of the inspection were announced, the operations officer called me into his office and said, "Well, it is just you and me. I am the department head and you are the division officer for all of the divisions. As we rebuild the manning of the department, I will take your recommendations as to who should assume specific division officer responsibilities. Until then you have them all." That was something of a shock, but I committed to do the best I could.

My plan for implementing the maintenance of the GCA unit was for the maintenance personnel and controllers assigned to Adak augmented by technical personnel from Vallejo, would totally upgrade the spare channel of the system, install the repaired channel and repair the other channel, then take the system off the air for a maximum of one hundred hours to repair/replace single points of failure systems such as antennas, etc. The technical folks from Vallejo told me that it would be impossible to do, but I told them that I had total confidence in my sailors, and they would get it done.

When the work started we had about two feet of snow on the ground. My sailors, men, and women, were dismantling equipment, grinding metal, and painting running gear as required. The effort exhibited almost equaled the performance I saw while we were installing the system in Fallon. The civilian technicians became excited by the effort and commitment of the active duty folks and worked equally hard. We completed the EFM and the associated commissioning flight check with a down time of 97 hours. We not only saved the taxpayers a lot of money, the effort developed a sense of camaraderie within the division that would stand us in good stead during the coming months.

The third weekend I was assigned at Adak was my first command duty officer watch. Things were going well until about four P.M. on Friday afternoon. I received a panic call from the commanding officer informing me that a large group of sailors were marching on his house and that I should do something about it. I had to ask where the commanding officer lived. After obtaining directions, I drove my duty truck to his house. I passed a mob of sailors, about 150 personnel, walking on the road as I made my way to his residence. When I arrived the skipper and his wife and children were in the yard and everyone was very worried. He said, "What are we going to do?"

I responded with a wise ass remark, "What is this we shit sir? This is not my house." After that statement, I asked him what was going on.

He said that an unannounced inspection had occurred that afternoon and a lot of booze and a small amount of drugs had been confiscated. The sailors said they had a lot of gripes in addition to the inspection effort and wanted to discuss these issues with the skipper.

I immediately called the assistant duty officer and asked him to break out the duty section and dispatch them to the skipper's house.

He said, "All I have are the folks either on watch or those scheduled for watches," and he recommended that I contact the commanding officer of the Marine Barracks for assistance. I made that call and was informed that the Marines were assigned to protect the weapons storage compound, and that I was on my own.

I informed the skipper of these developments, and he said, "What are we going to do now?"

I said, "let me go down the hill and meet with them and see what I can negotiate."

He said, "Okay."

I drove down the hill and stopped in front of the crowd. I asked for the three senior men to step forward and identify themselves. After a bit of shuffling around three first-class petty officers came forward. I introduced myself and asked them what was going on. They started telling me about grievances they had, which covered a lot of territory. I could relate to some of their complaints because of my enlisted background and my three weeks aboard the command. I said, "There is no way you guys are going to march on the skipper's quarters, hold him and his family hostage, and get anything done. All of you know that we cannot tolerate that, and instead of getting something done, you will all destroy your careers." They were sensible enough and senior enough to know that I was correct. After giving them a few minutes to think things over, I said, "If you guys will break this mob up and send them back to quarters, the skipper and I will meet with you three in his office at one P.M. tomorrow to discuss your concerns." After talking it over between themselves for a few minutes, they agreed and began to break up the mob.

The next day at one P.M. the skipper and I met with the three petty officers. They gave a detailed briefing on concerns they had and indicated that they spoke for the majority of the enlisted personnel assigned. The skipper took all of their concerns aboard, committed to address those things within his power with the understanding that he would not tolerate drugs and alcohol abuse in the command. They all understood his position. To finalize the meeting, the skipper assigned me an additional duty of human relations officer, responsible for identifying and rectifying the reported deficiencies as well as others that I might observe. That appeared to satisfy all concerned, and the meeting broke up. After they left, the skipper complimented me on a job well done and told me to come directly to him if I did not get command support in rectifying the complaints we had noted. (Is this not a great way to start off an unaccompanied tour?)

The next significant event was a major drug bust. Since I was the division officer for all of the divisions in operations, I was spread pretty thin. One of my responsibilities was the air terminal. Since Adak is totally isolated, any illegal substance that arrives on the island must arrive by air through this terminal. I noted that a number of my controllers worked in the terminal on their off-duty time. The vast majority of cargo and mail was delivered to Adak by civilian contract carriers. Fresh produce, milk, bread and the like was brought in by logistic flights of the U.S. Air Force. If illegal substances were coming on the island they must transient through the terminal. I placed a number of cameras and a small number of personnel from the security force around in the terminal, and sure enough, we caught a number of my personnel receiving packages addressed to fictitious addresses. They would pull these packages from the incoming mail and divide the contents among the participants, who would then distribute the drugs around the base.

When I brought this to the attention of the captain he said, "What are we going to do?"

I said, "We have to court martial these folks and do what is right."

He said, "That is obvious, but how are you going to provide Air Traffic Control when so many of your folks are involved?"

I said, "We will manage."

Overnight, my division went from twenty-two personnel to ten, six of which, including myself, were qualified. Thank God the six folks were the cream of the crop. We continued to provide uninterrupted service until we received a number of top-notch personnel as replacements.

One of my favorite memories of Adak was the setting of road conditions by the command duty officer. In Adak one of the responsibilities of the duty officer was to constantly review the status of the roads during adverse weather and advise the command when the roads appeared to be too dangerous to travel to conduct routine business. They had various conditions, the most serious being road condition Alpha. In Alpha, all personnel not on watch were confined to quarters. Civilian employees not in quarters were to be dispatched immediately to their homes and essentially stay in quarters until the road condition was upgraded. Obviously setting Alpha was serious business, as all work stopped. The command was very serious about setting Alpha. While the duty officer could recommend, the only official that could actually implement Alpha was the commanding officer or the executive officer.

My first opportunity to become involved in this exercise occurred on my second CDO watch. I was traveling the roads in my two-wheel drive pickup and was constantly slipping and sliding on the road. I worked my way to the Administration Building and proceeded to the executive officers office where I recommended that we go to Alpha.

The XO looked out the window and said, "I think you are over reacting. The roads look good to me."

I told him that looks were some what deceiving and suggested that he go out and give them a road test.

He said, "Okay," and got his hat and coat. (The XO was a native of Wyoming; I was a native of Louisiana.)

When we got outside the building he began to go to his four-wheel drive Dodge Power Wagon.) I said, "Not so fast, XO, almost anyone can drive on these roads if they have that type of vehicle. Very few folks here have the luxury of four-wheel drive. Let us try the roads in my two-wheel-drive pick up."

He said, "Okay," got behind the wheel, started up the truck, and promptly slid into a ditch. After getting a tow out of the ditch in the parking lot he promptly slid off the main road into another ditch. He looked at me and said, "Lieutenant, point well made. Set condition Alpha." To his credit, the next day he turned in his four-wheel-drive truck and drew a standard pickup for his personal official transportation.

In addition to my other duties I was also appointed as the snow king. In this assignment, with the help of 24 Construction Battalion (CB's), I was responsible for keeping the runways clear of snow and ice and ready for flight operations. This was a challenge, considering the weather conditions at Adak. Thank God my wife and I had made the decision not to bring the family to Adak, as I would have never been home. In certain times of the year at Adak, from November to late April, the snow-removal job was continuous. I had a lot of dedicated personnel, but I knew that if I was out on the runways with them, they would do a better job.

At the end of the snow season a research of the records indicated that for the first time in history the runways at Adak had never closed for weather conditions. I was proud of that accomplishment and contacted the commanding officer of the deployed squadron to inform him of this feat. In recognition of their dedication, he had a plaque made describing the accomplishment and coordinated a ceremony with me to present the award. When the presentation was made, one of my Seabees yelled out, "Fuck the plaque, Lieutenant, where is the beer?" This brought out a chuckle but three days later an aircraft arrived from Moffett field. Shortly after its arrival the commanding officer drove down to the GCA unit and dropped off four cases of Coors. I contacted the leading chief of the See Bees and asked him to bring our snow removal crew down to the unit. When they arrived, I told the senior chief what had happened, gave him the beer, and those suckers sat down in my ready room and drank all four cases. (This story is provided for the readers who do not have a military background.) It is amazing what a group of men can do when their morale is high and no one is attempting to get credit for their performance.

I have previously indicated that when a bunch of folks are essentially isolated in a remote location some interesting and often humorous developments occur. Adak was no different.

We had a salty old CWO-4 assigned to the command as the administrative officer. His name was CWO-4 Williams. Mr. Williams had been in the Navy a long time, knew a lot of folks, and had seen a lot of things. We received word that a senior captain was coming to Adak to conduct an inspection. This inspection was to cover all administrative matters, the Human Relations Program and related issues. Needless to say, the command was not looking forward to this visit. We had an all officers meeting where the CO and XO cautioned all of us to make sure that we and our personnel were on good behavior. The visiting captain was met at the air terminal when he arrived by most of the senior officers in the command. After grips and grins, he was loaded into a staff car and taken to the bachelor officers quarters (BOQ) where he would be berthed in the Very Important Person (VIP) suite. Much to the surprise and initial dismay of the skipper, when the vehicle arrived in front of the BOQ CWO-4 Williams opened the door of the vehicle, snapped off a textbook salute, and then proceeded to throw the visiting captain to the ground where they rolled over in the snow like two first graders on school break. I really thought the skipper would have a heart attack. He attempted to break them up, apologizing to the visiting VIP while simultaneously giving Williams the chewing out of his life. Finally, these two rascals came up for air and the visiting captain began to explain. It seems that CWO-4 Williams had been the leading chief of a division headed by the captain when the captain was an Ensign. They had been stationed together for seven years in various assignments and were best friends. Finally, the captain began to understand and joined in on the joke but I really believe he never forgave CWO-4 Williams for not sharing their relationship before he arrived. If the captain thought that this was the end of their celebration he was in for more surprises.

The BOQ at Adak is collocated with the Officers Club mess and bar. At the end of the day, after the evening meal, the visiting captain, CWO-4 Williams, and I retired to the bar where they began to exchange life stories and commence some heavy drinking. When the captain left to go to the head (bathroom), Williams said, your job is to entertain the captain when I leave for a little while, and under no circumstances are you to allow him to have another head break. Not understanding what was going on, but knowing it was something that might be good, I agreed. About thirty minutes after the captain returned, Mr. Williams excused himself and said he had to take care of some official business and would be back in a short while. While he was gone, we exchanged some sea stories and generally had a good time. When he returned we continued to talk until the bar closed. Each time the captain attempted to go to the head, Williams would start another story. Finally, the bartender announced last call, and we prepared to go to bed. I gave my respects, told both of them good evening, and entered my room. Williams escorted the visitor to his room and immediately came back to my door and pounded on my door. I opened the door and he motioned me to follow him. We proceeded to the door of the VIP quarters and Williams motioned for me to listen closely. I placed my ear against the door and almost immediately heard a blood curdling scream followed by a string of cuss words that almost embarrassed me. Williams was actually rolling around on the floor laughing as hard as he could. Suddenly the door was flung open and we had a captain standing in the doorway with the front of his trousers visibly wet, his fly open, and really pissed off. It seems as if Williams had covered the mouth of the toilet with Saran wrap. Being deprived of visits to the head, the captain's first order of business after entering his room was to recycle some of the beverages he had consumed during the evening. The Saran wrap served as a trampoline and vaulted the liquid back in the direction from which it came. Finally, after a few tense moments, he saw the humor in the situation and we all began to laugh. I figured that was the end of the tricks but the next evening proved to be equally entertaining.

The skipper hosted a dinner in his home for our distinguished visitor. Williams was invited because of his long-standing relationship with the visitor but begged off with the excuse of pressing business. I was not invited to attend because of my lack of seniority. As soon as the visitor left the BOQ area, Williams grabbed me by the arm and said, "Come with me." Not having a clue of what he was up to, I followed along to the VIP quarters.

When we entered the room, Williams began to strip the bedding down to the bare mattress. Once he had completed striping the bed he covered the mattress with strips of aluminum foil. When that chore was completed, he remade the bed making sure that he had short sheeted the bed in an acceptable manner.

The captain returned to the club after his social event at the skippers house and called Williams and my room and invited us to join him in an after-dinner drink in the club. The hour was late and our drink was not the first drink the captain had had that evening. After one drink, he pleaded fatigue and called it a night. As soon as he departed we very carefully followed him back to his quarters. We positioned ourselves outside his door and began to wait for the action to begin. As he made the normal preparations for going to bed after a long and eventful day we could hear him talking to himself. He checked the toilet to assure that a repeat of the previous evenings activities did not occur. We heard him say, "I know that old bastard has done something but I cannot figure out what it is." He turned down the bed, discovered the short sheeted prank and after fixing his sheets he turned off the lights and hit the sack. In a very few minutes we could hear his bitching about the heat. He said, "This place is the asshole of the world. There is four feet of snow on the ground and I am burning up." We were both rolling around on the floor. He began to toss and turn and the aluminum foil began to make a lot of noise. Finally he said, "What the fuck is going on?" and jumped out of bed and began to strip the blanket and sheets.

Williams opened the door to his room and began to laugh. The captain finally got down to the aluminum foil, considered the situation, looked up at Williams and said, "Rick, you are a real bastard." Laughingly, we assisted in making the bed, bid him a good night and made our way back to our personal quarters. The next day he left, after giving the command an excellent review of the inspection results. I have always wondered if the satisfactory inspection was based on the friendship between the captain and Williams or actual results. We missed him after he had left, for this was a welcome break in the normal humdrum existence of life in Adak.

The next memorable event also featured CWO 4 Williams. The Central Intelligence Agency (CIA) was ferrying their fleet of Air America aircraft back to the states from Viet Nam. This was a hazardous mission and because of the various types of aircraft and relatively short range of said aircraft they were required to transit the North Pacific via Adak. As I recall there were about 35 aircraft involved. When they landed at Adak, many of them were operating on fumes. A decision had been made that the aircraft and crews would lay over for a couple of days before completing the ferry operation into the Seattle area. The pilots were all billeted into the BOQ and were very good customers for the bar.

I was not aware of the fact that Williams' wife was a senior executive for the Orkin Corporation. She had provided a couple of jump suits with the Orkin logo to her husband to serve as casual wear during off-duty time. I was in the bar having a conversation with some of the air crewman when William' entered the room dressed in his Orkin outfit. He yelled for attention and asked to speak to the guy in charge of all of those old airplanes on the flight line. After a brief pause, the toughest one of the visitors said, "I guess that would be me. What is on your mind?" Williams said, "I was at home in Seattle on my day off, relaxing, when I received a call from my boss dispatching me to this hell hole to disinfect those old aircraft. God only knows what they have been exposed to, so I brought the most caustic chemical we have to disinfect these aircraft before they are dispatched to the States. This crap is so strong that it could damage and in some instances destroy any paperwork or exposed instruments in those aircraft. The flight line is under guard, so I must have someone from your outfit survey those aircraft and remove any classified or valuable contents." In a very short period of time the room had been cleared of Air America visitors. Rick went over to the bar and ordered a drink when they left. I sat there in shock anxiously awaiting their return and the obligatory ass kicking that would occur.

In about an hour and a half the Air America folks began to return. The senior guy approached Rick, still in his Orkin attire and said, "I have been fighting wars around the world for the last 25 years. I have been almost everywhere and done almost anything you can imagine. Once we got to the flight line, I began to think, called our headquarters, explained out situation. They contacted Orkin and they denied any knowledge of your presence. I contacted the captain and he asked me if the Orkin's representative was named Williams. I said, 'yes,' and he said, 'Welcome to Adak. CWO Williams is our number one character, and we have a lot of those folks up here.' He wanted to know what I wanted to do about this, and I told him that this was the best practical joke that had ever been played on me during my entire career, and if it was all right with him, I would assure that you did not have to buy a drink for the rest of the time we are here." Everyone began to laugh and giggle and a good time was had by all. This was just another day in Adak. Sometimes you have to do dumb things to maintain focus.

I have previously indicated that after the unsuccessful NTP inspection I became the division officer for all of the divisions in the operations department. One of my jobs was to identify prospective reliefs for each of these divisions from the personnel reporting for duty. The most troubling division other than the Crash/Fire division was the ships division. We had three tug boats assigned ,and in addition to performing duties associated with tugs, i.e., assisting transiting ships into and out of the harbor, etc., the tugs served as a lifeline for some of the natives living on islands relatively close to the island of Adak. The members of the division were not bad guys, but they were a salty bunch.

An older female LTJG by the name of Ann Rice checked into the department. She along with her husband, also a LTJG, were a very impressive team. I was impressed by her can-do attitude, no-nonsense approach to everything, and most of all, her maturity. After observing her in action for a two-week period I approached the operations officer and recommended that LTJG Rice be appointed as the ship's division officer. Initially the boss was not in favor of the idea. I finally persuaded him to give her a chance. He agreed, and I took her down to the ship's division spaces for an introduction. LTJG Rice was a very attractive, mature woman. The men in the division were delighted. I pulled the senior chief aside and told him that if he or his folks gave the LTJG a hard time, they would answer to me. He said, "Don't worry boss, we will take care of her."

Later that evening we received an emergency call from a representative of an Indian Tribe that lived on one of the small islands about one hundred miles from Adak. They had a medical emergency and required assistance. The only way we could respond was with a tug boat. I alerted the ship's division and got dressed to make the trip. When I arrived, LTJG Rice was already aboard, all decked out and ready to go. I called her aside and attempted to talk her out of the trip since it would be difficult and the water was extremely rough. She said, "I either am or am not the division officer. If I am and they go into harm's way, I go with them." I could not argue with that so I wished her a pleasant journey and with deep feelings of apprehension went back to my room.

The trip to the islands was long and dangerous. Radio contact was lost shortly after the tug departed Adak. Frankly I sweated blood. All the next day we attempted to contact the tug to no avail. All of our helicopters were either down for maintenance or not equipped to fly in the type of weather we were experiencing. The morning of the second day I drove through base housing on my way to work to see if Mrs. Rice had returned to her quarters. As I approached the house of the Rice's I observed a sign. The sign said, "Home of Tug Boat Annie and her Spouse." I knew the crew had successfully returned, and I also knew that LTJG Rice had won the hearts and minds of the folks in her division. I called the senior chief and he told me that she was seasick for the first fifty miles, then began to recover. On the way back after successfully picking up the ill passenger, she got totally qualified as a helmsman and crewman. He said, "Boss, this lady is a trooper, and we will all go to hell if she is leading the way." I informed the operations officer that he had no worries about the ship's division, as it was in good hands.

I was rapidly approaching the end of my tour. We had accomplished a lot of things, all of the responsibilities of the various divisions had been transferred from me to qualified folks, and frankly, I was ready to leave. The captain called me in and said, "You have done a hell of a job. You promised me that you would give me three years of work in one year, and you have delivered. I have one more thing I want you to tackle before you leave."

I said, "I appreciate your kind words, but as you know I had some fine folks helping me do this job."

He said, "I understand. We are approaching the two hundredth birthday of our nation, and we need some kind of celebration. How about thinking about it and getting back to me with some ideas?"

The next morning I called on the captain and suggested that we consider doing something that not only would be memorable but would be exciting for the folks living in Adak. He asked me what I had in mind, and I told him that including dependents, Adak had a population of approximately three thousand folks. The military members were there for one or three years but many of the civilian employees and their families had been there for fifteen or twenty years. Those folks had children; many of those children had never had a McDonald's hamburger and french fries. My idea, in addition to the normal parade, was for him to allow me to go to Anchorage and propose the idea of having McDonald's provide the makings of their products for the citizens of Adak. We would need to persuade the contract airline (Reeves Aleutian Airlines) to provide transportation for the fixings, and transportation for me and others involved to and from Anchorage. He gave me the go ahead, and the next day I caught a flight to Anchorage after calling the McDonald's folks and making an appointment.

When I arrived in Anchorage I was met by a representative of McDonald's and taken to the local corporate headquarters. After a series of introductions I made my pitch. The reception was overwhelmingly positive. The senior representative told me that he would have to coordinate with higher authorities, but would have me an answer within two hours.

I killed some time by walking around in town and returned at the stated time. When I walked in, he asked me if I had solidified the support for transportation from Reeves. I told them that they had expressed a willingness to do whatever was necessary to make the event happen. He said, "Corporate has given me the go ahead to dispatch three personnel and Ronald McDonald along with the makings for twenty-thousand hamburgers and fries to Adak to assist in the celebration of America's two-hundredth birthday." I was overwhelmed. He said that I would have to solicit volunteers to assist in preparation and provide some type of cooking capability, as well as tables and so forth to assist in preparation. I told him I could do that, and left to catch the next flight back to Adak.

On the morning of July 4, 1976, a flight arrived from Anchorage with four personnel from McDonald's including one dressed as Ronald. They had the meat, bread and fixings for 20,000 hamburgers and orders of fries on board. We unloaded the groceries from the aircraft and proceeded to a hangar where I had thirty grills, twenty-five tables, and 60 volunteers, including the captain's wife, standing by. After a one-hour lesson on how to prepare the food the McDonald's way, I declared us ready for business, and went to open the hangar doors. I have never seen anything like that in my life. There must have been over one thousand folks standing in line, with more coming.

The crowd represented all segments of the population. Young sailors desperate for a taste of home, grizzled old veterans, young families, and families with teen age children that had never had the taste of America's favorite food. We were totally out of food at three P.M. Some families were ordering food by the bag. I am sure many of them took their hamburgers home and put some in the freezer to eat at a later date. Others just sat down and devoured this treat. Needless to say, the event was a roaring success. Everyone involved had a special memory of celebrating America's two-hundredth birthday. I believe the folks at McDonald's enjoyed the celebration as much as we did. At the end of the day, the captain expressed his appreciation to McDonald's for their support, and the command gave out a loud and long cheer of celebration. I am sure that McDonald's made life-long customers of a bunch of folks stationed a long way from civilization. After cleaning up the hangar and escorting the McDonald's folks back to the air terminal for their flight back to Anchorage, I hit the rack and slept like a log. I really believe this was a special event, and it is high up on my list of good memories.

I had orders for transfer to the Naval Air Station in Dallas, Texas, and departed Adak on 9 July. After boarding the aircraft and taxiing to the departure end of the runway, the aircraft came to an abrupt halt. After a brief delay, the pilot requested that Lieutenant Calhoun report to the cockpit. I entered the cockpit and the captain said, "take a look." I looked out the forward window and saw a Navy pick up with the front bumper placed solidly against the front nose landing gear. I saw one of my sailors waving a sign that said, "Lieutenant Calhoun." He said, "What is going on?"

I said, "I don't have a clue, but if someone will open a door I will find out."

One of the side doors of the aircraft was opened, and I approached the opening. The leading petty officer of the air terminal division was lifted on a fork lift to the opening and passed me a package. He said, "Boss, we worked for a week on this, and was late in finishing. We could not let you leave with out it. Please take this as a token of our respect and appreciation for the support you have given us during your tour of duty." I thanked him and he left the area. The truck backed away from the aircraft, the door was closed, and we began our take-off roll. When we reached altitude, all of the passengers on the aircraft, especially those close to me, began to demand to find out what was in the package. Finally, with a bit of concern I opened the package and began to cry. Those crazy lovable sailors had fabricated a flag. They had used red and white striped canopy cloth, drawn a snake diagonally across the material, and printed "DON'T TREAD ON ME." In smaller letters but equally important to me were the words, "AND NO WAY ON MY PEOPLE." This was my payback for all of the twenty four-hour days, the stress and worry and separation from my family. This token remains one of my favorite and most treasured mementos of my career.

CHAPTER XV

NAVAL AIR STATION
DALLAS, TEXAS

I was excited about my upcoming tour at Dallas. I knew that I would have some difficulty in becoming reacquainted with the pace of activity on a reserve air station that I had been exposed to during my tour in Atlanta, but Dallas was close to home, we had bought a nice house, and my family and I would be together. I anticipated that the Dallas tour would give me an opportunity to slow down the pace I had been following for a number of years. Boy, was I wrong.

When I departed the plane at Dallas/Fort Worth airport, the temperature was 109 degrees. After being in Adak for a year this was like getting hit with an over-hand right. The temperature would not go below 100 degrees for the next five weeks. I worked my way to the base and traveled to the Operations Department office spaces. When I entered the building, the first person I saw was senior chief Air Traffic Controller John Bowman. Chief Bowman had been one of my students, and was as sharp as a tack. I knew he was the leading chief of my Air Traffic Control Division, and I was extremely glad to have him in my organization.

We shook hands, exchanged pleasantries, and then he said, "Welcome aboard. The division is in pretty bad shape. There are only two things that will get you in trouble here: illegally eating a box lunch or fucking up a quiet hour. If you will keep from doing that, I will cover your back and keep you out of trouble." Little did I know that he was right on the mark. I did not eat any box lunches, but I did screw up a couple of quiet hours, and needless to say, the skipper was not happy.

I completed my check in on the base and sat down with Senior Chief Bowman to receive a briefing on the division. His briefing was thorough, and I was dismayed to find out what the issues were, what we were doing about them, and what the future held. A contract had been let to tear down the control tower. A new tower was under construction, but was not scheduled to be completed before the old tower was scheduled for demolition. The GCA unit was undergoing an Extensive Maintenance Program but was behind schedule. The temperature was forcing work to be stopped at 11 A.M . each day, and the Army was becoming a tenant on the base and had constructed a 800-foot landing area for their helicopters that was parallel to the primary runway at Dallas. The issue was that the contractor had no idea what they were doing, so they had installed all of the taxi way blue lights in cluster with the white runway lights. This led to confusion for pilots, since there was no taxiway to that landing area. While the helicopters did not really need a taxiway, it would have been impossible for a crash vehicle to reach a helicopter in difficulty on that landing area, since that landing runway was elevated twelve feet above the surface of surrounding terrain. Finally, the controls for the lighting of that landing area, a responsibility of the ATC Division, were located in a hangar owned by a civilian tenant of NAS Dallas (LTV.) The GCA unit had been off the air for two months; thus, no one in the command was currently qualified to provide ATC services in adverse weather conditions. Needless to say, I had my work cut out for me.

I began to address these problems by persuading the public works officer to provide space in one of the hangars to allow my folks to complete the repair work on the GCA unit in the shade. Next I negotiated a reallocation of the lights on the helicopter landing area to reflect a standard configuration, worked with the contractor and the fire chief to develop two egress/ingress ramps for emergency vehicles to the landing area, negotiated a relocation of the lighting controls to the new control tower, and renegotiated the contracts with various firms regarding the dismantling of the old tower to coincide with the commissioning of the new structure.

Once these tasks were completed, I began to feel pretty good until I had an opportunity to evaluate the operational aspect of the organization. The Navy had committed in writing to the FAA that NAS Dallas, would close when the airport known as DFW opened. Dallas is approximately 4 ½ miles south of DFW, and the runway alignment is identical. The airport at DFW was designed with the understanding that NAS Dallas would not be an obstacle to the free flow of civilian aircraft. The problem was that the folks that made the commitment to close NAS Dallas, had overlooked two important factors: NAS Dallas shared the runway with a major defense contractor LTV, and NAS Dallas, was the reserve drilling site for a very senior member of

Congress, Senator John Tower. Once these facts were known, there was no way Dallas was going to close, so we had to mitigate the impact on traffic flow at DFW caused by flight activity at NAS Dallas.

We finally completed the repair effort on the GCA unit and placed it on the pad in preparation for a commissioning flight inspection by the FAA. We did all of the voltage calculations, sighting criteria, etc, and began the flight inspection process. We began flight checking the approaches from the north and passed with flying colors. We recalculated our documentation and began flight inspection of the southern approaches. Despite our best effort we could not satisfy requirements. This went on for a three-day period. On the fourth day, when I reached the GCA site, I was informed that the technical representative from Vallejo, the guy in charge of this maintenance effort, had departed the area the previous evening and returned to California. I appreciated that this effort had been exhausting, but I had to get that GCA unit in an operational status. We had exhausted our personal technical expertise. In desperation I contacted a long-time friend who had retired from NAVELEX and was working as a consultant for the chief of Naval Air Training in Corpus Christi, Texas. I explained my problems and asked him if he could travel to Dallas and see if he could resolve our difficulties.

He said, "Can you pay?"

I said, "How much?"

He said, "Pay my travel expenses and I will do the work for free."

I said, "I can do that."

He said, "I will be there tomorrow."

The next morning he arrived at the GCA site at approximately eight A.M.. We immediately proceeded to the GCA unit where he reviewed all of our calculations, voltage settings, and compliance with sighting criteria. He said, "These are all correct. Let us take a ride." I got into the follow-me vehicle and asked him where he wanted to go. He said, "Let's go to the reflector site." We proceeded to the site and dismounted from the vehicle. He proceeded to the reflector and pointed out that we had a three-inch-diameter tree growing adjacent to the reflector between the reflector and the GCA trailer. As the result, there was no way we could accurately align the unit with that reflector because the tree blocked the signal. I immediately called for an ax, cut down the tree, and we realigned the unit. I had one of the local-area aircraft fly an approach and the line up was perfect. I contacted the FAA and they dispatched a flight inspection aircraft to the site. We passed in flying colors, I paid the expenses of my friend out of my pocket, he departed for Corpus, and we placed the GCA unit in a fully operational status. (I reviewed the past history of the unit and discovered that we had not conducted a southern flow instrument approach within the previous eighteen months. I never found out how we passed periodic flight inspections, but the lesson learned was never to assume that something is correct without investigating every aspect of the situation.

Dallas was an interesting assignment. I was uncomfortable with the Naval Reserve Environment. The captain, ground electronic maintenance officer, and I were the only commissioned, active-duty personnel on the base. The vast majority of enlisted personnel were Training and Administration of Reserves (TARS.) I did not question their dedication, but the laid-back approach to mission accomplishment was something I could never get accustomed to. My saving grace was a hard nosed commanding officer who shared my attitude. He was a problem-solver who had little interest in being popular or politically correct.

The skipper was appalled at the appearance of the base. The vast majority of structures were wooden, in need of paint and minor maintenance. Resources to address these deficiencies were limited. The captain made the decision that we would rectify these deficiencies with a "self help" effort. He called for an all-hands meeting on a Sunday afternoon and announced that on the upcoming weekend, Monday and Tuesday, he would meet with all volunteers and begin a clean-up, rehab effort on the barracks. He instructed the public works personnel to pre-position paint, rollers, brushes, scrapers, etc., at one of the barracks so we could begin work without delay. The next morning when we mustered, the only personnel that showed up were all of the enlisted personnel from my division and that of Ground Electronics not on watch, and the three active-duty officers, including the captain. He was shocked and said, "Well, folks we will get this barracks knocked out today and that will end the voluntary portion of this exercise. Next weekend, except for those currently present, all personnel assigned to this command, regardless of rank or pay grade, will be chipping and painting." We finished the barracks just before dark, and the skipper bought everyone lunch and drinks. (When I look back on the Dallas tour, my first memory is the disappointment I saw on his face when he realized that Dallas, his command, was not impressed with his "can do" spirit.)

One of the amazing events that occurred during my tour of duty at Dallas involved the crash of an F-8U in the traffic pattern. When the aircraft entered the break the aircraft became uncontrollable and crashed in one of the barracks areas. We were extremely lucky in that the barracks was unoccupied at the time of the crash. Immediately after the crash, things were extremely busy. The phone on my desk began to ring, but I was involved in drafting messages announcing the crash to higher authority. Finally, in frustration, I picked up the phone. The caller was a retired Marine aviator living in the Dallas/Ft. Worth area. He indicated that he knew the cause of the crash, as it was similar to two accidents he had investigated while on active duty. He even recalled the number assigned to those accidents and suggested that I call the Navy Safety Center and obtain copies of the accident reports. When things quieted down I placed the call, and in a few days copies of the accident reports arrived in the mail. I cannot recall the specific part that had broken off the aircraft causing the crash, but the details associated with those accidents were very similar to what had happened in Dallas. We had an all-hands searching party comb every inch of the base looking for the missing part. There is a small lake immediately south of the runway environment at Dallas. When the search proved negative we assumed the missing part had landed in the lake and was unrecoverable. Approximately three months later, we had a significant rain storm in the Dallas area. A large leak appeared in the mess hall. When the rain let up, a working party was dispatched to repair the roof. The cause of the leak was the missing part from the F8 stuck in the roofing material of the mess hall.

Dallas was a very difficult tour. Our commanding officer was a hard-charging, regular Navy officer with an impressive record of accomplishment. He wanted to turn his command into a show place in the Reserve Training command and could not understand that the vast majority of personnel in his command were more than satisfied to just be average folks. He knew that he could depend on his regular Navy personnel to adopt his point of view but could not motivate the TARS to follow his lead. The TARS, on the other hand, were extremely jealous of the attention the skipper gave to the regulars. This situation resulted in the development of a us against them philosophy.

All of the personnel in the ATC division were categorized as Watch Standers. What that meant was that their normal work schedule was comprised of rotating watches. The remainder of the command was on a five-section watch bill, and my folks were excluded. The TARS began to complain to the XO (a reserve captain.) He investigated and made the decision that my folks would no longer be exempt from station watches. What that really translated to was that the folks in the ATC division would never get a day off. On the days off allowed by the division watch bill they would be assigned station watches. Obviously this was not fair. In addition to the fact that everyone needs a day off occasionally, this was "shore duty" for the regular Navy folks, a bit of a break from the challenges of "sea duty." Since the reserves would never be assigned to "sea duty," it was a difficult point to make.

After being briefed by the XO on his decision, I requested to discuss this issue with the skipper. He not only disapproved my request, he gave a direct order that I was not to either officially or unofficially discuss this issue with him. Since I was driven by my concept of *Mr. Roberts*, and I had done everything in my power to right a wrong, I elected to retire. I drafted the retirement request and interviewed for the job as the senior Junior Naval Reserve Officer Training Course (JNROTC) instructor at Crowley High School in Crowley Louisiana. I passed the interview with flying colors and made the tentative decision to retire.

A few days later I received a call to report to the captain's office on the double. When I arrived and entered the skipper's office he said, "I received a call from Admiral Lawrence in the Pentagon today. He indicated that he had been the flag officer in charge of the Light Attack Wing Pacific in Lemoore when you were in Fallon. By accident he saw the request for retirement that you submitted. The reason he called was to tell me that he did not know what in the hell I was doing here in Dallas, but if it was so bad that it forced Calhoun to retire, it was wrong, and I had better get it fixed. Now that the background is out of the way, what in the hell is going on?"

I said, "I would love to discuss it with you skipper but I have been ordered by the XO not to do so."

He said, "That is a bunch of crap," and called out for the XO to come into his office.

After a brief delay, the XO entered the office and asked the captain what was going on.

The captain said, "That is what I am trying to find out, but Lieutenant Calhoun said he had been ordered not to discuss this issue with me by you. He has submitted his retirement papers. I received a call from the Pentagon to find out why."

The XO said, "Lieutenant Calhoun is not happy with a decision I made regarding placing his people on the station watch bill. I knew he would discuss it with you, and I knew your bias for the regular Navy folks would encourage you to override my decision. In an effort to avoid a confrontation, I ordered him not to discuss the issue."

The captain asked me if that was my interpretation of the events.

I said, "Yes, if I cannot protect the welfare of my personnel and cannot discuss issues with my skipper, I have no reason to stay in the Navy, so I have elected to retire."

The captain stood the XO at attention and told him if he ever deprived any member of his command from a personal audience with him, he would fire him on the spot. Additionally, the skipper directed the XO to take immediate action to remove watch standers from the station watch bill. After these comments, he excused the XO from the meeting as asked me if I was satisfied with his decisions.

I replied, "Yes sir."

He said, "Would you agree to pull your retirement papers?"

I said, "Yes, sir, but you know if I stay here it will be a constant fight between me and the XO, and not only is that not in my best interest, it has the potential to destroy what you are trying to build here in Dallas."

He agreed and gave me permission to begin negotiating for orders. He said, "If you are not satisfied with what they offer, let me know and I will get involved." I thanked him for his support and went back to the division to withdraw my request for retirement and begin negotiating for my next duty station.

When I contacted the detailer he informed me that he had been briefed by Admiral Lawrence and my skipper on the situation. He said, "You are an unplanned transfer, so I do not have much to offer. I can give you a one-year tour as sort of gap filler, and then make it up to you after that tour is completed."

I said, "I know this is an unplanned event and will accept anything you have to offer."

He said, "The command will not like this, because they believe their best interest is served by personnel on a three-year tour. That said I can pull it off if you can take the heat."

I said, "After Dallas, I believe I can take anything."

He said, "Okay, you will receive orders for a one-year tour as air traffic control and assistant air operations officer to Naval Support Forces, Antarctica."

I said, "Is that Operation Deep Freeze?"

He said, "Yes, I will transfer you 1 September. You will check in no later than 15 September and deploy to the Ice on 27 September."

I said, "Sounds good to me. Why do they need me in Antarctica?"

He said, "They run a shoe-string operation down there and need someone with experience to evaluate their procedures, equipment, and training program. They have received a chunk of funds to refit their ATC capability and need someone with your background and experience to assist them in this modernization effort."

I said, "Sounds good to me."

That evening I had to break the news to my wife and children. Since we had only been living in our new house for one year, and the children were all set in the local school system, we decided that they would stay in Dallas until my Antarctic tour was completed. Once again I left them high and dry and proceeded on my merry way to the next set of challenges.

CHAPTER XVI

NAVAL SUPPORT FORCES, ANTARCTICA, OPERATION DEEP FREEZE

I checked into the summer home stateside of Operation Deep Freeze located in Port Hueneme, California. The majority of the senior leadership of the command had already departed for Christchurch, New Zealand, but the core of the ATC and Ground Electronic Division were aboard. I met with those folks and discovered that my old friend Petty Officer First Class Frank Mason was a member of the division. That gave me a high level of confidence that whatever the challenges were, we would be able to work them out.

The few days I had in southern California before deploying to Antarctica passed very fast. We caught a contract flight out of Pt. Mugu California with stops in Oahu, Hawaii and the Fiji Islands before landing at Christchurch. The flight proved to be long but uneventful. I was totally amazed with Christchurch. They were approaching spring while we back in the states were entering the winter months. I could not believe the rural nature of the countryside and the backward development of the area. That is not intended to be critical. In fact, of all the places I have been privileged to travel, New Zealand is only place outside of the United States that I believe I could live.

During the few days I had been in the command before we left the states I had made a number of close friends. Since we would have eight days before we left for the ice, some of us decided to attempt to tour the country side rather than do the normal sailor things like hanging around bars and getting drunk. We were billeted in a hotel in town because of a paucity of quarters and took advantage of the opportunities.

The first time I saw someone jogging was in Christ Church. I saw my first cricket match and observed the daily debates about political events held in the town square. I finally made contact with a local resident who hired his American sized vehicle out for tours. We struck a financial deal and spent four days touring the south island. Never saw so many sheep in my life. During our tour we ran into a tour bus filled with ladies touring from Australia but that is a whole lot of different stories.

One of the stories about our trip to Christ Church was the dinner we had the night before we departed for the continent of Antarctica. I and the three folks that accompanied me on the tour of the south island saw a sign in a restaurant advertising a steak dinner for two with all the trimmings for $14.00. We had no idea what kind of food we would have once deployed and thought we would take advantage of this final opportunity to eat a good meal. After sitting down to a nicely appointed table the waiter approached us for drink orders. One of the guys suggested wine. Despite my tour of duty in Rota, I know nothing about wine. (Frankly Ripple and Boone's Farm is call brand to me.) I was elected to order the wine. After a careful review of the menu, I ordered Blue Nun. I did not know anything about it but did recognize the name. The meal was exceptional; the wine was so good we ordered a total of three bottles. Much to our surprise when the bill was delivered the total exceeded $100.00. I demanded an explanation. The water explained the wine was responsible for the majority of the charges. Once the explanation was completed we understood that imported wine was more expensive than domestic. (Lessons learned are sometimes expensive.)

After eight days in Christchurch we had been outfitted with our cold weather clothing, saw the local museums and were ready to go south. The flight in Navy C-130 aircraft took about eight hours. When we landed on the ice runway at McMurdo the outside temperature was minus 73degrees. Most of the billeting was in one large building that contained not only billeting but messing areas. We were living in three-man rooms and found out quickly that this would be a different experience.

The normal work day for all personnel assigned was 12 hours on and 12 hours off, seven days a week. The mission was to support the National Science Foundation in scientific efforts. Most of the folks were engaged in keeping the place running while the aircraft were tasked with resupply of all outlying camps with food, fuel, etc. We also were responsible for getting the sponsored scientific parties to the various areas they were required to go to conduct their scientific experiments. My controllers were responsible for providing ATC services and flight following for all of the American activities that occurred on the continent. In addition to the flight activity, the operations department was responsible for tracking all of the cargo both air and surface that arrived at McMurdo or departed from McMurdo to one of the outlying camps.

I had controllers on Williams Field, a site that would be used when the strength of the ice on the ice runway would not support logistic aircraft. I also had controllers manning the control tower/radar unit on the ice runway, at the Air Route Traffic Control Center (ARTCC) in McMurdo and the tower/radar facility at the South Pole. In addition, we were going to install navigational aids at Siple Station as well and conduct maintenance on the navigational aids at Byrd Station.

One of my primary responsibilities was to draft the weekly situation report message that tracked the activities of the command for the previous week. This was vitally important, as we had to make sure that each outlying site had sufficient fuel/food, etc., to assure survivability should adverse weather conditions inhibit resupply efforts.

The best way to describe the tour at Antarctica is to compare it to an organized camp out in cold weather conditions. Everyone worked extremely hard, but because of the isolation, there was plenty of time for pranks and everyone took maximum advantage of those opportunities.

After we had been on the ice for approximately one week, one of my roommates, a warrant officer photo mate called me into the room and asked me to take a look. He pulled a container out from under his bunk and displayed a gorilla suit. I said, "What in the hell is that?"

He said, "That is what we are going to have a lot of fun with." He indicated that he had bought the suit to entertain at parties and thought it would be a hoot to have something like that in Antarctica. He said, "The gorilla's name is Ralph. If you want to participate you can be Ralph's trainer." Sounded like a good deal to me so we began to plan for Ralph's coming-out party.

The first appearance was very brief. The next day the camp was abuzz with conversations about the gorilla sightings. The scientist was all excited about the possibility of a new form of life on the continent. The warrant officer's name was Dale Cramer. He had mastered all of the gestures of a gorilla and was exceptionally talented. Approximately two weeks later, Ralph made his formal appearance in the dining facility. This appearance brought the house down, and in a very short period of time Ralph became the unofficial mascot of the command.

Approximately two months into the deployment we ran in to difficulty in attempting to commission the new Tactical Air Navigation (TACAN) system at Siple station. My senior technician, Petty Officer Mason, who had served with me at Fallon, had performed all of the steps essential to commissioning a TACAN. We discussed the problems a number of times and could not figure out our next step. I suggested that he contact the chief engineer of the station and attempt to locate a set of blue prints for the station. He discovered that directly beneath the planned site for the TACAN was buried a sled loaded with expended Jet Assistant Take Off (JATO) containers. Once this was known, I remembered a similar problem that I had encountered at Dallas. I searched the cargo area and located a roll of chicken wire. I dispatched the wire to Siple on the next flight, petty officer Mason encircled the proposed site with this wire located at the proper height and our problems were solved. (The wire barrier cancelled out the magnetic influence of the sled and JATO bottles.)

One of the interesting things that occured during Operation Deep Freeze is the annual fund drive to support New Zealand Charities. The week between Christmas and New Years is designated as the time when a number of varied campaigns are held with all of the proceeds going to various charities in Christchurch. These contests include the election of a Snow King (Ralph won without opposition), and various sponsorships to do various events. Ralph and I earned $7,200.00 in sponsorship by climbing a mountain 548 foot high covered with snow drifts up to six feet deep. In addition, I had to carry Ralph's pet dog granite on this journey. Granite was a 56-pound rock.

The biggest money maker was an accident. My secretary, YN2 Valerie Russell worked in her off-duty time as a disc jockey on the Armed Forces Radio. She came up with the idea of having people call in requesting a song. The starting price was twenty-five cents. This song would be played until someone else sponsored another song. When this occurred the price would double. One of my controllers made the first call. His requested song was, "Take this Job and Shove It." After hearing this song about ten times the commanding officer called in to sponsor another song. Immediately after one play, my guy, supported by the entire division again sponsored the Shove It song. Once again the captain requested another song. This went on until the price began to be pretty steep. After a few hours, the captain had an all-officers meeting and requested that we all pitch in to have that song taken off the air. The give and take went on into the wee hours of the night. When Petty Officer Russell called it off, we had collected in excess of $10,000 for charity. Needless to say, almost everyone in the command was broke, but we turned in the highest amount of funds in the history of the event at the end of the week.

I was consistently amazed at the science that was being accomplished during our deployment. Some of the ideas were truly cutting edge. Each Sunday a scientist would schedule a briefing for all interested personnel and provide an overview of their particular project. I am totally convinced that we get approximately ten dollars worth of science for each dollar spent in Antarctica.

Another Ralph story worth sharing was the visit of the Chairman of the National Science Foundation. He arrived with his secretary on an afternoon flight. Naturally the captain had a formal dinner party scheduled in his honor. We had a lot of visiting VIPs and the dinners were a part of the process. Attendance to these functions was rotated among the officers of the command. As luck would have it, I was scheduled to attend this particular event. Before I left my room, Dale told me to stand by for a surprise. He had made arrangements with the stewards serving the dinner to keep the back door of the captain's quarters unlocked and to let him know when desert was being served.

After everyone had been served their dessert, the back door opened and in rushed this gorilla. You must understand that no one outside of the command was aware of Ralph's presence on the ice. This included the chairman of the National Science Foundation and most certainly his secretary. Ralph rushed over to the secretary, swept her up in his arms and rushed out the door into the snow. The secretary was screaming loudly, in fact, according to Dale, she wet her pants. The chairman was in shock, and the captain, unaware of the plan for Ralph to appear was watching his career being flushed down the tubes.

After about a one-hundred-yard dash, Ralph laid the secretary down in the snow and removed his mask. She began to do a fair job of cussing, but the chairman saw the humor in the situation and began to laugh. This proved to be a highlight of the deployment and even today, 29 years later, Ralph's photos are displayed throughout the headquarters of the National Science Foundation located near Washington, D.C.

Initially I had a difficult time in establishing credibility in the command. The captain, as well as senior officials of the National Science Foundation was very concerned that I had been assigned without the normal vetting process. Additionally, my one-year tour was very disturbing since they believed, with just cause, that the first year was used to familiarize personnel with the tempo of operations and the challenges one faced in Antarctica.

Finally, the captain called me into his office and asked me point blank if I was a Naval Investigative Official (NIS.) I said, "Captain you have my word as an officer and a gentleman that there is nothing covert about my assignment. I have some expertise in ATC equipment acquisition and have been sent down here on a short tour to assist the command in identifying the best long-term solutions to your equipment requirements." He accepted my explanation and after that things went extremely well.

The tour in Antarctica was not especially challenging technically, but the environment, isolation and primitive resources made the tour memorable. I was somewhat amazed at the cold weather clothing that was issued in comparison to that issued to personnel assigned to Adak and Kodiak. While the weather in Antarctica was by and large more demanding than that experienced in Alaska, the differences did not justify the insufficient cold weather gear issued to personnel in Alaska in comparison to that issued in Antarctica. Guess funding explains the difference.

One experience that justifies sharing is the annual Urine Bowl experience. Each New Year's Day a flag-football game is held between personnel assigned to the Crash/Fire Division and the ATC Division. The temperature was minus 20 degrees at kick off. We were dressed in terminal underwear and cut-off dungarees. We used spray paint to paint numbers on the various players. The exercise was a welcome change, and while I forget the exact score, I am sure that ATC won the game. While we were playing flag football the senior officers in the command were playing golf, using orange-painted golf balls. Once again, when placed in isolated locations, American sailors, regardless of rank or position will find some way to keep themselves entertained.

I was under orders to leave the command soon after returning from the Antarctic deployment and report to the Naval Air Station Whidbey Island ,Washington, as the air traffic control officer. This was a plum assignment, as Whidbey was one of the major Approach Control facilities in the Navy. I also had been informed that it was excellent duty, and I had visited the place one time when we were making our tour while I was in the Squadron. The family appeared excited, not only at the location but the fact that we would all be together again.

CHAPTER XVII

NAVAL AIR STATION
WHIDBEY ISLAND

Unlike previous transfers, we left Dallas as a family. For the first time, we were traveling in style as I had procured a new outfitted van to make the trip. Once again, I planned on a leisurely trip across country with the family. Our vehicle was state of the art, I had a little money, and we had time to stop and see the sights. Things were going pretty well. I had wife, three children and our sheep dog, all very comfortable, well fed, and satisfied. Our plans included a stop in Los Angeles to visit Disneyland, another stop near Point Loma, California, to visit friends that had been stationed with me in Antarctica and Kodiak, and a final planned stop with lots of side trips to visit friends in Northern California that had been stationed with us in Rota, Spain.

I should have known better. As we approached the Eastern border of Arizona my wife began to complain about hearing a clicking noise coming from the rear of the van. I assured her that this could not be happening as we had a new van with less than 4,000 miles on it. For the first time we were traveling in a vehicle that should make a long trip without any problems. After all, we had made cross country trips in vehicles that should have never left a driveway must less made a long trip. After ignoring her for approximately 150 miles I finally pulled off at the Mohawk rest stop. This is located approximately 60 miles east of Yuma. After the normal functions expected of a family of five plus one dog, I decided to put to rest the alleged noise. Since I did not have a clue on how to troubleshoot anything mechanical, I decided to lay down on the pavement and let her drive the van over me. (She really missed her chance here.) I did not have any idea of what to look for or what to do if I saw something, but at least I was taking some action. After protesting my idea she got in the van and drove over me. I could not see a thing but I did hear an ominous noise coming from the area near the rear left wheel. Now that we had proved that my wife was correct, what was the next step? At that time this was very isolated country. It was desert. Since I could not determine if this noise was serious or not I was concerned about leaving the protection of the rest stop where we had shade and water and breaking down before we reached some center of population.

At wits' end I walked to the home of the local ranger. His wife answered the door and invited me in. The ranger came to the front room and asked me if he could be of assistance. I briefly explained my problem. He said, "I don't know a lot about automobiles but I have a couple of friends that are mechanics. They have a small repair shop (read shack under a tree) nearby and I am sure that they would come out and take a look if I give them a call."

I said, "I would really appreciate it. How long do you think it will be before they arrive?"

He said, "should not take more than twenty minutes unless they are engaged in some repair work that they cannot break away from."

I thanked him for his help and went back to the van to break the "good news" to my family. Three hours later a rust bucket of a car appeared out of the desert. There were two guys in the vehicle, both at least half drunk. They approached the van, offered me a beer and asked if I was the guy that was having car trouble. I said, "Yes," and explained the noise and my concern about traveling on until I had someone look at the wheel. They got out of their car and asked me to drive the van around.

Immediately after the car began to roll, they signaled me to stop. They said, "you have a frozen bearing on the rear axle."

I said, "Will it hold together until I can get into Yuma?"

They said, "Maybe, maybe not. Wish we had brought a wheel puller. We can't really tell until we get that wheel pulled off."

I said, "How long will it take to get your wheel puller?"

They said, "Well it is back at the shop. Should be able to get there and back in about one hour."

I said, "well go and get it and let us take a look."

After they left, my wife said, "Don't you think we should contact a Chevrolet dealer before you let a couple of drunks mess with this van? After all, it is under warranty."

Since I had never owned a new car with the exception of the one we bought when I was transferred from Rota, I had not thought about a warranty or what action would invalidate a warranty. I said, "Hell of a good idea. I will see if I can make a phone call from the ranger's house if there is a dealer in

Yuma." I went to the ranger's house and asked to borrow a phone after ascertaining that Yuma did have a Chevrolet dealer.

When I contacted the dealer he said, "Do not let anyone other than an authorized mechanic from Chevrolet touch that car or your warranty will be invalidated."

I said, "Well, that is great, and what do I do now?" He asked me where I was and I told him.

He said, "The best I can do is dispatch a tow truck out to the rest stop. I cannot do that until tomorrow morning."

I said, "Okay, I will be here when you arrive."

I went back and broke the news to my family.

My wife said, "Well that is just great. You have two loonies running around the desert, probably drinking beer; we are in the middle of nowhere without anything to eat, and we have to spend the night in a place that Setting Bull would not camp at overnight."

I said, "Well, I will figure out something."

The first order of business was to figure out what to do with the mechanics. Since I had them running all over the desert in an attempt to give me a hand, I felt I owed them something for not only their expenses but for their time. When they got back, less sober than when they left, I told them about the warranty issue and apologized for wasting their time and asked them if $100.00 would be a fair amount for the trouble they had been through. (This was in 1978 and $100.00 was a lot of money but I was in a bind.) After talking it over, they agreed that the $100.00 was fair. I paid them off and they left in a cloud of dust. My next problem was what to do with the family. My luck must have been running good. Approximately 30 minutes after the mechanics left a small camper van pulled into the rest stop. The occupants were a chief petty officer and his wife returning to the West Coast after a two-week vacation. After becoming acquainted, I told him my sad story. He said, "Well, we are going by way of Yuma. If your wife and kids don't mind, I can put them in the camper and let them off at the first motel I come to in Yuma." I discussed this with my wife. She would have agreed to almost anything to get out of the desert and began to pack a single suitcase with overnight gear for her and the children. After they loaded up, I expressed my gratitude to the chief and his wife and me and the dog settled down for a long night.

The next morning about nine A.M. a tow truck showed up. We hooked up the van and began the long, slow trek to Yuma. As we entered town I noted the first motel I saw. Needless to say, this was not a five-star establishment.

152

When we got to the dealership, they inspected the van while I called the motel. Sure enough, that was where my family was staying, so at least we could get back together. In a few minutes the maintenance manager came in and informed me that the bearings were frozen on the rear axle and that it could not be repaired. He said he would have to order an axle from Phoenix; it would be delivered by bus and would not arrive for two days. After arrival, he felt he could complete repairs in about four hours.

I said, "Well, do what you have to do. Do you have a loaner that I can use until the repairs are completed?" He said, "No, but I can have someone drive you to the motel. When the repairs are completed, I will send someone to pick you up."

I said, "Okay," and with my tail between my legs went to the motel to get a ration of crap from everyone in the family except the dog.

Needless to say, all of the big plans we had made regarding Disneyland and comparable stops of interest were changed. Instead of a normal vacation, we spent the next three days in a flea-bag motel eating fast food. At least they had a pool in the motel so the children had some fun. I had a lot of ear pounding, but as normal, it was deserved.

Finally the car repairs were completed and we were able to salvage an afternoon visit with our friends in the Point Mugu area. They wanted us to spend the night, but I insisted on pushing on. I decided to give the family a thrill by taking the Pacific Coast Highway. While the scenery was beautiful, it soon got dark. This is a very winding highway. Without visual reference traveling on this winding highway led to five cases of car sickness, wife, three children and one dog. Needless to say by the time we reached Seattle, my popularity with the family including the dog was at an all-time low. In fact, my oldest daughter asked me if the Navy would allow me to go back to Antarctica.

I decided to finish the trip to Whidbey via the Mukilteo ferry departing from Everett to Whidbey Island. The kids began to perk up when we drove on the ferry. After crossing the sound we began the winding journey up the island to our final destination. The scenery was beautiful, but I had a vehicle full of exhausted traveling companions. Despite my best effort I could not generate any enthusiasm for our new home.

As we traveled through the small town of Oak Harbor my oldest daughter said, "I cannot believe you have brought us here to the end of the world." I could appreciate her point of view as comparing Oak Harbor to the Dallas/ Fort Worth area was a difficult stretch. We finally reached the main gate of our new home, Naval Air Station Whidbey Island. The base was a mix of old and new buildings, and the view from the top of the hill entering the main gate was breathtaking.

After checking in through the main gate I drove over to the BOQ and asked if they had temporary housing. They said, they had some rooms set aside for reporting officers and their families and had reserved some quarters for us. We all began to unpack the automobile and take our possessions into the quarters.

After getting the family settled down I went over the housing office to see what kind of wait we would have before we could move into government quarters. I had observed some quarters as we were entering the base and was not impressed. They said, "We do not have any waiting list. We have a four-bedroom house reserved for you in officers housing." This housing was located approximately eight miles from the main base in an area referred to as the old seaplane base. This was good news, as it relieved me from the chore of looking for civilian housing on a temporary basis and anything would beat what I had seen so far as housing was concerned. They even gave me the address of our new home and directions. I checked on our personal effects (house hold goods) and found out that they had arrived in Whidbey the day before we arrived. This meant that we could move in as soon as I could make arrangements for delivery.

I went back to the BOQ and broke the good news to my family. They were excited about the house and it was apparent that four hours after moving into temporary quarters, they were ready to leave.

The next morning I contacted the personal property office and made arrangements to have our household goods delivered the next day. After that, I proceeded to the Administrative office and picked up a check-in sheet to begin the process of officially checking into the base. Before I started that chore I went down to the Operations Department to stick my head into the ATC Division spaces. Much to my surprise I knew at least fifty percent of the personnel assigned. Many of them were retired Navy controllers that I had taught while assigned as an instructor.

After meeting the captain I went through the process of checking in and returned to the division to begin the turn-over process. The guy I was relieving was set to retire in three days so the turn over process would be fast and furious. I was impressed by the area of responsibility of the division, the traffic load worked, and the apparent experience and talent of the personnel assigned. I was somewhat disappointed about some of the procedures being used but I had learned in other assignments that most things are the way they are for a reason, and until I discovered why, it would be foolish to implement changes.

The night before the pending retirement of the guy I was to relieve a message was received canceling his retirement. I was not only shocked, I was dismayed. I had accepted orders to Whidbey with the understanding that I would be the boss, and there was no way I was willing to accept a position as an assistant. At six A.M. Whidbey time I was on the phone to Washington. The detailer explained to me that the retirement cancellation was beyond his control, but he assured me that within a week orders would be forth coming to transfer the individual to the San Diego area. With that news I relaxed and began the process of learning about the provision of ATC services at Whidbey, the strength and weakness of assigned personnel, and making contact with personnel outside the division that would be supporting our efforts for the next three years.

The next shock that occurred was being informed that a lieutenant commander aviator was graduating from the ATC officers course and would be checking into Whidbey as the ATC officer. Once again, something was happening that was not in the script. I called my detailer in Washington, and he was surprised at the news. He said, I do not know anything about this, and if I had I would have never sent you to Whidbey. I said, I will discuss this with the captain and attempt to find out what is going on.

I made an appointment with the skipper and asked for an explanation. He said, we did not have a relief for your predecessor and the admiral became concerned. He pulled some strings and sent one of his EA-6 pilots to ATC School without my knowledge. I finally sat down with your detailer and hand picked you for this assignment. I only found out about the admiral's actions after you had been ordered here for duty. He said, I cannot do anything about it but when he checks in I will inform him that I consider you as the ATC officer and will transfer him from the division to another job as soon as one becomes available. Until then, you will just have to live with the situation. Obviously, this was not what I wanted to hear, but you do as you are told. When he checked in, we had a long meeting and he agreed that I would run the division and would keep him informed. I agreed and began to make changes as warranted. Looking back, I believe the ATC division at Whidbey may have been the best division I was privileged to lead during my career. Technically they were exceptional. Some of the procedures were dated, but other than that, traffic flow was timely and safe. Some of the senior personnel were a little too laid back for my taste, but they were only following the examples set by their predecessors. We turned that around in a very short time, and frankly the division ran on auto pilot for most of the remainder of my tour.

The smooth-running operation at Whidbey gave me the opportunity to begin writing letters and messages to higher authority highlighting areas that I felt needed improvement. I had started this campaign while assigned to Rota as an enlisted man and had continued in subsequent duty stations when time permitted. Some of these letters were accepted and changes were made. Others were either ignored, or the rationale for disapproving my suggestions were provided.

These letters were submitted via the chain of command and some of the ideas caught the attention of higher authority. I received a call from a member of the staff of the commander of Naval Air Pacific Fleet (COMNAVAIRPAC) inviting me to attend, on his dollar, a Naval Air Traffic Control, Air Navigational Aid and Landing System (NAALS) conference to be held in Brunswick Maine. He indicated that this was normally a meeting of engineers and technical experts and felt that the operational community was not properly represented. I told him that I would be delighted to go as his representative if he could clear it with my captain. He said, "That has already been accomplished; your orders are in the mail."

After receiving my orders and the associated funding data, I ordered my tickets, made motel reservations, and drove to Seattle where I caught a flight to Portland, Maine. I had a friend, the ATC officer at Brunswick who had worked for me in Fallon, meet me at the airport and take me to the meeting site in Brunswick. After spending the night in the motel hosting the meeting I was the first to arrive at the conference room.

When the meeting began I was somewhat amazed at the attendance. I knew a lot of the attendees by name but the only individual I personally knew was my old adversary from the school command and Kodiak, now a master chief. I do not know how his promotion happened, but he was now assigned to the staff of the CNO in the office with oversight of ATC programs.

When the meeting began a lot of discussions were being conducted about ATC equipment, procedures, priorities, etc. What was disturbing to me was that all of these discussions were being led by engineers and technicians with little if any input from the operational community, i.e. controllers. I listened to this dialog during the morning hours of the first day and knew that I could not allow that to continue to happen. After all, the only reason I had wanted a commission was to be able to articulate the controller prospective on issues like those being discussed and I felt if I did not begin to stand up and be counted, not only was I letting my community down, I was not doing the job that COMNAVAIRPAC had funded me to do.

When the meeting reconvened, I interrupted the conversation by stating, "Folks, I have listened to your discussion, recommendations and decisions for a half day. I am somewhat amazed that this group is making operational decisions without the input of operators so effective immediately this crap will stop. I appreciate that I am only a lieutenant but I am the senior controller present, and you will either dismiss me from the meeting and explain your decision to my sponsor, COMNAVAIRPAC or you will take my input on every issue, including those issues you have already made decisions on. In addition, when I get back to Whidbey, in my trip report, I will explain that these operational decisions are being made by well-meaning but unqualified technical experts and that either meetings such as these will be cancelled or the membership of your organization will be expanded to include operators." The senior CNO representative (A civilian Employee) asked the master chief what he thought of this idea. Before he could respond, I said, "Perhaps you do not understand; a lieutenant is senior to a master chief. It is not important what the master chief thinks. Your choice is to either take my views into consideration or dismiss me from the meeting and take the repercussions for that action."

After that comment, a break was called and voting members of what was referred to as the NAALS council took place. After the vote was completed, the remainder of the attendees were recalled to the conference room and the chairman announced that membership of the NAALS council had been expanded to include members of the ATC operational community representing all upper echelons of the chain of command. I expressed my appreciation for their decision and said, "With that detail out of the way, let's get to work." (Looking back, that may have been the most important single thing I accomplished during my almost forty-year naval career. For the first time, operators had a say in how the community would be run. After that, if it was screwed up, it was at least partially our fault.)

When I got back to Whidbey, the word had spread about my actions. The community had the word and controllers at all commands ashore and afloat began to forward ideas and suggestions. Over night, we became a source of information. Additionally, instead of receiving equipment upgrades on a hit-or-miss fashion based on the ideas of someone, we were able to structure priorities that satisfied fleet requirements, not personal agendas.

One of the interesting things that occurred during my tour at Whidbey was the receipt of an invitation to attend an ATC symposium hosted by the facility in Lemoore. Symposiums were held on an annual basis and the host responsibilities were transferred from site to site on a voluntary basis. I had planned to attend this shindig because it was a golden opportunity to exchange information throughout the community and see old friends. What made this invitation so interesting was the announced guest speaker was the Air Minister from the Soviet Union. I could not believe that something as trivial as a symposium of Naval Air Traffic Controllers could entice such an important visitor; remember, this was around 1980, and relationships between the two countries was, to say the least, somewhat cold.

I contacted the facility officer at Lemoore and quizzed him about the validity of the guest speaker. His name was Tom McMahon, and he was a full commander, one of the leaders of the community. He swore to me that the invitation was legitimate. Based on his assurance I briefed my captain on the opportunity to see, first hand, a representative of the Soviet Union, one that had considerable influence on Soviet Aviation. He was excited about the opportunity and committed to go with me.

Shortly before we left Whidbey for Lemoore to attend the symposium I received a call from my skipper indicating that late-breaking developments would make it impossible for him to attend the symposium. He expressed his regrets and asked me to give him a full debrief when I returned. Disappointed, I hit the road for Lemoore.

Upon arrival I proceeded to the site for the symposium, met old friends, made some new ones and waited anxiously for the big night featuring the guest speaker to begin.

We had an excellent dinner and sat around waiting for the show to begin. The guest speaker came in and began to speak. His English was a bit rough but understandable. He began with a brief background on his personal role in Soviet Aviation, flashed a copy of Pravda featuring an article highlighting his accomplishments and then began a diatribe highly critical of the United States of America in general and the Navy in particular. You could have cut the tension with a knife. The crowd was becoming very unsettled. I noticed that one of the attendees had left their chair. He had worked for me in Fallon, was a bit of a hot head, and totally committed to the goals and ideals of America. I began to become concerned and spread the word to be on the look out for this guy.

A disturbance occurred at the entrance of the meeting room. I noted that my guy was being man-handled by four or five personnel. I rushed over to see what was going on. They had taken a pistol from him as he entered the room. His stated goal was to shoot the bastard that was insulting his country and his way of life. We finally got things settled down and the master of ceremonies introduced the guest speaker as an entertainment act from Las Vegas. One of the senior members of the ATC facility at Lemoore had caught his act and persuaded the facility officer to tender an invitation. I must say that his performance was convincing. In fact, if he had known just how convincing it was, he probably would have made that his last appearance. While I was relieved that nothing serious had happened, I was equally relieved that my captain had cancelled out his appearance, as I don't know how he would have taken the act when he was persuaded by me that it was the real thing.

Speaking of personal agendas, either I had one or the XO had one. I will admit that my agenda was driven by my desire to have the command in general and the Navy in particular, bestow the respect for limited duty officers (LDOs) and warrant officers (WOs) that had been present when I had first joined the Navy. Obviously, in our particular technical areas of expertise we were listened to, and most, if not all of our recommendations were followed. This level of respect did not spill over to the military side of the issue. It is true that our previous experience as enlisted personnel was considered when we were assigned station watches, but we were referred to as junior officers and given mundane assignments normally assigned to ensigns and/or lieutenant junior grade, folks fresh out of the Academy or flight training. I along with my peers took exception to this practice, and I made a vow that I would bring it to a head.

The opportunity to challenge the system was presented when the XO scheduled weekly junior-officer meetings in his conference room for each Wednesday at nine A.M. I persuaded all of the LDOs and WOs in the command not to attend and promised that I would take the heat if it backfired. Sure enough after the first scheduled meeting the XO made some calls and identified me as the culprit. He called my office and directed me to come to his office immediately. When I arrived, he said, "What in the hell are you doing leading a revolt against my JO meetings?"

I said, "XO, I believe that every JO in this command attended your meeting. LDOs and Warrants are not JOs. You discuss such things as career planning, relationships with wives and snotty noses and how to wipe them at these meetings. The LDOs and WOs are running divisions and departments. We don't have time for that kind of crap. If you want to have a meeting to determine how to solve problems or run this command in a more efficient fashion, we will be the first ones in the door."

He said, "I will discuss this with the skipper and get back to you." About one hour later, he called and said, "Effective immediately, the junior officer meetings was not mandatory for LDOs and Warrants."

Our next conflict occurred over zone inspections. I, as well as all of the officers assigned, LCDR and below, on a rotating basis drew assignment as zone inspection officers. While this was a pain in the butt, a good zone inspection program was an excellent tool for measuring the material condition of a command. I drew a zone that included the BOQ, recreation facilities, and the dog kennel. I spent about 3 ½ hours inspecting my zone and turned in approximately five written pages of discrepancies. Six weeks later I drew the same zone for inspection. I began the inspection at the BOQ and noted that all of the discrepancies I had reported on a previous inspection were still discrepancies. I continued through the zone and when completed I had a list identical to that I had turned in six weeks previously.

When I had completed the inspection I went to the XO's office and verified that in fact, follow-up on zone inspection discrepancies were a direct responsibility of the XO. I pointed out the lack of action and requested to see the captain to discuss the waste of time zone inspections if, in fact, nothing was being done to rectify the deficiencies. He asked me not to do that and promised that he would give greater attention to zone inspection reports. In subsequent inspections I noted that all previously reported discrepancies were rectified. (Did not make me a friend but did improve follow up)

Our last conflict was related to alcohol abuse education. I had a pretty good workload and was identified as the last officer in the command to attend this course of instruction. I received a terse note from the XO pointing out my lack of attention to detail and demanding that I attend the make-up class. While I was not looking forward to this one week of pain and agony I was smart enough to know what side of the bread was buttered so I changed my schedule to accommodate this course of instruction.

On the scheduled date I reported to the classroom for instruction. I was the only officer in the course but we had a large number of senior petty officers in attendance. On schedule, a door opened into the class room and a senior chief petty officer entered the room, introduced himself as the instructor for the class and began by stating his name and that he was an alcoholic. After a round of introductions, the instructor asked all personnel in attendance if they would acknowledge their feelings about hiring a recovering alcoholic to work in their particular work center. A number of hands were raised signifying that they would not object. The instructor then asked how many individuals in the class would not object to employing a practicing alcoholic in their work center. Again, a number of hands were raised. The instructor noted that I was the only one in the class that had not responded to either question. He pointed that out and asked me what my feelings on the issue were.

I replied, "Senior Chief, I need more choices. If you asked me those questions, but the third alternative would be that I hire an individual that had never had a drinking problem that would be my choice. Since you insisted that I focus on folks with a problem, I cannot hire those types of folks to supply ATC-related services." He considered my response for a couple of minutes then placed the class on a break. He asked me if I would remain for a brief conference. When the room cleared he said, "Lieutenant, I know you don't want to be here and frankly, you do not need to be here. If you will agree, I will log your attendance for the entire course of instruction and you can go back to doing what you are being paid to do." I felt that was the mature way to address the issue and thanked him for his consideration. Obviously the XO was briefed but I never heard anything about it.

I do not mean to imply that the relationship between me and the XO was a constant state of warfare. He was an excellent officer but not accustomed to working with LDOs and Warrants. He had an excellent mind, good leadership qualities ,and was a great administrator. His major fault, other than lack of respect for former enlisted personnel was his total lack of a sense of humor. I saw an opportunity to pull his chain and with the assistance of the skipper I set the trap.

At that time, priorities for receiving new equipment to support the ATC mission was for some reason made in alphabetical order. Since Whidbey started with a W, we were at the tail end of the pipeline, despite the fact that were either the first or second largest approach control facility in the Pacific Fleet. I received official notification that Whidbey was on the list to receive a new capability. The capability was the Automatic Terminal Information Service (ATIS). ATIS was designed to provide a communications relief for controllers at busy locations by recording the prevailing weather information. A pilot scheduled to land would tune in a preset frequency and listen to this recording. The pilot would notify the controller on initial contact that he had received this information thereby relieving the controller from repeating the information over control frequencies. The first two stations on the priority list were Adak and Agana Guam. I had been stationed at one of those locations and flown in and out of the other. I knew that the traffic at those locations was light and therefore controllers were desperate to have something to talk about. Automation of routine communications was not their highest priority.

Armed with this information, I drafted a memorandum to the skipper via the operations officer and the executive officer. I attached the priority list and reflected that since equipment priorities were made in alphabetical order, the only way Whidbey could get needed equipment in a timely fashion was to change the name of the command from NAS Whidbey to NAS Aardvark. The operations officer was cut in on the prank, and he forwarded the memorandum to the skipper recommending approval. When the XO received the memorandum he spent at least ½ of a day justifying the reason for his disapproval. He pointed out the expense of changing the letter head on official command stationary, the cost to change all of the charts and publications, updating command briefs and the public affairs effort required to make everyone aware of the name change. When the captain received the memorandum including the endorsements he called me, the operations officer, and the XO into his office for a discussion. He played the game out by being the devil's advocate on the XO's position. The longer he talked, the more frustrated the XO became. Finally, before the XO broke down in tears, the captain said, "XO, we are pulling your leg. Have a nice laugh and get back to work." (I really don't think the XO forgave me for this stunt but the skipper liked it a lot.)

Despite my conflicts with the XO, things were going well in the division. Controllers were being trained, service was being provided, personnel were being promoted and morale was at an all time high. The ATC division was selected as the outstanding ATC Facility in the Navy by the Rotating Beacon Association. My family and I had moved from base quarters to a beautiful rental home adjacent to Deception Pass.

Just remember, when things are going well, stand by for a ram. This ram came when I was assigned command duty officer duty (CDO) on a Sunday. I had a deal with the senior watch officer that I would stand CDO watches on the weekend, preferably on Sundays. This would allow me to perform my normal duties during the week without interruption. This agreement was normally beneficial to all but I had second thoughts after that particular Sunday.

I relieved the watch at approximately 7:15 A.M. At approximately 7:45 Mt. St. Helen erupted. Whidbey is slightly northwest of Mt. St. Helens, but the initial reports indicated that we would be in for some serious damage as the result of fallout. I immediately attempted to contact the CO or XO. Since it was a Sunday morning, they were not at home, so I had the responsibility of getting the base in shape to ride out the storm. My first concern was the security of the water supply. Next was to get all of the aircraft either undercover in hangars or some type of coverage over the jet intakes. I did not have a lot of personnel resources to get this job done but the ones I had performed yeoman-like service.

Not long after the initial eruption I was notified that Whidbey would escape most if not all of the damage because of favorable wind conditions. That information led to Whidbey being the fly-away location for all of the military aircraft and a significant number of civilian aircraft in the Pacific Northwest. This information led to more problems, i.e., food and billeting for all of these transient personnel. We put all available personnel to work by opening closed berthing facilities, recalling all off-duty cooks, mess cooks, etc.

After a twenty-hour day I went in to brief the CO/XO on the day's events. I started by telling them that we did not have a station instruction detailing actions to be taken in the event the top of a mountain blew. The CO said, "Well, when you finish your log entries we will have one. Good job; go home and get some rest." I told him that everyone had done an exceptional job and staggered out of his office and home to a well-earned rest.

One of the major events of my life occurred while we were stationed at Whidbey. I received a call from my sister-in-law in Louisiana informing me that my mother had passed away. I cannot explain the impact this news had on me. She was a saint, my personal hero, and the one individual in my life that had made the biggest impact. When I was very young, my father was off fighting World War II. She and I had some tuff times but she was always there. When my father and I had disagreements, which occurred infrequently, despite the circumstances, she always took my side. She never had material possessions but she had a deep faith, a strong character, unbelievable strength, and most of all, she believed that the sun rose and set in her son. I would have gladly taken a bullet in her defense, and would have given up an arm and leg before disappointing her. She was the motivation for any success I might have achieved. I wanted to become someone for my mom.

I immediately made arrangements to fly to Louisiana and assist my sister in making funeral arrangements. I knew we had to have two funerals since most of the folks in our hometown viewed her as a saint as I did while North Louisiana where most of the relatives were had to be the place where, along with my dad, she would be buried.

When I got home, I was relieved and delighted that my sister had the arrangements well under way. Our hometown had a population of 800 folks and two funeral homes. Rather than fight between the two organizations they agreed to jointly handle the arrangements at no cost to the family. In addition, the hamburger joint (Panther Den) that she had run for so many years was being demolished. When the contractor was informed of my mom's death, he stopped work and said, work would not commence until she had been laid to rest

The funeral was an event. Next to a football game, this may have been the largest crowd ever gathered in this small town. The caravan from the church to the graveyard in North Louisiana numbered approximately 100 cars. It was obvious that not only had Judy and I lost a mother, the town had lost a pillar of the community.

After the burial service, I returned to our hometown and with Judy's assistance began to wrap up her details. Because of the lack of organization when my Father died, Mom was determined that her affairs would be in order. She had every thing logged in a dog-eared spiral notebook. I went around settling affairs, receiving condolences at every stop. I held up pretty well until I got to the little branch bank. This bank was housed in a house trailer in the center of town. I had not noted the contents of the bank book. When I handed it to the teller she checked the account number and said, "O, this was Mrs. Calhoun's 'Going to Whidbey' account."

Mom had never flown. I had begged her to come visit us. She promised me when we left for Whidbey that she would overcome her fears and make the trip. This little account with a value of $117.29 was her attempt to live up to her promise. I can tell you that I broke down and cried like a baby. In fact, as I write this, I am once again remembering my hero. I just had to share this with all of you.

I have avoided this subject thus far but now it is time to introduce air shows. Because of the position held by the Air Traffic Control Facility officer one of the collateral jobs that comes with the position is the coordinator for air shows. Air shows are routinely held on an annual basis at the majority of the major aviation shore commands in the Navy and Marine Corps. The purpose of the air show is to gain publicity for the Navy on a local and national level, enhance recruiting and provide a positive benefit to the morale of active duty personnel and their dependents.

The commanding officer at Whidbey had been the previous skipper of the Blue Angel commander. On a very short notice an air show featuring the

Blues in the Pacific Northwest was cancelled. The Navy has a long-standing commitment to conduct an air show in the Seattle area, so the Angles were already in the area. As a favor to his old boss the skipper of the Blues contacted my skipper and said, "If you can have an air show put together by next weekend, we will appear." The blues had not made an appearance in Whidbey in a number of years, so my skipper was excited about this opportunity.

He called me and said, "Can you put together an air show for weekend after next?"

Obviously he knew the level of detail required to plan and host an air show, but it was important so I said, "I will give it a try."

When I got back to the division I put all hands not actually on watch contacting various organizations that historically participate in air shows. We offered them the opportunity to be a part of a show featuring the Blue Angels. I called all of the local fleet activities and some of the fleet organizations that hosted aircraft not available at Whidbey. Considering the short-fused nature of the request, I was totally amazed at the positive response. I had units from all of the services volunteering to participate as static displays. (Whidbey is a nice place to visit.) I had flying fleet units participating. This was desirable as it was extremely important to me as well as the captain that we were able to provide a show for the dependents that reflected what their husbands and wives actually did while deployed.

Supporting the performance of the A-6 aircraft was fairly simple. We just buried some explosives in the ground between the runway and parallel taxiway and when a flight of A-6s flew over the area, we electronically detonated the explosives and simulated a bomb drop. The EA-6B was a different story. This aircraft does not drop bombs or shoot bullets. It is essentially an electronic warfare aircraft that jams enemy radio and radar signals. How were we going to demonstrate this capability? I discussed the issue with a chief from the Ordnance Division and he came up with a solution. We found old radar setting in a salvage yard. We relocated the radar behind a small hill adjacent to the runway environment and set a charge in the antenna. In addition to jamming radar signals, the EA-6 is armed with missiles that not only identify hostile sites, they destroy them.

During the air show I was acting as the moderator. When the EA-6 aircraft approached the center point of the air show I gave a signal and the explosive in the antenna went off like clockwork. Everyone was wondering how we would be able to demonstrate what the EA-6 actually did. When the explosion occurred the crowd, especially those representing the EA-6 community, went wild. This would have been the crowning event if not for a scheme I set up in the static display area.

This was at a time when discussions about stealth were essentially the rumor of the day within the Department of Defense. Some were proponents of stealth-type paint while others believed that a total redesign of aircraft using composite components was necessary if the desired level of stealth was to be realized. With this in mind, I had some folks assist me in developing a scam. We recorded the noise generated by an F-14 Tomcat taxiing into the parking ramp from the taxiway. I got a couple of personnel to weld some tie, down chains together to reflect tension. We reserved a parking place for this Tomcat in the center of the static display area.

Just prior to the start of the air show I announced that there might be a slight delay because of a late arriving stealth aircraft. I stated that the interest in this technology justified any delay to give all concerned the opportunity to observe this technology. After the announcement, I reported that the aircraft had just landed and turned the recording on. The crowd could hear but not see the aircraft. I had the flight line personnel rush to the designated parking area, give ground signals as appropriate to guide the pilot to his parking area. They had the chains and chocks with their ground-handling equipment. After the signal to shut down engines these folks rushed to pre-marked positions on the ramp and appeared to tie this aircraft down. When they left the area, the chocks and vertical tie-down chains marked the spot where the aircraft was parked.

I was splitting a gut to keep from laughing. People were approaching the parking area. Some were saying "I cannot see any thing; this stealth crap is really good." Others were saying, "Not so good, I can make out the outline of an aircraft." No one thought about the fact that the background was visible. No one thought about the fact that while an aircraft might be stealth, no one had solved the stealth pilot issue.

Finally, the captain walked up to me and said, "This is bullshit isn't it?"

I said, "Yes, sir, but it sure is entertaining a lot of folks."

He said, "You are a complete nut. Good job."

Bottom line, the air show went off without a hitch. The Blue Angels performed superbly. Fleet units more than met expectations. The show was the talk of the town for the next few weeks. There was a lot of speculation about the stealth aircraft but no one actually identified it as a hoax.

While things were going well at Whidbey and in fact, throughout the Naval ATC community, on a national scale that was not the case. The civilian controllers union, Professional Air Traffic Control Organization (PATCO) had made a decision that they would challenge President Ronald Reagan over salary hikes and benefits. The president essentially called their bluff and gave them something like forty-eight hours to return to work or lose their jobs. The union felt and persuaded their membership that the ATC system could not function without them so they stayed on strike. What the union did not know was that the Administration had developed contingency plans in the event of a strike. This plan was centered on the augmentation of the FAA work force that did not strike with military controllers. I had identified five controllers from Whidbey that would be assigned to the FAA if the strike did occur. Throughout the military in all services similar actions were taken. When the controllers did not come back to work the augmentation of their work force with military controllers did occur. After a brief slow-down period, the ATC system began to function to an acceptable level. (To be fair, the PACTO position as advertised in the media was more about the lack of supervision and upward mobility than about benefits and salaries, but union leadership underestimated the will of a president and the talent of non-strikers and military augmentation. As the result of this miscalculation a lot of careers of very good people were destroyed.)

Because of my actions at the NAALS conference in Brunswick and the revitalization of the community as the result, I had become well known in the community. As the result, a tentative decision was made, predicated on my being selected and promoted to lieutenant commander that I would be assigned to the staff of CNO to work on ATC-related matters. Board results reflected that I had been selected for promotion but at that time no vacancies were available for me to fill. Instead, I would be assigned to a troubled ATC facility at Lemoore, California, with instructions to fix the problems and essentially stand by for a vacancy on the CNO staff.

My family was very happy in Whidbey. They did not look forward to moving to what my wife referred to as that God-forsaken place in California. I understood her concerns but I saw Lemoore as a challenge, since the base had been designed to support extremely high levels of air traffic but since commissioning, the goals had not been met.

We left Whidbey with mixed feelings. It was a model command, the division was exceptional. We had made friends thorough out the community that would last for a lifetime. The division threw a beach party in honor of our departure. Despite the fact the roasted pig did not get thoroughly cooked, a good time was had by all. It remains one of the fond memories of my career.

CHAPTER XVIII

NAVAL AIR STATION
LEMOORE, CALIFORNIA

The trip from Whidbey to Lemoore proved to be uneventful, uneventful that is if you overlook the shock to my family of leaving the beautiful, green, cool climate of Washington, Oregon, and northern California and entering the desert like climate of central California. You also have to overlook the frozen wheel bearing on a small trailer I was pulling, the shock of seeing grapes drying on sheets of brown paper lying between rows of grapevines, and the refusal of my wife to enter the base because she thought it looked like a concentration camp. (I chased her for about eight miles before I could get her to come to a stop and turn around.)

Finally we entered the base and signed up to live in the Navy Lodge motel until I could either identify on-base quarters or find a place to live off base. Again, the family was not happy. I immediately went to base housing and found out that there was a six-month waiting list for housing. I went back, picked up my wife and we went to the big town of Lemoore. At that time the town of Lemoore was difficult to describe. I am sure that if it had been paradise my wife would not have been pleased, as she really did not want to leave the Pacific Northwest. We did find a house that was sufficient for our needs. It was in a sad state of repair but the property manager informed me that if we were willing to do the work, primarily clean and paint, the owner would pay for materials. I agreed to that, and since I had a couple of weeks before I had to check in for duty I knew we had time to get the place looking shipshape.

Our household goods arrived, and my wife and family began to turn a house into a home, a feat they had achieved countless times before. I focused on cleaning and painting the outside of the dwelling, ably assisted by my son. I took one day off and went to the base to let the leadership in the division know that I was in the area and would be checking in a few days. I was pleasantly surprised to find out that a number of assigned personnel were either previous students of mine or had worked for/with me at previous duty stations. I requested that a get-acquainted meeting be scheduled to begin at eight A.M. on the day I checked in. After spending a few minutes shooting the breeze with old acquaintances I went back to our house, picked up my paint brush and continued with the facelift on the house.

I arrived on base at 6:30 A.M. and proceeded to the air-operations building. In addition to housing the control tower and radar room, this building was the administrative headquarters for the entire operations department with the exception of the aircraft maintenance division. After approximately one hour of shooting the breeze and receiving an informal briefing of the status of the division I was ready to meet my troops. I essentially introduced myself and shared with them my philosophy, goals, and expectations.

After the all-hands meeting I met with the senior leadership of the division and received a thorough briefing. Frankly, I was shocked. The division had 102 enlisted personnel and eight civilian controllers assigned. Of this number only nine personnel were fully qualified, eight civilians and one active-duty personnel. This did not make sense. I asked the leading chief, an individual who had been a non-rated man in my first squadron, if he could explain. He said, "Well, about five years ago we had a captain who did not like civilian controllers. He came down here and essentially told them that one of his goals was to eliminate the civilian jobs. The civilian controllers took this to heart and essentially have refused to qualify active duty personnel. I believe that is a job-security action, but as you know, you have to be qualified to qualify someone, and we only have an E-6 that is fully qualified."

I said, "Give me a roster of the civilian controllers." He provided the information and I noted one name that had been stationed with both the leading chief and me in our first squadron. I asked the leading chief to have the individual report to my office. When he arrived, we renewed acquaintances and I told him that I needed his help. I explained the situation and told him that it was a Navy approach control and we must have qualified Navy personnel.

He said, "What about our jobs?"

I told him that no one qualified would have their job cancelled as long as they were performing up to standards. I identified that one of those standards was becoming active and aggressive in the training of Navy personnel. I also asked him the name of the Navy individual that was the closest to being qualified. He named one of the chief petty officers.

I said, "Effective immediately, your job is to qualify that chief. You have three weeks to do so. At the end of three weeks he will be qualified or terminated. If he is terminated we will start on the next-best qualified. If qualified, he will immediately be designated as the training chief responsible for the training and certification of all personnel assigned."

He said, "Because of our long-term relationship and your reputation, I will take this for action." I told him that I appreciated his confidence and dismissed him from the office.

My next stop was to make my official call on the commanding officer. I had 30 minutes scheduled. His first comment after welcoming me aboard was to ask me why in the hell I wanted to be in Lemoore. I told him that I had always been curious about the inability of the command to provide the level of service one could expect from a location designed to support massive numbers of aircraft. I also said, "Based on brief discussions with senior leadership in the division I believe I have at least some of the answers." He responded by calling his secretary and canceling all of his remaining appointments for that day. After that, he said, "What have you found out?"

I said, "Well, first of all, we do things ass backwards here. The wing has dictated that departures have priority over arrivals, you have entry points that conflict with visual recognition for pilot to pilot identification, and perhaps most of all, the weather conditions here are Visual Flight Rules (VFR) for nine months per year, then the fog rolls in and no one can see anything for three months. No one demands that pilots exercise Instrument Flight Rules (IFR) procedures for nine months, and then one day, the visibility and ceiling is zero and no one, pilots or controllers have a clue of how to work traffic."

The captain explained the justification for some of the procedures, but I was able to persuade him that his justification was crap. He finally said, "Change as you see fit, and I will fight the battle with the wing. What are you going to do about the VFR/IFR?"

I said, "I am going to request that the wing identify a different squadron each week to be the duty whore. By that I mean that for the designated period, all flight activity by that squadron will be fully IFR regardless of the weather. That will not only keep the cutting edge on my controllers, it will, after the rotation is completed bring the skill of IFR flying back into the cockpit."

He said, "Glad to have you aboard. Get on with it and let me know if you need assistance."

I returned to the division, sat down with my senior leadership, and we modified the course rules and procedures to comply with the information I had given to the captain. I left for home at the end of the day and was very well satisfied with what I had accomplished.

The next morning when I arrived at work the leading chief informed me the FAA had gone on strike and Lemoore had been tasked to provide eight controllers for augmentation. I asked him to get with the branch chiefs and section leaders and identify the folks we could spare. I told him that I did not want to send our very best, but I did not want to send shit birds either, as our reputation was riding on their performance.

About two hours after we had identified the augmentation personnel I was informed that the chief controller at Fresno had offered jobs to five of the eight civilian controllers we had at Lemoore. Four of those had accepted. (Lemoore-qualified controllers would be qualified at Fresno since the airspace was identical.) I said, "Okay, give me a list of the FAA controllers assigned to Fresno." I read the list and saw the name of an individual who had been stationed with me in Rota. I called him and asked if he was happy with what was happening in Fresno in particular, and the FAA in general.

He said, "No, but what choice do I have?"

I said, "Are you qualified to control traffic here at Lemoore?"

He said, "Yes."

I said, "Do you have any other FAA controllers that are qualified to work Lemoore traffic and are unhappy with the current situation?"

He said, "Yes."

I said, "Use your judgment and identify to me three controllers not including yourself that would be willing to leave the FAA and come to Lemoore and work for me."

He said, "Will do."

About two hours later he called with the names and qualifications of the personnel I had requested. I contacted civilian personnel, explained what I wanted to do, obtained permission, and hired those four folks. Once that was completed I called the chief controller at Fresno, explained what I had done and told him we could either call a halt on personnel raids or continue until I had replaced all eight of my civilian controllers with eight of his. He agreed with me that this would be foolish, so the war was over.

Things were going pretty good in the division. The new procedures had been implemented, and the runway acceptance rate increased dramatically. The rotating squadron concept had improved the operational readiness of squadron pilots and my controllers. Things were looking up. I had modified the watch bill to have a three-section watch bill rather than four, with the fourth section working from midnight to eight A.M. on the approach-control trainer. The civilian controllers were aggressively training their active-duty contemporizes and the training pipeline was beginning to show positive results.

One of the more interesting developments that occurred during my tour of duty at Lemoore had to do with my concern about drug use by personnel in the division. I attribute this high level of concern to the experiences I had encountered with my controller workforce in Adak. The division in Lemoore was comprised of one hundred and eight personnel. The ages of these folks ranged from seventeen to fifty-five. I was very concerned that at least some of these folks were at least casual users and wanted to make my point that such use would not be tolerated.

In today's environment, I probably would be relieved for cause should I pull this stunt in the politically correct era, but it worked very well for me in the early 1980s. I wanted to send a signal that would make a lasting impression, especially on the younger members of the division. To this end, I requested that the helicopter pilots during their routine training mission locate and bring me a dried skull from a dead cow.

About one week after my initial request a helicopter crewman came to my office with a skull in tow. He looked at me a little bit funny but said, "Commander, my pilot in command asked me to deliver this to you." I told him how much I appreciated it and to pass on my appreciation to the pilot. I took the skull home with me that night and painted it bright red. On the forehead of the skull I stenciled the words "EX AIR CONTROLLER DRUG USER."

The next morning after consultation with my leading chief, we hung the skull on the wall in a prominent position in my office. I asked the master chief to arrange for each member of the division, E-5 and below to be called into my office sometimes within the next two days. Since he was as old as me, remember we had been young petty officers in the same squadron he attacked this chore with enthusiasm. He took great delight in escorting these young folks into my office and placed them at attention in front of my desk. I would pretend to be occupied with paper work and allow them to stand there for a period of time before recognizing their presence.

When I did acknowledge their presence I would give them the order to execute a left face. When the movement was completed they would be approximately three feet from the skull with the message being silently transmitted loud and clear. I am proud to report that we did not have one incidence of drug abuse in the division during my tour at Lemoore.

In retrospect it seems that I had to pull some type of scam at every duty station. Lemoore was no exception. The lounge furniture in the break room of the Radar facility was a disgrace. This furniture was long overdue for the dump. The material condition featured torn upholstery, dirt beyond repair, missing legs, scared surfaces on the wooden furniture, etc. I approached the supply officer and asked him for some assistance. I knew he had a warehouse somewhere on the base loaded with excess furniture. He said, "Well, I do have some stuff but I have to keep it in the event of an emergency." I tried to persuade him that my situation was an emergency, but my plea fell on deaf ears.

Lemoore is actually two bases. The administrative part of the base along with base housing, supply, public works, security, etc., is located adjacent to the main gate while the operational side of the base is approximately six to eight miles away. This isolation kept us out of the direct oversight of the skipper thus the operations officer was essentially a separate command.

I received a call from the captain's secretary informing me that the skipper was hosting a visiting group of civic leaders to discuss noise abatement issues. Since we were the cause of that noise he felt it appropriate to have the meeting in my office followed by a tour for the visitors to the radar room, control tower and flight line. I saw this as a golden opportunity. At the end of the working day preceding the scheduled meeting, I directed my folks to take the furniture from my office to the radar ready room and bring that furniture down to my office.

The next day when the captain and his visitors entered my office I could see the shock on the captain's face. He apologized for the facilities and indicated that this was a sign of a declining budget. After the meeting he called me aside and said, "This furniture is a disgrace and should be carried to the dump." I agreed with him and told him that I had approached supply for replacement furniture but was informed that we had a limited supply and it was being saved for emergencies. He said, "This is a fucking emergency." With that, he picked up the phone, called the supply officer and directed him to send a working party to pick up the furniture in operations, take it to the dump and replace it with something reflective of the importance of operations to the mission of his command.

Approximately two hours later a flat bed loaded with furniture and a working party appeared in the parking lot. The furniture from my office was replaced with new stuff. After they left the area, I had my folks take the furniture to the break room and return my original furniture to the office. The next time I saw the supply officer he said, "You should have made a better case. I looked over that junk my folks picked up from your office and it was indeed ready for the trash pile." (I swore all of the members of the division to silence.) I suspect the skipper would have had a cow if he had known.

When I arrived at work the next day I was informed that I had received a call from the Bureau of Naval Personnel. The purpose of the call was to inform me that I had been selected to be a member of the selection board for limited duty and warrant officers. I was very pleased to have this opportunity as I had always been curious about the selection process. I informed my wife that I would be going to Washington for six weeks of temporary duty. Needless to say, she was not pleased with the news.

I made arrangements to fly to the D.C. area and caught a flight from Fresno. I arrived very late in the evening and since I had never been in that area I was at a bit of a loss. My orders indicated that quarters had been arranged at a motel on Columbia Pike. I did not have a clue of where that was located but thankfully found a cab driver who did know. I arrived at the motel, checked into my room and immediately went to bed.

The next morning I met some of the folks who would be serving on the board with me. As a group we proceeded to the Naval Annex for a briefing on the board process. This was quite a group. All of were excited to be a part of the process. When we arrived we were escorted to a conference room. The limited officer detailer, a classmate of mine in knife-and-fork school, gave us a briefing on what to expect, the hours we would be working, and the board process. When he completed this in brief he said, "In addition to your board duties, I have been tasked to task some of you to assist in structuring an organizational chart for your particular community. The justification for this tasking is the fact that the Navy was building to a 600-ship force and the existing organizational structure would not accommodate such growth."

I viewed this as a golden opportunity to finally organize the ATC community in a structure that would not only best support fleet requirements but would place an ATC expert on the staff of every major staff in the aviation shore community. The organizational structure that I submitted was implemented and remains essentially in place today, 23 years after implementation.

The selection board was one of the most memorable events of my career. I am convinced that the selection process of the Navy is head and shoulders above that of any other service. I was totally blown away by the quality of the candidates, the meticulous process of assessing individual records and the commitment and dedication of the board members. This was not a boondoggle. The first couple of weeks we worked six days a week, 12 hours per day. Every record was screened at least twice by different reviewers. I believe all of us had the same thought: *How in the hell did I get selected for promotion from this process?*

On Friday afternoon of the third week, the president of the board announced that we had worked hard, were ahead of schedule and therefore he was securing us for the afternoon and for the weekend. Some of the board members decided to go into D.C. Since I thought we were in D.C. I elected to go to the Pentagon and meet with the folks that I would be working for/with when/if I were assigned there for duty as promised.

I arrived at the Pentagon and called the office. An escort was sent to accompany me to the work center. I am fairly sure that if they had not have provided an escort, I would have never found the place. My first impression was, *This is a big building.* My second impression was that working conditions in that place were horrible. Back at Lemoore as well at all of my duty stations since I had obtained a commission I had a private office. In the Pentagon I was junior to everyone in the organization except for the master chief, and all personnel assigned, with the exception of the branch head shared a common office separated by artificial walls forming cubicles.

After becoming acquainted with the folks in the office I was directed to the branch heads' office for what turned out to be an interview. After initial introductions he said, "I understand that you are interested in coming here for duty."

I said, "Yes, sir, and I just finished a restructure of the ATC community organization and established an O-6 billet on your staff. I know that you know that there are no LDOs 0-6s but we do have a few 0-5s and the detailer can fill billets with individuals either one pay grade below or above the billet requirement."

He said, "Well, you are a 0-4 but by all accounts you are the best qualified to fill the job if I decide to bring an LDOS into this office. Why, in your opinion should I do that?"

I said, "Well, captain, this is the sponsor for the ATC community. The office is responsible for training, equipping and manning the Navy and Marine Corps. Since every platform sponsor in the organization is represented by a member of that platform, it seems logical that the ATC community should have the same representation."

He said, "That makes sense. I will let you know what I decide."

I left the office not knowing if I had made a good or bad impression, but at least I had given it my best shot. We finished the board action approximately two weeks later, and all departed back to our home duty stations. After that first board experience I was honored to be on approximately fifteen more selection boards. The lessons learned from that first board and my insider knowledge of the selection process not only served me well throughout my career it gave me a heightened appreciation of the thoroughness and fairness of the selection process.

I returned to Lemoore and observed that the department and division was performing well. Shortly after my return, the captain called me up and informed me that I was the Master Chairman for the annual air show. He said, "The air show is a big deal here because of the isolation of the command, and you will have to relocate to an office adjacent to mine to organize the air show under my direct supervision."

I said, "Captain I was sent here to revitalize the ATC division and assist you in running a top notch department. I have organized many air shows during my career, and you have a staff that has put on a number of shows here. I would like to meet with them, discuss the process, get their ideas and historical records, and then decide if I need to be next to you or if we can depend on those folks to put on this show."

He said, "Well, for the last five years the coordinator has been up here, and I think things have gone well."

I said, "Again, I am sure that will work, but I would like to try it my way. If I screw it up, you can have my butt; if not then the staff will have proven that they can do the job without close supervision."

He agreed to give it a try. We had a lot of good people working the air show coordination. We were able to get a lot of good acts for the show, but for some reason the fleet, other than Lemoore-based units were not favorably responding to our request for assistance.

We had a commanders' conference on the base, and all of the aviation flags on the West Coast were in attendance. Obviously this was way above my pay grade. I received a call from the captain's secretary informing me that the skipper desired my presence in the officers club after normal working hours that day. Naturally I showed up. When I entered the bar area, the first person I saw was the flag from Whidbey. We renewed acquaintances and then I spotted the skipper talking to a three-star at the bar. I approached, and when he noticed, the captain said, "Vice Admiral Schultz, I would like to introduce you to my operations/ATC officer. He is a hard charger with a

176

bright future. I have tasked him with over all oversight of my air show and by all accounts things are going well."

Admiral Schultz acknowledged the introduction and said, "I have heard good things about you from a number of folks. If you have any difficulties in getting participation for the air show, call my chief of staff and we will intervene."

I said, "Well, now that you mention it, Admiral, we are having difficulty in getting fleet participation. When I follow up, I am informed that the decision not to participate is your decision and frankly, based on your reputation, I do not understand."

He said, "That is a bunch of crap. I know the value of air shows and someone is speaking for me. Resubmit your request. I am sure you will get a different answer."

I told him I appreciated his interest and began to leave.

He said, "By the way, I was informed that you will be transferred to Washington. So will I, and I believe you will be on my staff when we both report for duty."

I said, "I am looking forward to it, Admiral, and beat feet."

The following Monday the selection board results were released and my captain was promoted to commodore. We were all delighted with the news, as our skipper was first rate. It did present a slight problem as his transfer was two weeks before the scheduled air show

When his relief arrived I was one of the first officers he interviewed. He was concerned about the air show. I told him, not to worry, briefed him on the participants and schedule of events. He said, "Looks as if you have everything under control. Keep up the good work and let me know if I need to get involved in anything."

The day of the air show, I was on the flight line at the crack of dawn. We had a big day scheduled, and I did not want anything to go wrong. About ten A.M. I sighted a small LTV pickup driving around the ramp. I rushed over and stopped the vehicle. Much to my surprise a national hero jumped out of the vehicle and rushed over to introduce himself. I was honored to meet him. (I will not reveal his name for fear of being sued.) He said, "I just found out about the air show and was wondering if I could set up a stand and sell autographed copies of my novel." There was no way I could refuse this request so I began to attempt to find a site he could use. We finally settled down on a site that satisfied him.

He opened up the back of the little camper and out crawled two long-legged, blond-headed home wreckers. He said, "These are my assistants." I swallowed hard and assisted the ladies in unloading the camper and setting up tables, chairs, etc. In the middle of this activity I noticed the captain approaching. I immediately grabbed the visitor and took him over the captain for an introduction. He was delighted to meet a real national hero. I left them for a private conversation. I noted that the captain had a puzzled look on his face. The visitor left the captain and came back to sign some books.

I said, "Skipper, what is wrong?"

He said, "He asked me if he could berth himself and his assistants in the BOQ for the night. Since the air show is a two-day event, he needs a place to stay, and all of the motels in the immediate area are full."

I thought long and hard about this request, and my gut feeling was to recommend that this request be denied.

The captain said, "Well, you have to tell him, and if he pitches a fit, we will have to allow him and his assistants to stay."

I said, "Yes, sir, I will handle it." With that, I went over and informed our distinguished visitor that while we would love to have him and his assistants as our guests, the large number of transient pilots participating in the air show had exhausted our capacity.

He said, "I understand, but I had to try." (If you can read between the lines, his goal was to have his assistants provide some entertainment for a fee.) Think I saved the skipper's butt on that one. Guess it was worth it, as he retired as a three-star admiral about ten years later.)

One more air show story. I realize that what I am going to say is somewhat sacrilegious for a sailor to share about the Marine Corps. Despite the risk, the truth must prevail. In my opinion, based on forty years of experience and close observation, no organization, club, party, or click can compete with the Marine Corps in developing a team. A gunny can stick his head in a bar and call out the first eleven Marines he sees. He then can develop those men into a championship football team. The same can be said about anything from raising funds from a charity event to kicking the bad guy's asses in combat. I have always been in awe, and to be brutally honest, jealous about this ability. Despite my best efforts, I could come close, but I never developed this talent that seems to be ingrained in a Marine.

One of the events at the Lemoore air show was a half marathon. This 13-mile run had proven to be popular in the past, and I had put a slight twist on the one I had scheduled. I had an Air Force C-141 parked along the route with the tail and nose hatch lowered. The participants would be required to run through this aircraft as a part of the competition. We had a group of Marines assigned to Lemoore to serve as security. As was the custom, the Marine Barracks entered the marathon as a group. Every marine, not on watch would be participating. They would be led by their OIC, a young captain.

The day before the marathon I received a call from the Gunnery Sergeant. He said, "Commander, I hate to report but we have to cancel our participation in the marathon tomorrow."

I said, "what happened?"

He said, "the captain was involved in an accident yesterday afternoon. He suffered three broken ribs. We cannot participate without him."

I said, "please reconsider. We are really counting on you guys. If you don't participate, the retired marines in the community will really be disappointed and so will I."

He said, "I will discuss it with the captain and get back with you."

About three hours later, the Sergeant called back and informed me that the Marines would participate. The marathon was structured as a timed run. Each participant or group of participants was assigned a departure time.

I was at the starting line when I noticed a stir from the gathered crowd. I looked around and saw the marines approaching. When they got close I noticed that the captain was being borne by four young marines in a litter. They carefully sat him down at the starting line. When the start gun was fired the captain took three or four steps followed by his marines. They then very carefully and gently lowered him on the litter and began the run. A long time later, the marines, in perfect step appeared. The captain, on the litter, was in the lead position. Approximately twenty feet from the finish line, the litter was lowered to the ground and the captain disembarked. He marched across the finish line followed by his marines in perfect step. Their time did not qualify for a prize, but I gave an Air Show Coordinator special award, one that I had to invent on the spot. (This is but one example of the pride, professionalism and teamwork I have observed.) Frankly I could write a book filled with similar stories. America should always be extremely grateful that we have these folks on our side, as they will never give in.

I have one more example of the Marine spirit which I must share. For some reason, the pay section of the Marine Corps got screwed up. As the result, the Marines stationed at Lemoore did not get paid. The first pay day missed caused some minor problems but nothing the senior marines could not address. When the second pay period was skipped the Marine captain in charge brought the issue to the attention of my commanding officer at the weekly all-officers meeting. My skipper asked the Marine what action he had taken. In addition to numerous phone calls he provided copies of various messages he had sent describing the problem. The captain immediately asked all of his officers to either chip in with a donation to assist the marines in their time of difficulty or provide a personal credit card that could be used by the marines to assist their personnel in meeting family obligations as well as purchasing quality-of-life items. Everyone chipped in to the maximum of their ability. When the next pay period rolled around, again there were no checks for the marines. The young captain sat down and wrote a two-page message directly to the Commandant of the Marine Corps. This message briefly laid out the issues and requested his personal attention in resolving this matter. (I have misplaced my copy of that message, but believe me it was a dozer.) The next day we received a flight plan for a transport aircraft out of Washington with a distinguished visitor aboard. When the aircraft arrived, out stepped the Commandant of the Marine Corps with his traveling party. Ground transportation was provided to the Marine Barracks area. All of the marines assigned were mustered in formation. The Commandant personally trooped the line and personally handed each marine the over-due pay he deserved. After a short speech essentially apologizing for the difficulty, the Commandant returned to the flight line and departed the area. Needless to say, this young captain had gained the admiration and support of every marine assigned to his charge. (I often thought that he had seen either *Mr. Roberts* or *The Sands of Iwo Jima*.)

After the air show, my orders came in for transfer and reassignment to the Office of the Chief of Naval Operations, Washington D.C. I was excited about the opportunity, but somewhat concerned about filling that position when we had five full commanders and three lieutenant commanders senior to me in the community. I called all of them and received their assurance that I would have their full support. With that concern addressed I spent the last few weeks in Lemoore, polishing off procedures, making sure that proper praise was given to deserving people, and briefing my relief. In looking back on the Lemoore tour, we got a lot of things corrected. We declared peace between the civilian and active duty controllers, developed a training pipeline that was spitting out qualified controllers, and revised course rules and procedures that enhanced the traffic capacity of the command. We had survived a raid by the FAA on our personnel and streamlined the arrival and departure procedures for the airport. In addition, we had managed the transition from the A-7 to the F/A 18 without a glitch.

CHAPTER XIX

OPNAV STAFF PHASE I

The trip from Lemoore to Washington D.C. via Louisiana was long but uneventful. Some of the stress normally associated with a transfer was relieved because I had made arrangements to rent the home of the guy I was relieving, Commander Bill Wotjowski. The home was very near Mt. Vernon and very close to the high school. Access to the George Washington Parkway and the Pentagon was very simple. Commander Wojtkowski had even arranged for me to be in a car pool from our house to the Pentagon with one of the men I would be working with in the office.

My first day in the Pentagon was an adventure. I believe if I had not had an escort I would still be checking in. After the mundane event of checking in was completed, I was called into the office for a guidance meeting with the boss, Captain Don Sumner. Captain Sumner was a highly decorated combat pilot who commanded the respect of juniors and seniors alike. He started the meeting by stating, "Despite the favorable impression you made on me and my staff during your visit and the establishment of a LDO billet in the office, the decision was made to bring you in based on the unqualified recommendation of Master Chief Jackson. [Jackson had replaced my old adversary, the chief I have referred to as a prick.] The master chief said that you could do the job of everyone in this office, and provided me copies of communications you had written over the years on the subjects of Air Traffic Control and Air Space Management. After I completed this review I went up to the Naval Annex and pulled and reviewed your record. Finally I received a call from Vice Admiral Schultz raving about your capabilities. You have impressive credentials, but you have to know that in this office, we must always be looking at the big picture. We always have three file cabinet's full of requirements and one cabinet of resources. In an effort to evaluate your ability to see the big picture I have had the staff set on ten letters you have written over the years. These letters identify deficiencies and recommend solutions. I want you to review this correspondence and provide me an OPNAV level written response tomorrow morning."

The next morning I turned in my homework. After about one hour the captain came out and said, "You have passed the test; welcome aboard." I had disapproved seven of the ten letters and provided rationale for the decision. After the captain left the office, Commander Wojtkowski gave me a document and asked me to take it to security and return. After a few false turns I found the security office, delivered the document, and returned to the office. When I opened the door Wojtkowski was standing in the entrance. He said, "Well, obviously you know your way around the place, so I stand relieved." That completed my turn over, and I was ready to go to work.

The first three days I spent reviewing the files and getting up to speed on various issues. I was well aware that I really did not have a clue of what I was doing or expected to do and recognized that I would have to have a lot of help. I was confident about my knowledge and understanding of Air Traffic Control but did not have a clue about how paper work was processed in the building, style, substance, format or even the process of gaining approval prior to release.

The solution for most of these problems rested in the hands of the secretary, Mrs. Kay Moreland. Mrs. Moreland had been the secretary in the office for approximately fifteen years, knew everything there was to know about correspondence, security, filing, and message traffic, and was highly respected not only in the office but throughout the organization and the fleet. The only problem was that she appeared to hate my guts. I reviewed the interactions we had had and could not identify anything or series of things I had done to piss her off. I realized that I came off headstrong and aggressive, but if you are in over your head you must put up a brave front.

My chance came on the first Friday afternoon after I had reported aboard. There was an all-hands meeting that I begged off from. After everyone had left the office I approached Mrs. Moreland's desk and said, "Lady, I do not know what I have done to piss you off. Whatever it is, I am sorry. You have been around a long time, and I know how committed you are to your job and to the ATC community. Like it or not the Navy had made the decision to send me here to represent that community at this level. I do not have a clue about the process required around here. If I cannot figure it out, I will fail. It is not important that I as an individual fail, but it is extremely important that my failure does not have an adverse impact on the community you and I both love. I am begging you on bended knee to teach me what I need to know to get along around here, and if possible, succeed. Without your help, I am doomed to fail. Please think about it." With that, I returned to my desk and began to work.

In a few minutes, she stuck her head around the corner and said, "Well, Commander (I was just a lieutenant commander but that was okay by me), I will give it a try." From that moment I could not have asked for more professional help. Any success I had early on in my tour was the direct result of her efforts on my behalf.

I found out very quickly that there was no spool-up time for the new guy in Washington. I was overwhelmed at the volume of work, the commitment of the workforce to do a good job, and the complexities of the issues we were required to resolve. One of the most disturbing things I noted early on was the cavalier attitude everyone had when talking about large sums of money. In my meetings with representatives of the Naval Electronic Systems Command (NAVELEXSYSCOM) I was blown away by the discussions involving millions of dollars. It appeared to me that they had lost sight of the value of a dollar, how hard taxpayers had to work for that money, and how little money folks had in the fleet to support the systems fielded for their use. I knew that I did not have the credibility or prestige to turn this around early on in my tour. After all, I was the new guy in town and was totally unfamiliar with the budget process, how things were funded, what kind of decisions were made regarding priority, etc. I had to do something flashy to get their attention. We had a meeting to discuss budget issues scheduled for nine A.M. I carried a flight bag that I used for a brief case. On the way to the meeting I stopped by the Navy Federal Credit union and applied for a signature loan. The largest loan I could get on my signature was for $2,000 dollars. I asked for the money in one-dollar bills. When the meeting started and we got to the money portion of the agenda I said, "Well, folks, you all are discussing funding in terms that are above my head. I personally have never had any money. For the last fifteen or so years I have been trying to run an Air Traffic Control Facility with approximately $1,500.00 a quarter. I believe that some of you have lost sight of the value of a dollar and I thought I would refresh your memory." With that, I opened my flight bag and tossed the $2,000 out on the table. I said, "That is all I could come up with. To me that is a lot of money, and I expect in your personal lives, it may be a lot of money to you, also. From now on, I would appreciate it if we spent the taxpayer's money as if it were our own. I don't want to deprive the fleet of anything they need to accomplish their mission, but I want us to focus on 'got to have' instead of 'nice to have.'" I can truthfully say that the message was well received. We continued to spend a lot of money because things cost a lot, but I am sure that waste became a thing of the past.

Early on in my tour I became concerned that the organizational structure within the office discouraged cross talk. The artificial walls within the office isolated individual action officers. Master Chief Jackson and I exchanged views continuously and we were the only Air Traffic Controllers in the office. Other folks were working issues and making decisions that affected our community, but often we were made aware of these decisions after the fact. I knew that the community was looking to Jackson and me to represent their interests, and often we were failing. I also noted that the book shelves in the office were filled with engineering documentation, studies, schematics, etc. I also noted that the documentation associated with Air Traffic Control and Airspace both nationally and international, were conspicuous by their absence. I did a little research and discovered that we did not have an engineer in the office. That translated to me that no one in the office could read nor understand the contents of these books.

Being an action type of person, I came into the office on a weekend and dismantled all of the partitions that isolated individuals into cells. I also threw out approximately 90% of those unused books. On Monday when everyone came to work I informed the captain of what I had done and the reasons for my actions. He said, "I would have appreciated it if you had discussed it with me before rather than after the fact, but I agree that it was the right thing to do." With that, he called an all-hands meeting and informed everyone that I had taken action based upon his direction. (That made him one of my heroes.)

It did not take me long to figure out that the Air Force dominated the building. They had by far the largest staff and their Public Relations (PR) arm put that of the Navy and Army to shame. The Marine Corps were another issue, but for the most part the Navy funded all non-tactical issues for the Marines, so their massive and effective PR effort was expended on issues not associated with my small piece of the pie.

I was determined to put the Navy brand on issues that justified our participation. My first meeting of the Department of Defense Policy Board on Federal Aviation (DoDPBFA) gave me an opportunity. This organization was the single focal point between the DoD and FAA on Joint Service issues. I had never heard of the organization until I got to Washington. After introductions and brief discussions on a number of minor issues the subject of Tactical Air Navigation (TACAN) was discussed. The issue was to develop a response to the FAA regarding their desire to decommission Federal (non DoD) TACANS in the National Airspace System (NAS.) Their justification was that TACAN was a requirement of DoD, not civilian aviation, therefore they should be relieved from the funding burden of the system. After a round of discussions, the executive Secretary, Mr. Tom Falatko announced that the Air Force would take the lead in developing the DoD response. I sat there for a couple of minutes in shock. Finally I said, "Mr. Falatko, that is bullshit. The Navy invented TACAN. We not only know how the system operates, we are well aware of the FAA responsibility to support the DoD when operating in the NAS. I have listened to the agenda for the last 1 ½ half hours, and every action has been assigned to the Air Force. If this is the way this organization is run, I will recommend to my flag that we terminate our membership so I can do something important rather than waste my time."

He looked at me and said, "Never before has the Navy stepped up to the plate to take the lead. If you want to become an active participant in the process, welcome aboard. You have the action." I felt this was an important step in gaining visibility for the Navy on a national stage.

The next major event that I can recall was our initial involvement in the National Airspace System Plan (NASP.) This plan, developed in isolation by the FAA, was a plan to modernize the civilian air traffic control system. The initial plan, referred to as the "Brown Book," was a packaged proposal to spend 11.7 million dollars over a ten-year period to upgrade the system. Included in the plan were all currently funded programs and all programs that were either in late or early stage of development. I reviewed the plan and immediately identified a number of issues that if implemented could be damaging to the interest of DoD.

The FAA announced that they were hosting a meeting in Cape May, New Jersey, in early January to discuss and brief the NAS plan. DoD was invited to attend. I was selected to represent the Navy/Marine Corps in this meeting. (The FAA Technical Center is located near Atlantic City. The FAA was concerned about the perception of hosting a major meeting in a highly desirable tourist location, so Cape May was selected.) Just an example of the bullshit that one must put up with.

I had never been to New Jersey but had heard about Atlantic City. I had to fly from Washington to Cape May via Atlantic City. When I left the Pentagon to go to Washington National to catch a flight I had $3.00 in my pocket and two government checks, one for $300.00 (travel advance) and another for $37.00.) I knew when I landed at Atlantic City I could get those checks cashed and catch a cab or rent a car to go to Cape May. (Distance about 15 miles.)

When I arrived at Atlantic City in a puddle jumper and stepped off the plane, I was in a total shock. I expected a large air terminal with banks, rental car booths, restaurants, etc. Instead, the terminal was a Quonset hut. There were no ground services. I asked a ticket agent where I could find a bank to cash a check. Remember, I had only $3.00 in cash. He said, "If you walk down that road about 1 ¼ mile you will find a branch bank adjacent to a bus station." I was dressed in Service Dress Blues, no pea coat, carrying a fairly heavy bag. It was snowing, with a brisk wind of approximately 20 miles per hour. I began the trek. (I hate to mention it, but folks in Atlantic City do not pick up sailors, regardless of the weather conditions.)

After a difficult journey that reminded me of my tour in Antarctica, I located the branch bank. I was glad to get in out of the weather and walked up to the teller, presented my government checks and government identification card. She looked over the material, gave me a particular hard look and said, "We cannot cash government checks. There has been a lot of theft of government checks in the area, so the bank has established a policy that we will not cash government checks for people who do not have an account with us."

I said, "Ma'am, I am in a bit of a bind. I told her my sad story."

When I finished, she said, "I will let you talk to the branch manager."

I told her I appreciated it and she took me into the office of the branch manager. She was an attractive young lady who listened intently to my sad story. She said, "You are in uniform, you have a picture ID. While I am breaking bank policy, I will cash your small check. This will give you the funds to catch a bus to Cape May."

I said, "That will be fine. Do you have any idea of the bus schedule?

She said, "Yes, the bus stop is directly across the street. It runs every four hours and there it goes now."

Needless to say, the next four hours in the snow appeared to be much longer. I passed the time by talking to a bunch of folks drinking out of paper bags and complaining about bad luck. At long last the bus showed up and I got aboard. This was a local that stopped at every intersection and cross walk. As we approached Cape May I moved up close to the driver and asked him if he could let me know when he got close to the hotel I was scheduled to stay in. He said, "As you will see, Cape May essentially closes down in the winter. I am amazed to hear this hotel is open this time of year. I can drop you off at the board walk which is located six blocks from the hotel." When we got to the board walk, the snow was really coming down hard. Adjacent to the ocean, the wind speed and spray was impressive, to say the least.

I completed the walk, located the hotel, and entered the foyer. I walked up to the desk clerk, identified myself and asked if they had my room reservation. She checked the roster told me the room number and welcomed me to Cape May. I said, "is your dining room open?" I left Washington at six A.M. and am getting a little hungry.

She said, "I am sorry we only opened the facility as a favor to the FAA. Our dining service will not be available during your stay."

I said, "That is in keeping with all of the other developments of this trip. Is there any place in this town where you can get something to eat? It looks like a ghost town."

She said, "Yes, this time of year most folks have headed south. There is a Seven-Eleven store six blocks from here. As you know, they sell packaged sandwiches, coffee, hot dogs, etc." I thanked her, took my luggage to my room, changed clothing and struck out for the Seven-Eleven.

I bought a couple of cups of coffee, two hot dogs, a bag of chips, and a sack of groceries to eat later. I also took this opportunity to shop. I purchased bread, meat, chips, cookies, etc. I had no idea how long this torture was going to last, but I wanted to be prepared. After devouring the hot dogs, chips, and coffee, I proceeded back to the hotel with my bag of goodies. When I arrived I noticed a sign on a bulletin board announcing that the FAA would be providing transportation to the Technical Center the next day beginning at seven A.M. That worry satisfied, I left a call for 0530 A.M. and went to bed.

The next morning when I arrived at the Lobby I saw a number of folks that I was acquainted with. The hotel had provided coffee and pastry, so things were looking up. Someone yelled out that the transportation had arrived, so we rushed to the door. The transportation was a cargo van with only a seat for the driver. The driver was an old friend, Dave Tuttle. Dave, as a civilian, had had my job in the Pentagon when I attended the first NAALS conference. He had a fight with the branch head and left the DoD for the FAA. We renewed acquaintances, and I said, "I see you have come up in the world."

He said, "Don't be a smart ass; I have seat on this bus and you are sitting on the floor." He had a point. (Dave's talent soon became apparent. He had a very successful career in the FAA and retired as a member of the Senior Executive Service.) We all loaded up in the bus and became better acquainted than anyone really desired during the trip to the technical center. My uniform was a mess, but so was everyone else's. The first order of business after arriving at the technical center was to arrange for better transportation.

The meeting was chaired by Mr. Jerry Thompson. Mr. Thompson was a senior engineer in the FAA and was actually the father of the NASP. What was amazing to me was the lack of understanding of the contents of the plan by the attendees. The engineers understood the technical issues and the controllers understood the operational issues, but very few personnel outside of the working group Mr. Thompson had used to develop the plan had a clue of the contents and the impact those projects would have on ATC services if implemented. I recognized this confusion early on in the debate and asked Mr. Thompson if I could serve as the translator. He welcomed my assistance with open arms. (Jerry Thompson was one of the true geniuses that I met during my career. He had vision, a total grasp of technical issues, and I consider him not only a pioneer but a true friend.)

We spent a very exhausting week at this NAALS conference. I was able to persuade Mr. Thompson and the FAA that it was imperative that DoD be given a formal invitation to participate with the FAA as this plan matured. I told them that DoD would make a formal comment to the FAA via the Secretary of Transportation on our view of the NASP and the impact and benefits to the DoD of its implementation. I began to draft the DoD response during off-duty hours in Cape May. After all, there was nothing else to do.

I returned to work, drafted the DoD position on the NAS plan, and briefed my seniors that this was not a one-time thing. In my view, the DoD had to get aboard with this program, accept the elements we could live with and challenge those that would harm DoD flight activity. I said, "this plan will cost the DoD some money but failure to modernize in concert with the FAA will be a disaster." They agreed with my assessment and we began to work on other things.

One of the key elements of the initial NAS plan was the development of a concept referred to as the Area Control Facility (ACF) project. The FAA announced that they were hosting a concept exploration of the ACF concept in Lawton, Oklahoma. Mr. Falatko appointed me to be the DoD member of the Systems Requirements Team (SRT) for this concept.

I traveled to Lawton via Oklahoma City. We were all housed in barracks-type buildings that served as student housing when the college was in session. The FAA used this site as a management-training center; therefore, the facilities, berthing, and food were all in place.

The ACF concept was essentially a plan to consolidate major Terminal Approach Control Locations (TRACONS) with Air Route Traffic Control Centers (ARTCCS.) This concept would take advantage of emerging technology and reduce overhead staffs in a measurable way. The initial plan called for a total of 23 ACFS with special designation for the New York area and Puerto Rico. It was obvious to me that the concept would never be accepted. While technically sound, the political opposition of relocating a large number of highly paid government employees from one congressional district to another would never pass muster. In addition, I was concerned about the increased vulnerability of the system resulting from consolidation and the requirement for DoD to either join in on the concept or be left as isolated islands in the system. I knew if I was forced to place DoD controllers as members of the FAA workforce isolated from the support infrastructure they enjoyed on a military base and the associated camaraderie, I would be the victim of cherry picking. The FAA would naturally recruit my best and brightest, and I would be left with, at best, second-level controllers to deploy overseas and aboard ship. I pointed out all of these issues during the debate, but when the meeting was over they had a plan for implementation. (For the reasons I stated and budgetary considerations the ACF concept was later abandoned.) Paramount among other things was the upcoming budget. Competing for resources in a very competitive environment is the primary responsibility of the requirements officer. I worked around the clock with the folks in NAVELEX, personnel in the fleet, and anyone else that I felt could be supportive of our efforts. I knew the issues cold, had reviewed all relevant documentation, and based on my instructor experience and basic extroverted personality felt that I could compete with anyone for the resources we required to continue uninterrupted service provision to the fleet ashore and afloat.

The big day came, and I made my presentation to a room full of folks. All of them were senior to me, but I knew my business and was able to answer every question asked in a timely and thorough manner. At the conclusion of the presentation, I was told that I had done well. I went back to the office feeling proud of myself and of the folks who had supported the preparation of the presentation.

This good feeling lasted until about three P.M. that day. At that time, we received a print-out of the decisions made on the budget presentations. I had not received one dollar to support the resolution of the ATC deficiencies. I was totally destroyed. I had given it my best shot and failed miserably. While this was a disaster for me personally, the real tragedy was that I had let the community down. The system had sent me to Washington to take care of the needs of my community, and I had failed. I was, to say the least, devastated.

After briefing my captain and office mates on my total failure I walked around for a few minutes and then went to the head. I cannot recall if I needed to go to the head or just needed some place private to cry. While I was standing at the urinal Vice Admiral Schultz walked in. He asked me how things were going and I said, "Admiral, we really screwed up by bringing me in here. I am totally over my head."

He said, "What is the matter?"

I said, " As you know, we had first cut budget hearings this morning and I gave, what I thought was a factual, honest, and thorough briefing. I answered all of the questions asked, and felt that I had done well. We were just informed that I received absolute zero dollars. I have not only let you and Naval Aviation down, I have let my community down. Obviously, this is not the place for a LDO to be stationed, as we are not educated enough to be competitive in this environment."

He said, "You are telling me that you received zero resources in the budget hearings?"

I said, "Yes, sir."

He said, "Are you aware that if you are totally unsuccessful in the budget process you can request a hearing with the boss to discuss your issues?"

I said, "No sir, I am not familiar with that."

He said, "What are you doing at 5:30 P.M. today?"

I said, "I have nothing scheduled. I will be in your office with brief in hand."

At 5:30 sharp I presented myself to the admiral's secretary with briefing material in hand. She said, "He is waiting for you; go right in."

I entered his office and said, "Admiral, I am here to present a briefing on ATC requirements for your consideration."

He said, "My executive Assistant (EA) will be sitting in; you may begin."

I went through the briefing with the vigor of a southern preacher. After all, this was my religion, and I felt this was my last chance to salvage something for the community. When I finished the briefing, he said, "Very well done. Is your third alternative your bare bones requirement?"

I said, "Yes, sir, if we are funded at this level we can maintain our current tempo. We will postpone some needed upgrades but we can survive."

He turned to his EA and said, "Direct the head of the budget committee to fund Lieutenant Commander Calhoun's issues at the bare-bones level. I know him, and I know that he is honest and is not an empire builder." He turned to me and said, "Jim, we unrestricted line aviators do not really understand what you folks do for us. We know it is important but do not have a total grasp of that importance. I promise you that if you do not make a pest of yourself, I will fund you at the level you indicate is essential. Once every 20 years or so, come to us with a big request and we will support it. In the meantime, keep it affordable."

I said, "Yes sir, I will do that, and I and the ATC community appreciate your support." (I know now there was no policy for briefing the boss as a last-ditch effort.) I also know that his commitment to me was made a pass-down item for his relief and subsequent reliefs, for I never was funded at less than I indicated was essential, and when I requested a big chunk of money for modernization in concert with the FAA, that request was approved.

In addition to all of the Air Traffic Control issues, I was involved in airspace issues. The DoD requires airspace that is free of civilian aircraft to conduct training, weapons-systems development, and testing. The FAA Act of 1958 designated the FAA as the manager of all of the airspace within the United States. In order for the DoD to be delegated airspace it must petition the FAA. This request, along with justification, is circulated throughout the system. Civilian aviation interest, both commercial and private flying, views delegated airspace as an obstacle to the free flow of air traffic. The negotiations can often become hot and heavy as each interested party defends its position. I must admit, the FAA does an excellent job in managing the airspace, and for the most part, with proper justification, the DoD is delegated the airspace it requires to support the DoD mission.

Often conflicts about airspace are between services. All services have different concepts of operation. The ideal is for the DoD to share airspace between all DoD services, but sometimes that is not as easy to do as one would imagine.

Such an event occurred with the airspace known as Restricted Airspace (R-2508.) This airspace overlies Edwards Air Force Base, Naval Air Station China Lake, the Army Training Center at Fort Irving, and at the time, George Air Force Base. (George was later closed as the result of a Base Realignment and Closure (BRAC) decision.) The geographic location of the R-2508 complex almost due west of Los Angeles Airport is a serious obstacle to the egress/ingress of civilian aircraft into the Los Angeles area. In recognition of this, as well as the vital importance of this airspace to the DoD, the FAA and DoD in a joint effort, modernized the control, surveillance, and communications capability of the complex. The funding for this initiative was split between the Air Force, Navy, and FAA based on a traffic count formula existing at the time the modernization effort was accomplished. A part of this package was the assumption of the control responsibilities within the complex by the FAA. The DoD committed to funding the annual cost of the complex with a formula identical to that used to defray the modernization cost.

I was approached by my Air Force contemporaries in the Pentagon with the suggestion that the Air Force assume the control responsibilities in the complex. My initial reaction to the proposal was negative, but before I gave them an official position I coordinated with the Navy personnel in China Lake. They were violently opposed to this idea. Armed with the fleet position I addressed the Air Force and indicated their proposal was a non starter. I indicated that when civilian interest made a raid on the airspace under the existing arrangement, the DoD and the FAA could rebut their request from a joint position. If the Air Force assumed jurisdiction, the DoD would be isolated in their defense of the resource. I also indicated that the operational philosophy of the Navy and the Air Force was so different that if Air Force assumed responsibility the capacity of the airspace would not satisfy capacity requirements.

Despite my stated position, the Air Force called for a meeting at Edwards AFB to discuss the issues. Before I left, Admiral Schultz and my immediate boss, Admiral Dunleavy instructed me to protect that airspace at all cost.

After a long flight and a rental car trip across the desert I arrived at Edwards. I had been there before while I was stationed at Fallon but had little knowledge of the base. The next morning at eight A.M., the meeting began. Meeting attendees were 12 personnel from the FAA, 67 personnel from the Air Force, and one lone lieutenant commander from the Navy. The Air Force delegation was made up of senior civilian employees and a large number of colonels and lieutenant colonels. They also had four senior enlisted personnel to provide subject-matter expertise. During the first day, all of the discussions centered on how the facility would be run after the Air Force assumed control responsibility. I sat in the meeting in total shock. I knew the Air Force was aware of the Navy's position, but in their arrogance they were totally ignoring our concerns. At the end of the normal working day a decision was made to break for the evening meal and reconvene at later in the evening. During the break period I had a long talk with myself and made a decision.

When the meeting reconvened I started off the conversation by stating, "For an entire day, I have heard discussions about how this complex will run after the Air Force assumes control jurisdiction. For those of you that do not know my name is Lieutenant Commander Jim Calhoun. I speak for the chief of Naval Operations. The Air Force staff at the Pentagon has been provided the Navy position on this issue. I will now restate that position, unless an analysis of the issues proves that the operational capability of this facility will be improved as the result of the proposed change, there will be no change. If you read the charter, any change made in the operation of the R-2508 complex must be a unanimous decision. I will support an analysis of the operation, but when the data is finalized, I will look to the local command, China Lake for a position. If they agree, I will take that position back to the Pentagon for a decision. If they determine that maintaining status quo is in the best interest of the Navy, that is the decision." Needless to say, my comments broke up the meeting.

At four A.M. the phone rang in my room. The caller was Vice Admiral Schultz. He indicated that the senior Colonel in the meeting had called the Air Force chief of staff and reported my actions. The chief of staff called the CNO, and since he was a submariner he referred aviation-related issues to the deputy chief of Naval Operations, Air Warfare Vice Admiral Schultz. Admiral Schultz informed CNO that I was doing exactly what I had been instructed to do. This message was relayed back to the Colonel at China Lake. Admiral Schultz terminated the conversation by stating, "Keep up the good work."

The next morning the attitude was totally different. A decision was made to collect and analyze data associated with the complex and debrief the information for a decision. At the end of thirteen days of driving and walking around the desert, we met for a decision. After the briefing was completed, I turned to the China Lake representative and asked for their position. Their captain said, "Based on the facts collected, complemented with our knowledge of how this complex actually works, China Lake's position is to maintain status quo. With that, I relayed that the Navy position was to maintain status quo. I move that the meeting be adjourned. The skipper at China Lake seconded the motion, and without a vote, the meeting was adjourned.

Just because you are out of the office on Temporary Additional Duty does not mean that the work stops while you are gone. When I reported to the office, the first action was to get a briefing on the status of issues being worked from the individual covering my issues while I was gone. Initially the briefing was standard. At the conclusion of the briefing he said and we have one really hot issue with senior flag officer and secretary of the Navy interest.

Immediately curious I asked him to describe the issue. He said, "Vice Admiral Schultz called him and the captain into his office and said the Secretary of the Navy had directed him to procure an Instrument Landing System (ILS) for a little airport in the southeastern United States."

I said, "That is crap. It is illegal for us to spend DoD money to procure a landing system for a civilian airport."

He said, "I tried to explain that, but the admiral was not in a 'receive' mode."

I said, "I have it for action." I began to investigate and discovered that the Airport in question was previously an outlying field declared excess by the Navy and turned over to local civilian authorities for civilian use. Any aircraft coming from the north or east to that airport would be required to transit training airspace used by student naval aviators operating from either NAS Pensacola, or NAS Whiting Field, Florida. Not only was this illegal, it would create a safety hazard by encouraging civilian pilots with various degrees of experience to operate in an area where young naval aviators were learning to fly.

I called Admiral Dunleavy and asked for an appointment. He said, "Come right over." I went to his office and explained the issues. He said, "Let's go and see the boss."

We made an appointment with Vice Admiral Schultz, and I told my story. He listened and then said, "You folks just don't understand. My tasking was from the Secretary of the Navy. He had lunch with a senior representative from a southern state. The representative indicated that the good citizens of his state had named the airport after him and had lengthened the runway. The only thing keeping that portion of the state from turning green was the lack of reliable air transportation. He said this deficiency could be addressed by providing an ILS for the airport. Now before you tell me no, I would like to remind you that I have requested special consideration from the Navy for my state for the last two years. Both times my request was ignored. In the near future we will be voting on funding an aircraft carrier and the number of F/A 18 aircraft you procure. If I do not get the ILS, you will not get what you want." Admiral Schultz concluded by saying, "Folks, this is a high-risk issue that I cannot take. Go buy the ILS."

I said, "Admiral, I believe I can satisfy the congressman's requirement without procuring an ILS."

He said, "How?"

I said, "The book allows me to provide a surveillance approach to an airport located within 20 miles of the antenna site. I have measured the distance from the radar at Pensacola to the approach end of the runway at that airport. It is 18 miles. All I have to do is raise the antenna at Pensacola by a height of ten feet, negotiate airspace from the FAA, develop a surveillance approach, and have flights check it. If it all works out, the congressman will have an instrument approach. It will be under Navy control. This control will assure that civilian aircraft transiting to that airport will not get tangled up with Navy training flights."

He said, "Work it out and come back to me."

I said, "Thank you, sir," and went back to the office to complete the work. I had it all completed in about four hours, and once again went back to the admiral's office.

He listened and said, "Take your proposal to the congressional liaison. He is a very good friend of the congressman. Make your pitch to him. If he feels it has merit, continue. If he does not, get your ass back to your office and buy an ILS."

Admiral Dunleavy and I went to the office of the flag officers serving as congressional liaison. I made my pitch, and he blew his top. He said, "Don't you guys know the risk we are running on this issue? The congressman wants an ILS. He will provide the funding in our budget. Just accommodate him and buy the damn equipment."

That was when I lost my temper and should have been fired. I said, "With all respect, Admiral, you and I have been in the Navy about the same amount of time. I have successfully competed and been promoted 17 times. You have been promoted a total of eight times, but most of those were non-competitive because you are a Naval Academy Graduate. I do not advise you folks how to fight and win a war. I would appreciate it if you would give me the same courtesy by not telling me how to do my business."

If I thought he had been angry before, I had seen nothing. He actually began to froth at the mouth. He yelled in my face, "All right, wise ass. I am going to schedule a lunch for you two with the congressman tomorrow. If he likes your proposal, fine. If not your ass is fired."

Without batting an eye, Admiral Dunleavy stepped forward and said, in a loud and clear voice, "Admiral, before you fire him, you have to fire me first." (I had always had the utmost respect for Admiral Dunleavy, but after that, there was nothing he could have asked me to do that I would not have done.

This was a fast-track flag officer who put his career on the line for an illiterate LDO.)

The next day we met the congressman for lunch, and I made my presentation. He asked a couple of questions for clarification and then said, "I love it. We get what we need for the citizens of my state, and it is all legal and above board."

We went back to the Pentagon and debriefed Admiral Schultz. He said, "Good job," and we went back to our respective offices. In the next two years the Navy received three letters from the congressman expressing his appreciation for the support the Navy provided to the citizens of his state. (I have left out some names to protect the guilty. You would be amazed at how often things like this happen in the Pentagon.)

Things were going extremely well at work. I was enjoying my job and getting more comfortable and confident with each passing day. Things were not so good on a personal level. My wife's back had gone out and she was confined to the bed. This caused her to lose her job, so once again money was a factor. I looked at the promotion opportunities, and they were grim. Each year it seemed they pushed the possibility for consideration for promotion out one more year. While I loved the Navy and my job, my ability to remain on active duty was beginning to be doubtful.

While my concern about finances dominated a portion of my thoughts, the fact that the FAA was beginning to make a significant move in the modernization of the ATC system was another. I knew this would be a significant development, one that if not carefully worked by the DoD could result in the FAA assuming all of the ATC responsibilities in the United States. If that occurred, I felt that DoD would not receive the priority it needed for launching and recovering aircraft, nor would their access to airspace be timely. Bottom line, this was a big deal, and I wanted to be a part of it. One more factor that held my attention was the move afoot to legalize the promotion of LDOs to the grade of 0-6 (Navy captain.) I did appreciate the added prestige of a 0-6 and the increase in salary, but I felt the LDOs job was to serve as technical advisors to the unrestricted line, and as an interface between the enlisted and officer community. I believed and still believe that good LDOs do not have to have rank to justify their position; thus I could not justify the 0-6 concept. Despite my opposition, legislation was introduced and passed to raise the promotion ceiling for LDOs from commander to captain.

After considering all of the alternatives and discussing them with my family I made arrangements for Commander Tom McMahon to come from

COMNAVAIRPAC as my relief and put in my retirement papers. My wife was delighted with that decision, I was not.

Shortly after I received a retirement date and Commander McMahon received his orders to relieve me, in desperation I took my wife to a chiropractor. I did not have personal knowledge of this form of medicine but we had tried every type of conventional medicine with minimal results. I drove her to the office and carried her up the stairs to the office. Thirty minutes later she walked back to the car and except for some brief periods of pain rectified by exercise she has been fine since. She was able to find a job and go back to work within a week. That took care of the financial worries.

The next week the Air Force sponsored an initiative to create an office in FAA headquarters to work with the FAA on NAS modernization issues. Their plans far exceeded those envisioned by the Navy. My boss, Admiral Dunleavy called me on the phone and said, "I realize that you have requested retirement, but I need you."

I said, " Cdr. McMahon is in receipt of orders. He has sold his house and is on the way. I cannot screw over him."

He said, "We just had a billet open up in the FAA as the Department of the Navy Liaison to FAA Headquarters. This billet has always been held by a pilot but I feel that an LDO Air Traffic Controller, especially you, would be a better fit. Just say the word and I will have your retirement orders cancelled and have you assigned to that billet. In addition to working the liaison position you will be the Navy lead on this NAS modernization issue. I expect you to continue working the budget issues on any program associated with this modernization effort."

I said, "Will I continue to have a code in this office in addition to the FAA job?"

He said, "Yes."

I said, "You know that I will do anything you ask; therefore, make your calls. I need to help McMahon become familiar with the budget when he arrives, and I will work both jobs until he is checked out."

He said, "Consider it done, and thanks."

When I got home that night and broke the news to my wife, needless to say, she was not happy. In addition to me staying in the Navy, I was turning down a high-paying job with the firm of Booz Allen and Hamilton. She saw this as the opportunity to finally own her own home, and knew we would never be able to swing that in the Washington D.C. area on my lieutenant-commander salary.

The Air Force initiative to create a 50-person office in FAA headquarters was the subject of much debate between the services. After a series of briefings, the Army and Navy persuaded the Air Force to decrease the size of that commitment and provide fifty thousand dollars from each service to hire contractor support for the effort. After this agreement was reached, a meeting of the flag officers from each service, along with technical experts, was convened to finalize the decision.

This meeting was chaired by Mr. Tom Falatko, the executive secretary of the DoDPBFA. After a series of discussions resulting in apparent agreement, a vote was scheduled. Before the vote, the Air Force principal once again raised the idea of the 50-person office. Admiral Dunleavy allowed the Air Force General to complete his pitch and then said, "The Navy has fifty thousand dollars and Jim Calhoun. That will be our contribution to this effort. In return, he will be given a letter authorizing him to call upon all assets within the Navy and Marine Corps he requires to assure Naval Aviation Interest are protected." With that statement the decision was made that the Air Force would provide a colonel and a lieutenant colonel, with the colonel as the chief of the office, the Navy would provide me and any assistance I required, and the Army would provide a senior civilian ATC expert. The Navy would also select the contractor to support this effort. I was designated as the deputy chief of the office.

Before the meeting was adjourned, the chairman, Dr. Tom Cooper, asked the question, "How long will it take to develop and provide a report on the impact of this elephant referred to as of FAA modernization on the DoD? After some debate between the various attendees, the response was one year. He paused for a moment and said, "Wash its ass and get me a report in four months. We cannot wait a year before we start budgetary action.

Mr. Falatko was ill. His age, complemented by the increase pace of activity between the FAA and DoD and his illness mandated that he retire. He selected a young transportation expert working for the Air Force at Andrews AFB as his relief. The Air Force was paying for this billet, so the other services had no say in this selection.

When he reported aboard I was in shock. He looked to be about thirty years old and did not know a thing about the FAA, Airspace, or Air Traffic Control. His name was Frank Colson. He proved to be one of the most intelligent men I have ever met. He not only knew he did not know anything, he was willing to learn. In addition, while I have always prided myself on my work ethic, Mr. Colson was the hardest working man I have ever known.

The first time he and I had a private meeting he said, "Mr. Falatko told me that if I was to succeed in this job I had to pick your brain and depend on you until such time that you and I felt comfortable that I could go solo. Would you be willing to do that?"

I said, "Yes, sir, but we have to do something. Your position is currently that of a GS 15. Your peers in the FAA will all be high-grade senior executive level (SES) personnel. They respect rank and position. I cannot ask one of my admirals to accompany you each time you go to the FAA for a meeting or conference. I am sure the other services cannot provide a General for the same purpose. The first thing we have to do is beef up your job description and process the paperwork for an upgrade. To do this, we have to change your title from 'Executive Secretary' to 'Executive Director.'" He said, "Naturally I am all for that."

I said, "Let us get it done." Hindsight suggests this was one of the most important decisions we made associated with NAS modernization.

Commander McMahon checked in, and I began the turn over. Things had changed a lot since I had reported aboard. His position now was expanded to include all aspects of air traffic control ashore and afloat, assistant to the air space officer, and to be frank, he became the trouble shooter for all functions of the office. The transition for him was a shock. I appreciated that, for I remembered the shock I had when I checked in. My primary focus was to get him up to speed on the budget. I could not leave until both he and I were comfortable with his understanding. My transfer day came and went. I was required to, for administrative purposes, check out of the Pentagon and check into Naval Air Station Andrews AFB Washington D.C. I would have no duties at that command, but for record purposes that was my official assignment. When my transfer date passed I was put on eight days' leave until I could check in to my new command. That was the only leave I took during my first assignment on the OPNAV staff.

CHAPTER XX

DEPARTMENT OF THE NAVY LIAISON, FAA HEADQUARTERS WASHINGTON D.C.

I finally was able to check into FAA Headquarters. I was acquainted with the major players in the FAA so the transition was fairly simple. I was also acquainted with all of the personnel from the services that would be working the NAS modernization effort. In addition, I was able to persuade the program office in NAVELEX to assign Mr. Bill Raynor to assist me in evaluating the contents of the NAS plan and reporting findings not only to the FAA but to DoD. Mr. Raynor, in my view, is the greatest unsung hero of the ATC community for the Naval Service. He was not an engineer, but he knew ATC systems better than anyone I have ever known. He was the prime supporter of the operational side of Naval ATC, often to his detriment. His no-nonsense defense of our actual requirements rather than those dreamed up by the engineers is directly responsible for the success we enjoyed during his long and fruitful career. I was delighted to lean on not only his technical expertise but his vast knowledge of Washington and how things really worked in that town.

We worked very hard in the assessment of the NAS Plan. Every project was evaluated with regard to need, cost, feasibility, and impact, primarily budgetary upon the DoD if implemented. The results of this analysis were bound in a report entitled the Blue Book. This document proved to be the template that DoD would follow for the next 15 years.

I was having a great time. There were some difficulties. I was a lieutenant commander, a GS-13 equivalent. The FAA authorized parking for GS-14s and above. I found this out when I applied for parking. They indicated that they would make special provisions for me, but I refused. I did not want to be obligated to the FAA for anything. The next issue was the lack of a dedicated office for me. I patiently waited for approximately two weeks with no results. I was hopping from desk to desk on a catch-as-catch-can basis. Finally I felt that I had given them sufficient opportunity to deliver and they had failed. I decided to take matters into my own hands.

The FAA Administrator at that time was retired Vice Admiral Don Engen. I had met the admiral, but we were not in any way close friends. I found a soft drink wooden case and an abandoned orange crate. I arrived at work early one morning and set my portable desk and chair up directly outside the admiral's office. He walked up and asked me what in the hell I was doing. I replied, "Admiral, I have been in this building better than two weeks. I do not have an office, even a desk and phone of my own. I have found my own office furniture, as you can see. If you will tell your secretary that I have your permission to use your phone, this will serve my needs."

He said, "That is a bunch of crap. Come into my office." I went in he called the head of building maintenance and asked him if I had submitted a request for office space.

He said, "Yes, sir, but I am having some difficulty in finding a space in the area where the rest of the military personnel are located."

The admiral replied, "I don't care who you have to move. It is eight A.M. Have him an office by 9:30, fully furnished with phone, computer, copy machine, etc., or I will assign your office for him until you can find an appropriate space for a senior Naval Officer." I told the admiral I appreciated his support and left his spaces. By the time I had located a cup of coffee, I had a fully furnished office. (This is provided as just another example of sailors taking care of their own.)

Perception of one's importance in FAA Headquarters is very important. The vast majority of personnel assigned were college graduates. They took great pride in displaying their credentials on the walls of their offices. I was a little short of certificates attesting to my higher education. I had to do something. My solution was to frame and hang a copy of my Elementary School and High School graduation certificates. In the center of this display I hung a picture of my boot camp graduation class. Needless to say, this was the source of comment throughout the building.

The longer I was attached to the FAA the more I was puzzled about how an organization can recruit and hire some of the best folks I have ever seen and by some magic trick turn them into under performers. I believe a lot of the difficulty lay in the lack of a defined chain of command between the regions and headquarters regarding who is actually in charge. Another factor is the oversight provided by the FAA from political interest in the congress and from bureaucrats in various administrations and the Department of Transportation. Don't get me wrong. Most of these folks have good intentions, but in their quest to "take care of their constituents" congressional members often manipulate priorities for equipment installation which may be in the best interest of their constituents but are not in the best interest of the system. Additionally, despite the success the FAA had in standing up to PATCO during the strike of 1982, those successes have been forgotten. Currently the Air Traffic Controllers Association (current union) have bullied and cajoled FAA leadership to the point where current leadership is left without bargaining room.

Despite literally thousands of studies on any number of subjects, the modernization of the ATC system continues to be behind schedule, over budget, and in some instances ineffective. The inconsistent budget stream results in the fielding of modern systems long after they have become obsolete. The constant change in requirements, often in an effort to chase emerging technology rather than achieve a stable baseline of capability, results in duplication of logistical support efforts, dissimilar equipment throughout the system, and most important, a detriment to morale of controllers, supervisors, and maintenance personnel.

The vast majority of my efforts while assigned to the FAA was focused on the modernization of the ATC system, attempts to assure that such modernization efforts would not hamstring the DoD, and if such changes would benefit DoD, acquiring the funding to facilitate such modernization efforts. The constant change in direction by the FAA made acquiring funding from the DoD difficult. The FAA would prematurely announce a technical breakthrough, the deployment of which was imminent. Action officers from DoD working the issues would be aware that this announcement was for Public Relations consumption and not based on fact would attempt to delay budgetary action until actually needed. This would result in a disconnect in budget strategy between the FAA and the DoD. These disconnects required a lot of explaining, all of which had to be carefully crafted to assure that we were not torpedoing the FAA effort while simultaneously attempting to budget to a realistic requirement rather than one driven by optimism rather than reality.

A decision was made by senior leadership within the FAA that the DoD would follow the lead of the FAA in the modernization of the ATC system.

This was an obvious decision to make, but the, "How are we going to do it?" was not so simple. The major issue was what service would have the lead for the DoD, and as the lead, who would stand up the program office. The two candidates were the Air Force and the Navy. Obviously I was in favor of the Navy lead while others favored the Air Force.

I believed the advantage the Navy had over the Air Force was a simple chain of command, centrally located in the Washington D.C. area, a cadre of top-notch technicians and engineers totally familiar with not only DoD equipage but that of the FAA, and a track record of delivering products on time and at cost. The Air Force insisted if the program office was assigned to them it would be located at Hanscomb AFB, outside of Boston. Additionally, while the Navy historically maintained their own systems with either active-duty personnel or government-employed civil servants, the Air Force depended on other types of maintenance and planning. In fact an analysis of maintenance between the services indicated that while ninety percent of maintenance performed on Navy systems was performed by fleet personnel on a local level and only ten percent in depots, the reverse was true in the Air Force.

Navy leadership was concerned about the cost in both funds and personnel if the Navy assumed the lead role. Since the lead service is responsible for all common Research and Development as well as the cost of employees employed in the program office, the Navy was reluctant to become obligated for this unknown cost. I felt the cost of the Navy's constant trips to the Boston area, the constant need for program office personnel to travel from Boston to Washington for planning and coordination purposes would be more expensive. Finally, the senior acquisition executive of the Air Force committed the Air Force to assume the responsibilities of lead service. I could not obtain a similar commitment from the Navy; thus the Air Force became service lead. (In my judgment this decision proved to be a big mistake.)

With the decision made regarding service lead for the NAS modernization program my attention was diverted to Airspace. The FAA airspace manager in the Southern Region of the FAA developed a briefing on airspace. The focal point of this briefing was slide nineteen. This slide depicted all of the airspace delegated to the DoD on one slide. While the dimensions of the delegated airspace were accurate, this depiction was a slanted view of airspace. This depiction presented every type of airspace including airspace that is restrictive to the flight of civilian aircraft as well as the airspace that is not restrictive. In addition, the portrayal gave the impression that the depicted airspace was active all of the time at all altitudes, which is totally misleading. Additionally, some airspace depicted was not delegated to the DoD, and other parcels were not under the jurisdiction of the FAA.

Needless to say, when this briefing became public there was hell to pay. The FAA Administrator at that time continued to be retired Vice Admiral Engen. Based on his military experience as well as personal knowledge as an aviator, he was aware that the briefing unfairly depicted airspace delegated to the DoD. In an effort to set the record straight and fend off an ugly confrontation with senior leadership of the DoD, Admiral Engen arranged to brief the members of the Joint Chiefs of Staff in the Pentagon.

Before a senior official either within the government or the civil sector briefs members of the Joint Chiefs of Staff, the individual staffs supporting the various members must bring their principal member up to speed on the issue. This fell to me and the Air Space officer within the Pentagon. We jointly developed a twelve-page briefing and began to brief up the chain of command. In the Pentagon when a briefing is developed, the first, most junior member of the chain of command receives the entire briefing. As you proceed up the chain of command the briefing is consistently reduced. Senior officials do not have the time to digest the background information. When the final level in the chain is reached, normally the issue is confined to a single page of salient points.

My partner in this effort was an excellent naval officer. He had been the commanding officer of an operational squadron and knew airspace extremely well. He had one problem. While very competent when interfacing with peers and seniors that he was familiar with, he became hesitant when briefing very senior officers. Finally with about an hour to spare before the briefing, we were given the opportunity to brief OP-60. OP-60 at that time was a very powerful position, and the incumbent was more powerful than most. He was a very large, three-star admiral, with the reputation of eating briefers for lunch. As the senior man began the briefing, it was obvious that the admiral did not have a clue about what we were talking about and was very close to kicking us out of his office. Sensing this, I stepped forward and said, "With all due respect, Admiral, perhaps I can clear this up."

He said, "It is about time someone cleared it up, as I was about to kick both of you out of my office." With that, I completed the briefing. He said, "Lieutenant Commander Calhoun, you come with me. Commander, return to your office." Following his lead I accompanied him out of the office, and we proceeded to the office of the chief of Naval Operations.

While I had been on the CNO staff for four years I had never personally seen this CNO. When we walked into his office, I was impressed. I was also scared to death. The CNO was a surface-warfare officer. He was also a huge man. He was sitting at his desk with his feet propped on the sliding shelf that was used to hold a typewriter. He had the single sheet of paper that was the Readers'-Digest version of the briefing. OP-60 began to brief the CNO. Approximately thirty seconds into the briefing he paused and said, "CNO, it is obvious that you do not understand what I am talking about. It is equally obvious that I do not know what I am talking about, Commander, Take charge."

I began the brief. Directly behind CNO hanging on his office wall was a clock. Time was running out. The formal briefing by Vice Admiral Engen was scheduled to begin in ten minutes, and I was having a difficult time in getting the salient points across. Each time I paused, the CNO would ask me what the briefing had to do with the Air Defense Identification Zone (ADIZ.) ADIZ is a charted zone around the coastal areas of the United States. Should an aircraft not preplanned to enter the area violate its boundaries, aircraft are scrambled to intercept the intruder. After the third interruption, and increasingly aware of the passing of time, as an instinctive reaction I said, "CNO, if you will just shut up and pay attention, I will have you ready for this briefing. It had nothing to do with the ADIZ."

As soon as those words left my mouth, I knew I was in deep shit. I just continued on after he took his feet from the desk, sat very straight in his chair, picked up a pen, and asked me exactly what points I wanted him to make in the briefing. I finished the briefing and pointed out the key areas for his consideration that were included in his brief sheet. He said, "I got it."

With those words, OP-60 escorted me to the door. On my way out of the door I noticed for the first time approximately 15 aviation admirals, one of which was my boss, standing in the back of the office. When we cleared the doorway, OP-60 said, "Go back to your office. After the briefing is over, I will call you for a debriefing."

I went back to the office and began to pack up my personal gear. I knew my career was over. Folks began to ask me what had gone on but I could not begin to tell. Finally my immediate boss stuck his head in and said, our boss just called me (our admiral), and indicated that you put on quite a show. I said, "Captain, I don't know if you would call it a show or not but I believe I have screwed the pooch."

About the time I finished packing my stuff, the phone rang. It was OP-60 calling me down to his office for a debriefing. I proceeded to his office, rerunning my career in my head. When I got in his office he looked up at me and said, "CNO said to tell you that for a minor issue yours was the best he had been prepared for since assuming this job. [I thought it was major.] As we were walking down to the briefing room he turned to me and said, 'Did that guy tell me to shut up and pay attention?' I said, 'Admiral, yes he did, and actually, you did shut up and pay attention." He said, 'You tell him he did a good job, but don't ever do it again.'" With that, he said, "Go back to your office and get to work. The CNO made all of the points you suggested, and the FAA administrator promised to take immediate action to clear this issue up. Good job."

The first thing I did after getting back to the office was to begin to unpack. The captain walked in and said, "Folks, I would like for you guys to meet the officer that told the CNO to shut up in front of every aviation admiral in the Navy and got away with it." (While I had a number of close calls during my career, I believe this was the best bullet I dodged.)

After the airspace briefing things got hot and heavy in the airspace business. I received a heads up that the General Accounting Office (GAO) was planning to conduct an audit on the airspace delegated to the DoD by the FAA. I knew better than most that the Navy was ill prepared for such an audit. I developed a briefing on our sad state of documentation associated with airspace and presented the briefing to the senior leadership of the Navy and Marine Corps in the Pentagon. The purpose of the briefing was to make them aware of the issues and solicit funds to support an independent study of airspace delegated to the Naval Service.

The briefing was well received and funding was provided. I contracted with the firm of Booz Allen and Hamilton to conduct this study. This firm was selected because of their performance in support of naval issues in other areas and the presence of an extremely well qualified cadre of personnel in airspace-elated issues on their staff. The study took approximately six months to complete. Its title was "Project Blue Air." I directed the contractor to report findings, good, bad and indifferent. When the study was completed, certain members of the firm was reluctant to release the findings because of the candor. I said, "I stand by your findings and will take the heat if there is any." The study was released, and with few exceptions the Navy received praise from both civilian and military organizations for its accuracy, candor, and completeness. I still believe that was one of the most important things we did during my tour in Washington.

One of the nay-sayers in response to the Blue Air report was the flag officer assigned to the Whidbey Island area. I had been assigned to Whidbey and was very familiar with the airspace structure in the area. The admiral at Whidbey called my flag officer and attempted to have the report changed to improve the image of Whidbey. My admiral called me into the office, informed me of the concerns of the Flag. I said, "Admiral, the report accurately reflects our management and mismanagement of airspace resources in the Whidbey area."

H said, "Very well, the report stands as is." I thanked him for his display of confidence and went back to my office.

I received a call a couple of days later from the staff of the Whidbey Flag. The individual said, "My flag is very disturbed by how your report reflected on his command. He directed me to inform you not to come west of the Mississippi or he would have your ass."

I replied, "What is to be will be."

The news of the Whidbey admiral's displeasure with my report spread rapidly throughout the Pentagon. Approximately six weeks later one of the commanders in my office laid a message on my desk. The message was a set of orders for the Whidbey Island admiral. His next assignment was to be on the OPNAV staff in the Pentagon. His position would be my direct supervisor. I said, "O, shit; I guess that is the end of me."

When an admiral reports for duty in the Pentagon, all action officers are required to provide him with an in-brief. This briefing is designed to bring him up to speed on every issue each action officer was working. I intentionally waited to be the last one in his organization to brief him.

When I walked into his office and introduced myself, he said, "Well, Commander, we finally meet."

I said, "Yes, sir, and it is obvious that you and I have a different opinion on airspace. I believe that I am right and you are wrong. One of my jobs will be to attempt to change your mind."

He said, "That will be the day."

I gave him the briefing on all of my projects and went back to my office. In the next eighteen months, this admiral became the strongest proponent of Airspace issues in the DoD. I had his support on every issue. He would accompany me to brief individuals in the congress, state officials, and senior officials in various special interest groups throughout the nation. We essentially led the DoD through troubling times with regard to airspace issues. I could not have had a more dedicated and informed partner in this endeavor. We became not only great partners but great friends. I rate this admiral as among the top three that I had the privilege to work for during my Navy career.

Even though my wife was back to work, money was still a problem. In an attempt to augment my income and stay in the Navy I opened an antique shop, open on weekends only. Antique shop is an overstatement, as it was actually a quality used-furniture and collectibles shop. Business was pretty good. I was clearing approximately $150.00 each weekend. One of interesting things that occurred, and there were several, was one Sunday afternoon about one P.M., a lady of Vietnamese nationally came into my little shop and began to look through a stack of dated Life magazines. I had no idea what they worth, so I had them priced at 50 cents each. After about an hour she brought one of the magazines up to the counter and offered me 25 cents for it. The cover was a Vietnamese man poling a small boat through a rice paddy. Normally I would have taken the quarter and have been glad to get it. In this case, perhaps because of a lingering distaste about the Vietnam conflict, I told her that my price was 50 cents and the price was firm. She bargained with me for about 30 minutes and finally left in a huff.

About one hour later I asked someone to watch my shop for me while I went to the Seven/Eleven shop next door for a cup of coffee, donut, and a package of cigarettes. When I entered the door, much to my surprise the clerk was my Vietnamese customer. I walked around the store picking up my coffee and donut. When I approached the counter I asked for a package of cigarettes. She found the smokes and totaled up my bill. It came to $2.46 cents. There was a fairly large crowd in the store. I told her that I would pay her $1.75 cents. She was confused and said, no, no, the total is $2.46 cents. I said, "You were in my shop earlier in the day and bargained with me for more than an hour over a 25-cent magazine. If you can waste my time, why can't I do the same with you?" I got a standing ovation from the crowd. After paying the full price I retreated to my shop and enjoyed the rest of the afternoon.

About one month later on a Saturday afternoon in my shop I looked up and saw an old friend, Lieutenant Commander Hose Turner. Hose was a legend in the aviation-boatswain-mate world, and he and I had served on a selection board together as warrant officers. He was one year senior to me, and I knew that he was awaiting the results of the Commander Selection Board. After a brief exchange of insults I asked him if there was any news on the selection board. He looked at me kind of odd and said, "You haven't heard?"

I said, "No, is the message out?"

He said, "Yes, it came out this morning and I was selected."

I said, "Congratulations; it is well earned."

He said, "Thanks. You really don't know do you?"

I said, "Don't know what?"

He said, "You were also selected. You are the first LDO in history to be deep selected for commander. The LDO community has been waiting for years for this to happen. Congratulations are certainly in order for you."

I cannot explain the joy I felt over this news. Not only had I been promoted, I could afford to stay in the Navy for a few more years. I called my wife and broke the news. Obviously, she was happy for me, but deep down inside, I felt that she was really disappointed that I would continue to stay in the Navy. In an effort to appease her concerns I promised that I would buy us a house. She was excited about that.

When I reported for work the following Monday, everyone was excited about the news. I received calls from all over the world offering congratulations. Naturally everyone in my sphere of influence in the Navy/ Marine Corps/Army/Air Force and FAA was equally graceful in their remarks.

Commander McMahon, now Captain McMahon, greeted the news by announcing that now that I had been promoted and would be around for a few years, it was time for him to retire and allow me to come back to my old job in the Pentagon. I knew that the issues we were working were too important to leave, and I also knew that after being in the Washington Area for almost eight years I would never be satisfied to take a job back in the fleet. All of the flag officers wanted me back in the Pentagon, so I agreed to come back to the best job in the Navy.

CHAPTER XXI

OPNAV STAFF PHASE II

My return to the Pentagon was made without incident. In a sense, I had never left. I had been involved with all of the budget activity associated with the NAS modernization effort and totally engrossed in airspace. One of the major changes was the reduction in staff. When I initially reported for duty the office was populated with ten active-duty and two civilian personnel. When I returned the manning of the office had been reduced to five active duty and two civilians. Additionally, the support infrastructure provided by NAVELEXCYSCOM had been changed by a BRAC decision to the Naval Air System Command (NAVAIRSYSCOM.) The engineering arm of NAVELEX had been decommissioned, and the function of that role had been transferred to engineering elements of NAVAIRSYSCOM and the Space and Naval Warfare Systems Commands (SPAWAR) in San Diego, California, and Charleston, South Carolina.

Thankfully, many of the dedicated personnel in civil service that had supported the ATC community from NAVELEX continued to support our requirements from their new commands. We had lost a significant portion of our engineering talent at the headquarters level, but the talent in the engineering centers of NAVAIR and SPAWAR proved to be capable of providing excellent support.

Personnel losses in the OPNAV office were a hit that was difficult to overcome. All of the action officers assigned during my tour in Washington were extremely capable and dedicated. These losses did not mean that the work load was reduced, as in fact, it had increased tremendously. The NAS-plan issue alone presented a tremendous workload. If the personnel from the Program Office and the Engineering Centers had not stepped up, we would have never survived. Perhaps the greatest loss was the secretary, Mrs. Kay Moreland. Not only was she the best office manager I observed during my almost-forty-year career, she was the corporate knowledge.

Kay's upward mobility was capped at the GS-7 level. In fact, her pay grade was one step higher than that normally found in a division head's office. She was very comfortable in her position, and despite the best efforts of many of the personnel assigned to the office, we could not persuade her to seek a higher-paying position. Finally, an opening occurred as the secretary of one of the flag officers in the organization. After a lot of persuading and serious lobbying, she applied for the position. To no one's surprise, she was selected and left our office for bigger and better things. This development proved to be important as subsequent events materialized.

My return to full-time status in the Pentagon gave me the opportunity to become more engaged with the issues involved in the fleet. The NAS plan was essentially the modernization effort for the shore-based equipment, and we were making giant strides in modernizing shipboard and Fleet Area Control and Surveillance Facilities (FACFACS) equipment. What was amazing to me was the ease with which our engineers identified problems and provided affordable and workable solutions in comparison to the difficulty realized by their FAA and Air Force counterparts. I believe the talent in all of these organizations was equal, but the Navy's philosophy of tasking individuals with issues and allowing them to work to solutions, rather than micro management, as exhibited by the other organizations involved in Air Traffic Control, was the difference.

On numerous occasions all participants were tasked with a problem, and invariably the Navy personnel came up with a solution that was fast, affordable ,and functional. In contrast, the FAA was constantly perusing the same problems with different solutions that invariably proved to be inaccurate. The Air Force was guilty of the not-invented syndrome. The solution to working with the Air Force, as previously mentioned, was to allow them to make minor, obvious changes to the proposed solution.

After that action was completed, normally the Air Force adopted the recommended solution as their solution, and we proceeded on. This did not normally work with the FAA, as the political influence of various members of congress or senior members of the administration in power would not allow the FAA to adopt the obvious course of action to follow.

My greatest ally in issues associated with Airspace and NAS modernization was the executive director of the DoD Policy Board on Federal Aviation, Mr. Frank Colson. After a slow beginning, he became an expert on equipment, procedures, and politics. He was a tireless worker who seldom made decisions based on any factor other than merit. I cannot overemphasize the contributions he made to the operational readiness of DoD and the FAA. His dogged attitude, friendly manner, and obvious passion for the job he was doing made him friends at all levels of the chain of command both within the DoD and the FAA.

Because of his Air-Force background, Mr. Colson was somewhat confused by the role I played in all of the issues. He could not understand why a Navy Commander had final say on issues involving the Navy and Marine Corps, while my Air Force counterparts, for the most part, full colonels, had to defer a decision until they could check with their bosses. While he liked and trusted me, he was concerned that he would take one of my recommendations and during the coordination phase, find out that the position I had fostered was not that of senior officials within the Department of the Navy but my own.

In his own politically correction fashion, he asked me to make him an appointment with my senior boss, Vice Admiral Dunleavy. I complied with his request and arranged a thirty-minute appointment. I accompanied Mr. Colson to Vice Admiral Dunleavy's office, made introductions and begin to make my way out of the office to give these two senior officials some privacy. Admiral Dunleavy said, "Where are you going?"

I said, "I thought I would leave the room so you folks could have your discussion in private.

He said, "Sit your butt down, and pay attention." I complied with this order.

Vice Admiral Dunleavy turned to Mr. Colson and said, "It is very good to meet you. Commander Calhoun has told me good things about you. I want you to understand that I am a very busy man. I have known Jim Calhoun for at least twenty years and have total confidence in him. He is the best I have, and while I apologize for that, it is a fact. The way I and the Navy work, is we put our best folks on an issue and leave them there until either the issue is resolved or they screw up. If the issue is resolved to everyone's satisfaction, we go to the next issue. If they screw up, we fire them. Pretty simple, isn't it? I realize that airspace and air traffic control are important; that is why Calhoun is assigned to these issues. What I am trying to impress on you is that he speaks for me and for naval aviation. No matter how stupid his position is, it is my position; therefore, there is no reason to ever check with me before you go forward. If he gets you or me in trouble, I will fire his ass. He knows that. Do you have any questions?"

Mr. Colson replied, "Admiral, after your comments, I don't believe I will have any reason to check with you in the future on any issue other than social.

I appreciate your time, and with that, I will return to my office and let you get on with your daily schedule."

We left the admiral's office and Mr. Colson said, "I have never seen such confidence expressed in any individual in my career."

I said, "This guy is my hero, and I will never let him or you down. More important than that is, this job is my life; my folks in the fleet depend on me, and more important than you and Admiral Dunleavy, is the reputation and trust and confidence they have in me." After this conversation, Mr. Colson and I made quite a team, and while we did on rare occasion disagree in private, our public positions were always presented with one voice.

One of my responsibilities was to essentially manage the careers of the LDOs in the ATC community. Essentially I allowed the system to detail individuals, lieutenant and below, to assignments identified as in the best interest of the Navy. Assignments for lieutenant commander and above received my personal attention. I attempted to review all records and question various individuals within the community about individuals before approving assignments. I felt it important to identify potential super stars and assure that they were given challenging assignments.

Normally this was fairly simple, but on occasion I had some problems. I had one lieutenant commander selectee that had an excellent record, but in my view he was wound so tight that I feared not only for his performance but his health. Since I had selected him for promotion initially, this was more than a professional concern: it was personal.

In a casual conversation with a captain assigned to the CNO staff I mentioned these concerns, for I knew that the individual in question had worked for him in the fleet. He said, "Don't worry about him. He worked for me on two occasions, once as an enlisted man and once as a junior officer. I was the executive officer on an amphibious ship. We pulled into New Orleans to be a part of the Mardi Gras celebration. I did not go ashore for the first three days in port but finally decided to take in the sights. About 30 minutes after I came ashore I noted a large crowd. I walked over to see what was happening. The young man you are concerned about was sitting on the curb with a set of marking pencils in his hand. He had a sign that said, "Tits painted, $2.00 each or a full set for $3.00." I relaxed. Anyone that could come up with that kind of scheme would do all right in a Navy career.

In addition to the normal routine, one of the major issues that occupied my time and attention was the decision to expand the three-mile territorial limit to twelve miles. On the face of this issue, it appears to be insignificant. In fact, it was very significant. Extending this limit would in fact extend the jurisdiction of the FAA from three to twelve miles. This extension would be at the expense of warning area airspace. Warning area airspace occupies most of the territorial waters adjacent to the coastal areas of the United States. In this airspace, the Navy and other services conduct a significant portion of their training. Surface, sub-surface, and airborne training is conducted in these areas. Providing the FAA with a block of airspace parallel to the coastlines of the United States could serve as an obstacle to military aircraft during egress/ingress to this airspace. In fact, the area is of sufficient size to allow the FAA to develop airways that parallel the coast line.

As the service with the greatest interest in this issue, the Navy took the lead in defending our turf. In many locations, we had activity that was actually launched from a shore-based command into the warning areas. If we could not either cancel the twelve-mile limit or negotiate exceptions, these commands would be in effect, out of business. The other services shared our concern, but it was not as great an issue for them as it was for the Navy. Not only did we have a problem with the proposal, we had a difficult time in identifying the sponsor of the issue.

After approximately six weeks of exhaustive staff work a high-level meeting was scheduled for the Pentagon. Since the Navy was the lead service in opposing this issue, I was appointed as the spokesman for the DoD opposition. When the meeting was called to order, I was shocked to see the CNO in attendance. I began my presentation by pointing out the adverse impact this issue would have on readiness and training, with particular emphasis on the Navy. We had Air Force and Army representatives to speak to their particular issues. After approximately fifteen minutes I observed CNO send a signal to the moderator, Mr. Colson, to take a break. I was puzzled by his action but naturally had no choice but to pause while Mr. Colson announced a fifteen-minute break. As I was reviewing my thoughts on the strategy I would employ to continue the briefing, CNO walked up to me and said, "See me in the passageway."

I said, "Yes, sir,"and followed him out of the room.

We walked about fifteen feet from the doorway and he said, "How dare you challenge an issue that I have sponsored? The reason for the change is hostile or potentially hostile submarines are following my submarines into their home ports. The twelve-mile barrier will allow my sub skippers to maneuver after they cross the magic boundary."

I said, "We in Naval Aviation had no idea that the Navy was the sponsor for this issue. I am sure you have reviewed the advanced briefing package provided you for this briefing and can understand the potential impact if this is approved. Did anyone on your staff coordinate with aviation prior to sponsoring this issue?"

He said, "Obviously not, but I am not going to allow a naval officer to speak in public against an issue I am sponsoring. After this meeting, you work with the FAA and the other services to mitigate the impact, but your public opposition will cease."

I said, "Yes, sir."

CNO returned to the room and, I contacted my Air Force counterpart and explained that my guns had been spiked and that he would have to take the lead in opposition. Thankfully we had worked together to develop the briefings, so he was familiar with the issues. After the meeting was completed, I called for a caucus of the primary players from the services and the FAA to develop a time line to identify and implement procedures that would mitigate the impact. Thankfully we were successful in this effort, but this is an example of incomplete coordination at the highest levels.

We continued to work the budgetary considerations associated with implementing the NAS plan. Since the Air Force was the service lead in this program, often we were forced to follow a course of action that did not make sense to the Navy. The cost continued to accelerate. Decisions on specific equipment to be procured were constantly changing. Costs were constantly escalating. Lead contractors were being changed. Bottom line, progress was difficult to measure. To compound the problems, money was getting tight in the Pentagon. The cost of everything was going up, and the search for improved technology, required or not, was endless. These factors combined to reduce the enthusiasm for funding the NAS-modernization effort by senior leadership of some of the services. This loss of support was especially visible in the Air Force.

It was an open secret at the working level in the Pentagon that the other services used me as the point man when we were working contentious issues associated with joint-service-interest issues. The selection of me as the point man occurred a number of times, but one time in particular deserves sharing. I continue to believe that my selection for the lead position was based on three factors: One factor was the service members had a great deal of confidence in my knowledge and understanding of the issues. Another factor was the total support of the Navy chain of command that I enjoyed. The third reason and perhaps the most important was that I was an LDO. LDOs, because of their background as prior enlisted, and the reputation of LDOs, rightfully or not, of being uncouth and ill mannered, allowed me to pull off a lot of things that unrestricted line officers would be crucified for.

We received informal information that the Air Force was seriously considering pulling out of their funding obligation for the NAS-modernization program. This obligation had been made during the negotiations regarding service lead of the program. The commitment had been made by the senior acquisition executive of the Air Force. When the rumor first appeared, the chief of staff of the Army sent a memorandum to the chief of staff of the Air Force stating his concerns about the pending action by the Air Force.

During the internal budget hearings of the Air Force council, my Air Force contemporizes arranged for my attendance. I was somewhat conspicuous in my Navy White's uniform surrounded by a sea of personnel dressed in Air Force working blue. A number of Air Force budget issues were discussed before the funding of the NAS modernization program reached the floor. When this issue was discussed, the chief of staff of the Air Force announced that he had received a memorandum from his contemporary in the Army regarding NAS-program funding and asked me if he could expect comparable correspondence from the CNO. Everyone in the room was waiting on the edge of their seats for my response. I paused for effect and then replied, "General, the Navy has no reason to question the integrity of the Air Force. Your senior acquisition executive made an iron-clad commitment for the Air Force not only to fund the Air Force share of this program but to fund all of the cost realized by being service lead for this program."

He paused for a moment and then turned to the other general officers in the room and said, "The commander is correct. We, as a service, are committed to this program. Programs must be cut to satisfy budget-ceiling requirements, but the NAS plan will not be one of those programs." He thanked me for my candor and attendance and dismissed me from the meeting. I proceeded back to my office and waited for the ax to fall.

About two hours later the working group members from the Army and Air Force came to my office and began to give me high fives. They said, "After I left, the chief of staff really read the riot act to his staff by overlooking a commitment, that if broken, would have brought discredit to his service." (This is an example of a routine occurrence in the puzzle palace.)

Despite my success in persuading the Air Force to maintain their participation in the NAS-modernization program I was beginning to become concerned about the escalating cost and program slippage, cancellation.

Additionally, some of the initial justification for Navy participation in the program had been changed. The transition from analog to digital technology had become a phased transition rather than an immediate change. The ACF concept had been cancelled. I pondered over these issues for a couple of weeks and then placed a call to a couple of my chief engineers for advice.

Essentially I felt we could digitize our fielded Surveillance Radar systems and conduct a planned product improvement to our fielded automation system. These changes would not only prepare the Navy to be in total commonality with the FAA modernized system, they would save the Navy millions of dollars. I proposed these changes to my engineers, and they agreed to go home and study the feasibility and cost of the alternative proposal.

In a few weeks' time they contacted me and asked for an opportunity to brief the concept. I set up the appointment for the next day, and when they arrived they had fleshed out my concept to a fully executable program. They had entitled the modified program, "Calhoun's Folly." This program was executable, and the cost was approximately twenty percent of the cost of the FAA/Air Force modernization effort.

We took this briefing to the Air Force and to the FAA. Both organizations were concerned about the impact on their particular program for modernization should the Navy follow a different path. The Air Force radars were not capable of being digitized, and the FAA could never get consensus among their work force to do anything but buy new stuff. The Air Force and FAA pointed out that if I pulled out of the Joint-Modernization program, the Navy would be required to reimburse those organizations for any additional cost they would incur from such action. Because of escalating cost and program slips I thought I could avoid those costs, but their reluctance to follow our lead in modernization caused me to delay action until it was too late in the program to execute. Hindsight suggests that my major error was naming the program alternative, "Calhoun's Folly." My reputation for opposition to some of their ideas set up a red flag. We should have executed the alternative. If successful, the Navy would have saved countless dollars and completed the modernization at least seven years ago. The program is still not fielded, and the cost has gone through the roof.

One of the most devastating developments that occurred during my second tour in the Pentagon was the infamous "Tail Hook" incident. Please understand that the following diatribe about Tail Hook is my personal opinion based on personal observation and does not reflect anything other than that.

I checked into the Pentagon initially in September of 1982. From that date until the aftermath of Tail Hook, the Naval Aviation Organization was the best place in the world to work. We, officers, enlisted, civilian employees, and support contractors were a team. We had some of the best flag officers in history leading us, and the morale and productivity of the workforce was not exceeded anywhere by anyone at any time.

Tail Hook was an annual event. It provided an opportunity in an informal setting in Las Vegas for senior leadership of the Navy with particular emphasis on aviation to share experiences and concerns with all ranks, from the most junior to the most senior aviator on the Navy/Marine Corps aviation team.

This particular Tail Hook was a prime target. A high level committee of a cross section of representatives from various special interest groups was in secession in Washington. The goal of that committee was to determine the adoption or rejection of Women in Combat. (I am not qualified to express an opinion on this issue, even though I have one.) Intelligence from the committee indicated that the vote would be close. In an attempt to sway the results of the committee to favor the combat role a group of personnel decided to set a trap at Tail Hook. During an open session chaired by the deputy chief of Naval Operations (Air Warfare), Vice Admiral Dunleavy was asked a question associated with what Naval Aviation was going to do to accommodate female aviators when they were authorized to operate in a combat role. Vice Admiral Dunleavy is an Irishman with a keen sense of humor. While he is a Yankee by birth, he overcame that by marrying a lady from Mississippi. His entire career was spent blazing a trail for those that followed in his footsteps. Instead of responding with a canned answer, like, "Future actions by the Navy will be driven by the decision made on this issue by a committee now in session," he responded with a flippant remark. This set the stage for the hell-to-pay that followed. I have read all of the reports and am personally acquainted with a number of attendees. According to their remarks, there was nothing out of the ordinary that occurred. The fact that all occurrences were reported, some accurately and some slanted, led to the debacle that essentially destroyed not only the careers of a large number of superior naval officers but damaged the morale of naval aviation with particular attention to the OPNAV staff to a degree that continues to hamper the productivity of the organization.

Despite my involvement in daily ATC issues, issues associated with Special Use Airspace essential to training and weapons systems development and the budget process not only for the NAS-modernization program but for all of the modernization or maintenance of fielded systems ashore and afloat not associated with NAS modernization, I was becoming increasingly concerned about the lack of upward mobility for LDOs not only within the ATC community but throughout the Navy. The rules essentially stated that a former enlisted person could serve, providing that they were being promoted within accepted parameters for the same amount of time as their unrestricted-line counterparts. This normally translated to thirty years of service, plus the time they had spent as enlisted or non-commissioned personnel. In my case that translated to a total amount of authorized service of the thirty years, plus the thirteen years of enlisted service, and the two years I had served as a warrant officer I. In other words, if I were successful in competing for captain (0-6) I could actually serve for forty-five years. This was fine for me, as I loved the Navy and felt that I was doing a good job. The problem was that if everyone stayed for the maximum time allowed, the upward mobility for the more junior personnel would be stymied. The rule for the junior LDOs was, if you had not been promoted or selected for promotion to lieutenant commander (0-4) when you had thirty years of combined service, you were forced to retire. Because of the high retention of the more senior personnel, many of the junior personnel were in a position where they would not even be considered for promotion to 0-4 prior to reaching the thirty-year service date.

I pondered this issue for several weeks. After I was sure that I had the facts correct I began to coordinate with various officials positioned in billets much more familiar with this situation than I was. They all agreed that the problem was serious and should be corrected. Not only was it unfair, it was beginning to have an impact on the number of candidates in the fleet applying for LDO selection.

After a great deal of thought I drafted a letter to the chief of Naval Personnel. In this letter, I briefly outlined the problem and proposed that legislation be adopted that would result in the mandatory retirement of all limited duty officers when they reached thirty-eight years of total service if they were 0-6s, and thirty-five years of service if they were 0-5s. I sent this letter to the LDO community manager and detailer for comment. The detailer was a good personal friend of the chief of Naval Personnel, Vice Admiral Mike Borda. Admiral Borda, later on the chief of Naval Operations, was a former enlisted man, and was very in tune with the issues addressed in the draft letter. He reviewed the draft letter and returned it to me with comments. He followed this up with a personal phone call to me. Essentially the comments and his conversation expressed admiration for the letter. He also said, "You realize that if adopted, this legislation will force you to retire. I know the last thing you personally want to do is leave the Navy, but if passed, this legislation will not allow exceptions to the rule."

I replied, "Yes, I understand, Admiral, but we must do something to put fairness back into the process. I have thought about this a lot, and this is the only fair solution I can come up with."

He said, "If you can get the letter through the chain of command to me, I will support your recommendation. It is the right thing to do, but I really hate to see you being forced to retire."

I said, "I appreciate your confidence, Admiral, but I have always been a fan of *Mr. Roberts*, and this is something I believe he would do."

He said, "I understand; go for it."

I smoothed up the letter and formally submitted it up the chain of command. My immediate bosses were violently opposed to the letter until I explained the issues to them. With great reluctance, they favorably endorsed the letter, and in about six months the proposal became law. Looking back, while I hated to retire, that letter may have been one of the best things I did during my career.

Professionally things were going well. We were defending our delegated airspace, funding for all of the ATC programs was being provided at an acceptable rate, relationships with the other services and the FAA were at an all-time high, and the training, recruitment, and retention of our work force was well above acceptable standards. On a personal level, things were not going so well. We had bought a home in West Virginia. The commute to Washington was a killer. In addition I had transitioned from an antique shop south of Alexandria to a shop in Inwood, West Virginia. Business was good, but the time and level of effort it took to run the shop, procure inventory, and refinish furniture for customers, was draining. I was totally exhausted, mentally and physically. To compound the issues, my wife's father became very ill with a heart problem. She, along with her sisters, began a bed-side vigil at the hospital in Houston, Texas that lasted six months. While I understood her commitment to her family, I became overwhelmed with all of the issues I was attempting to manage. Please understand, all of our problems were my fault. My commitment to the Navy was far greater than my commitment to my family. This was a mistake that I made, but looking back, I am confident that I would do the same thing again. The Navy had provided me an opportunity to excel, and my desire to become someone outweighed my family commitment.

At work, despite an ever increasing work load, I continued to lose personnel. A reorganization of the OPNAV staff resulted in me losing two additional billets, one 0-6 and one 0-5. This left me with myself, one Marine 0-3, a Navy E-9, and a GS-6 secretary. Thanks to a lot of assistance from the program office, the engineering centers, and the fleet, we were able to maintain control of our responsibilities, but the toll on everyone was severe.

My personal problems continued to fester. I actually had a choice. I could maintain my family by leaving the Navy, or stay in the Navy and lose my family. I chose to stay in the Navy and moved out of our home and took up residence in the Washington area. The commute was a vast improvement over the long train ride to West Virginia, and I was able to put in more hours at work. Slowly a relationship was established between me and Mrs. Moreland. This was legal, as she no longer worked in my organization.

I filed for divorce, and after a period of negotiation my wife agreed with the settlement I had proposed. The divorce became final on 1 November 1991. Mrs. Moreland and I were married on 11 November 1991. It was a day off, and I felt I would be able to remember the anniversary, as it was also Veterans Day.

The legislation I had proposed forced a modification of the eligibility for promotion of the senior LDOs in the Navy. The decision was made that all of the personnel that could be immediately affected by this legislation would be placed in zone for selection to O-6 or 0-5. Those selected for promotion would be retained in compliance with the legislation, while those personnel that failed to select would be forced to retire by 1 September of the year selection board action was completed. This meant that I, along with fifty-eight other senior commanders would be placed in zone for 0-6. Selection would allow continuation until 1 September of the thirty-eighth year of service. Failure to select would result in mandatory retirement. I felt confident of my selection potential, but I had one exceptional commander air traffic controller in zone with me. He and I had been running mates since the day we both were selected for warrant officer. Not only were we contemporaries, we were good friends. He had been one of my students when I was an instructor in the advanced school, and his performance had been exceptional. We both felt that the size of our community would not support the selection of two captains. We both felt that either of us would be deserving of selection, but the reality was that one of us would be forced to go home. This is the way it turned out. I was selected and he was not. To this day, while I believe my selection was warranted, his selection was also justified. The Navy in general, and the ATC community in particular, paid a price for this decision. He retired and continued to provide exceptional support to the ATC community as a private contractor.

When the selection results were announced, I was naturally overjoyed. While I continued to believe that the 0-6 selection for LDOs was not necessary, I was glad that I had been selected. The community was equally proud of my selection, as after all, I was their point man, and if I was successful it was a positive reflection on the entire community.

Since by law, I could not be promoted higher than 0-6, I had free rein to do what I felt was necessary for the best interest of the community. Since I had never considered promotion as a factor in my actions, there was little change, but I must admit the freedom from worrying about fitness reports was a relief.

While I had never experienced a lack of respect within the community or within the circles I worked in the Navy, the promotion to 0-6 was an obvious benefit while dealing with senior personnel in the other services and the FAA. Those organizations are much more attuned to seniority than is the Navy, so my reception by flag officers and senior executive-service civilians was enhanced by my promotion. Additionally, while I had been the spokesman for the ATC community within the Navy for a number of years, the reception of senior LDOs from other designators within the Navy was more open than it had been prior to my promotion.

One of the issues that occurred associated with the unfortunate shoot down of a civil airliner by the Navy bears sharing. Immediately after this incident, a hue and cry was raised about the cowboy-like attitude of the Navy when operating on the high seas. As the result of this visibility, action was taken to revise the handbook that describes operations on the high seas. After approximately one month of rewrite efforts by everyone involved, including all of the services, the Department of Defense, and the Department of State, Mr. Colson chaired a meeting to reach a consensus on the contents of the final draft. All of the action officers within the Pentagon had been working in concert with other to develop a draft that all of the services could live with. We approached the meeting with a high degree of confidence that we could achieve a desired result without a great deal of debate. Early on in the meeting, the State Department representative presented an eighteen-page modification to the basic document. His document essentially handcuffed the Navy from operating on the high seas. One of his proposals stated that the Navy would be required to provide forty-two days' advance notification before they could launch a flight. I went berserk. The State Department representative made some derogatory remarks about the Navy and our due-regard attitude, and I replied in kind to the panty-waist attitude of pansies employed by State. I summarized my comments by stating that it was obvious why he was in the State Department and I was in the Department of Defense. Mr. Colson resolved the argument by tasking me to draft the revisions to the document and submit them to all concerned for approval. I complied with his direction, and we were able to modify the document to please all concerned while maintaining the ability to operate unconstrained on the high seas of the world.

The longer I was in the Pentagon the more I was persuaded that the services did a lot of duplicate work. One of my areas of concern was associated with the training provided to Air Traffic Controllers. Each of the services had their own school, and the FAA also had a separate school. It appeared logical to me that if all of these schools were basically teaching the same basic skills, a significant cost savings would be realized if those schools were all or in part consolidated. I approached the training section of the CNO staff and proposed that such a study be commissioned.

This request occurred simultaneously with a BRAC initiative. Because the services were involved in identifying bases to be closed, the time was considered right for such a study; thus, approval was granted. Each service appointed representatives to participate in this study. The FAA also appointed personnel to represent their interest in this effort.

I must admit that since the Navy had just completed a move of the ATC school from Millington, Tennessee, to Pensacola, Florida, for all of the technical training in aviation, I felt the investment the Navy had made in Pensacola would make that the ideal location for a consolidated school for training Air Traffic Controllers.

When the ground rules were published, Pensacola was eliminated as a consolidated site because of the recent move. That put some obstacles in my path, but the idea continued to have merit, so the study went forward. It was amazing to me that the basic course of instruction provided by the Air Force was almost identical to that provided by the Navy. In fact, in thirty minutes we were able to modify the curriculums of these services to allow consolidation. The FAA was willing to consolidate with the Navy anywhere, but knew that political opposition to relocating their vast investment in Oklahoma City would prohibit such a move.

The most interesting thing we discovered was the minimal training the Army provided to their neophyte controllers. The Army exposed their personnel to the minimum information required to gain FAA certification, then sent them to an abbreviated course of instruction on ground-controlled-approach (GCA) procedures. At the end of this brief exposure, the Army sent their personnel to fleet units. I saw this as an opportunity to increase the education opportunities available to Army personnel. If all of the services were consolidated, the Army would be required to increase their investment in training. The Air Force agreed, and our report recommended this consolidation with the Army at Fort Rucker, Alabama with the understanding that the FAA for political reasons would remain in Oklahoma City.

Since the BRAC decision to relocate Navy training to Pensacola prohibited a move, the idea of consolidation was never implemented. I continue to believe that such consolidation would be in the best interest of the services, result in a better trained workforce, and save a significant number of personnel and resources. This development is provided as another example of the constipation of progress in a bureaucratic organization.

Things were going well. Funding was in place for all of our programs. Our relationship with the services and the FAA regarding airspace issues was at an all-time high, and the performance of our fielded equipment and dedication and commitment of the personnel in the fleet was at an all-time high. My world would have been perfect except for the fact that my mandatory retirement date was rapidly approaching. I not only had the best job in the Navy, I felt that I was doing a good job and did not want to leave. Because of that letter I had written associated with the thirty-five/thirty-eight year retirement, I was without options.

I began to attempt to identify my relief. Frankly, based on what I knew about the job and what I knew about the ideas, issues, and experience of personnel in the fleet in my community I was sure that no one was qualified to take the job. I realize that is self serving, but the facts were that the job had changed since I had arrived. The size of the staff and the complexities of the issues were far greater than those I had addressed when I first arrived. The experience of the support infrastructure in the program office and engineering centers did not approach the level that existed when I had arrived. Most of the experienced senior LDOs in the fleet had retired. That said, we had a lot of sharp younger LDOs in the community that were more than capable of growing to the demands of the job if given the chance to succeed.

I knew that a lot of folks capable of doing the job were not interested in getting in the pressure mill of the Pentagon. I felt that anyone accepting the job would be motivated by trying to lead the community, and more importantly, believing that the job was a path to being selected for 0-6. Based on my experience on selection boards, and being well aware of the records of the more senior LDOs, I knew that no one within reasonable reach of selection had a chance for selection.

I finally made my choice and informed the individual I selected that I felt he had the ability to do an excellent job, but if he were taking the challenge to make 0-6 he would not succeed. Obviously he reviewed the personnel in the community that had been selected in the past, including me, and felt that his record and ability gave him a competitive chance; therefore he took the job.

My pending retirement and the associated mental review of my career made me recognize that the philosophy of the limited duty officers and the role they play was changing. My personal feelings were the warrant/limited duty officer program was essentially the backbone of the Navy. In my view, chief petty officers actually ran the Navy, but if events exceeded their ability to rectify the situation, the Warrant/LDOS would fix what was broken.

I was so appreciative of the opportunity afforded me by the programs and felt that the historic role of being the connection between the mess deck and the wardroom was perfect. I was beginning to sense that some LDOs were dissatisfied with this historic role and were beginning to make click- like changes to the system. These changes were designed to generate command opportunities for selected designators at the expense of not only the unrestricted line officers, but also their peers. I contacted the LDOS program manager and shared my views with him. He agreed with me and asked me to write an article for the Limited Duty Officer/Warrant Officer Directory. I responded with an article expressing these concerns and warned that the historic value of the LDO/Warrant was being endangered. The article was well received, but despite my warnings, actions are continuing to occur that validate these concerns.

Prior to my approaching retirement date I had maintained sparse records. My excuse was that I did not have time to do all of the required actions and document those actions. Obviously, budget issues were a matter of record, and all of the various deals, agreements, and compromises with the other services and the FAA were documented in the files, but a lot of the actual agreements and actions taken internal in the Navy to support various requirements were missing. After realizing my shortfalls in this area, we began a massive effort to rectify these deficiencies. After all, no one could come in cold and do a job. I had to leave footprints for them to follow. Looking back, this was my greatest disservice to the community. I had attempted to make my efforts a one-man show rather than develop a team. I have mixed feelings about whether I could have done a better job. At the time, I felt what I was doing was correct but history will be a better judge.

Once a relief was identified and announced, the community began planning for a retirement celebration. Because of my long-time service in Washington, and the contacts I had made within the Navy, the other services and government agencies, and civilian consultant organizations throughout the DC area, it was mandatory that this event be held in Washington. I knew that an event would be scheduled concurrent with my retirement to justify attendance by a large number of senior civilian and military personnel, but that would not allow for the junior personnel to participate. Since everything I had done throughout my career was to support the requirements, goals, and ideals of the junior folks, I really wanted them to be a part of whatever occurred.

As always, the community came through. We had an annual planning conference scheduled for the ATC School in Pensacola. This conference drew attendees from every air station in the Navy and Marine Corps and every air capable ship not deployed. Without my knowledge, a ceremony was scheduled, and frankly a good time was had by all. The circle of honor by the honor guard with fixed bayonets scared the shit out of me, but that is another story.

Back in Washington, plans for a big blow-out were on-going. Civilian employees assigned to the Program Office were in charge of this event, and I must say, they did a bang-up job. Total attendance was two hundred eighty-seven personnel. I had friends and opponents from around the world attend. I think most of them were there to make sure I was actually leaving. The greatest single event that occurred was a number of the LDO's that I had trained got flat-top haircuts in my honor. A large number of the flag officers I had served throughout my career were in attendance. Needless to say, this event remains one of the highlights of my career.

At the conclusion of the day I was drained. More importantly I knew that the next day I would not have a home to go to. For almost forty years, the Navy had been my life. The system never told me they did not want me, and I can truthfully say that there was never a day that I did not look forward to going to work. I guess that you could say that I was the luckiest guy in the world. I found by accident my life's work. The example that *Mr. Roberts* gave to me was a positive one and if I was able in some small way to pass that example own to someone else, I am satisfied with the journey.

CHAPTER XXII

REFLECTIONS

When this effort began, my purpose was to document some of the developments that occurred during my naval career. I wanted to describe some of the major events that shaped me as a person and directed my actions throughout my career. I was amazed as I recalled specific events and personalities. I believe, based on personal experience, that if an individual is cursed or blessed with average intelligence and an inflated and somewhat unhealthy ambition to achieve, he or she can succeed if placed in an organization that recognizes commitment and passion to a cause. This document attempts to capture some of the circumstances and resultant actions I took to reach decisions.

A number of years ago, while living in West Virginia and commuting to the Washington DC area on a train, the Oliver North debacle was ongoing. This may have not resonated throughout the country, but in the Washington area, it was a big deal. Much of the discussion centered on the disbelief that a lowly Lieutenant Colonel in the Marine Corps could have accomplished all of the deeds, good or bad, reported and testified to about this issue. Based on my personal experiences, some which are described in this document, I can state without reservation that anyone in a military organization, based on a record of problem-solving, can accomplish most anything if they operate behind the scenes and take full responsibility for mistakes made, while giving total credit to their superiors for all successes.

On a number of occasions I have actually done someone else's job. I believe that I always gave the responsible individual the opportunity to do what was necessary; however, if he failed to act I stepped forward. In the almost forty years of my career, I was never chastised for doing this, if I made sure the responsible official received credit for a job well done.

In reviewing this diatribe, some thoughts stand out. I believe these developments should be highlighted similar to the justification for an

227

Executive Summary in official documents. I have no idea if anyone other than close personal friends and family members will be interested in the contents of this document. If there are interested readers, the reflections chapter will provide them with a quick review of the contents.

The single most important decision I have made in my lifetime was the decision I made to join the Navy. The movie *Mr. Roberts* served as the inspiration for that decision, and ultimately, my interpretation of his demeanor, commitment, and actions served as a checklist on my actions.

Anyone with average intelligence that finds him or herself in an organization that recognizes commitment and a desire to achieve can be a success in the Navy. I believe the Navy's philosophy of placing seemingly qualified personnel in responsible positions and allowing them to exercise their judgment and talent without external oversight is the basic difference between the Navy and other service branches. I also believe this philosophy, driven by the historic authority and accountability of officers assigned the responsibility of command at sea, attracts personnel that want to be measured by their actions.

I believe that the promotion system in the Navy is the fairest and most thorough of any organization both military and civilian. I am convinced that if people are blessed by having supervisors that allow them to perform and document their contributions fairly, they will succeed. I also believe that organizations that employ personnel that take advantage of the accomplishments of their employees rather than giving credit when credit is due is doomed to fail.

I am convinced the decision to become a career military person is one of the most selfish decisions one can make. The rewards for the individual are tremendous; the consequences for family members can be devastating. The spouse of the military member is essentially deprived of a career. Frequent moves based on the needs of the service or the ambition of the family member dooms spouses' careers. Children of professional military members are the greatest victims. They are constantly uprooted from friends and schools. They are deprived of developing roots with grandparents, cousins, aunts, and uncles. This lack of belonging damages their self worth and leaves them with a feeling of isolation when things go bad.

Success in the Navy depends more on circumstances than it does on personal accomplishment. I am convinced that any success I enjoyed was a byproduct of circumstances rather than planned. I will admit that the successful individual takes advantages of the circumstances offered, but the opportunities to succeed are accidental.

In my view, to succeed in the Navy you must position yourself to be the go-to guy in problem solving. Every command has a listing of problems that should be solved, but personnel resources do not exist to place these issues on a fast track to resolution. The successful individual will volunteer to take on some of these issues on a collateral-duty basis. As the list of problems declines, your worth in the eyes of your seniors increases. Not only are you contributing to the mission-accomplishment capability of the command, you are gaining notoriety as a valuable and trusted member of the organization.

In order to succeed in the Navy you must have heros. This hero can be anyone that you look up to and respect. Your goal is to become someone's hero. The greatest compliment you can receive is to observe your actions/demeanor in junior personnel. Your actions have so impressed others that they have adopted that trait as a part of their persona.

During my career I had a number of heroes. My first hero was my recruit training company commander. His professionalism and no-nonsense attitude established, in my mind, the traits I looked for in chief petty officers. I worked for and with a number of officers that had my total respect. Commander Don Clyncke, Commander Ernie Connor, and Lieutenant Commander C.T. Sanders in the ATC community were role models for me. I had equal admiration for the examples set for me by ACCM Fred Jackson, ACCM Jess Davis, ACCS Bill McPhaul, ACCS Bud Wills and ACCS Jim Brown. ACC Charlie Smith was also an inspiration. Each of these individuals along with many others was vitally important to me at various stages of my career.

I was blessed with working for some of the most outstanding officers ever produced by Naval Aviation. The best, in my opinion, was Vice Admiral Dutch Schultz. My respect for Vice Admiral Dick Dunleavy, Admirals Chuck McGrail, Fred Metz, Jeremy "Bear" Taylor, Robert "Boomer" Hickey, Commodore Mac Gleim, and Admiral Jim Seely is unlimited.

Many of the listed admirals were either my direct supervisors in the Pentagon or were commanding officers at various duty stations where I served. In addition to those listed, Captain Jim Foster at NAS Dallas, and Captain Boyd Muncie at NAS Fallon, were major contributors to my development and success.

In the civilian area, the folks that made a difference in my life either by actions or personal example included Mr. Hal Nordenburg, Mr. Frank Colson, Mr. Dave Hurley, Mr. Bill Raynor, Mr. Jerry Thompson, Ms. Edith Bibb, Ms. Debbie Cole and Retired Vice Admiral Don Engen.

Obviously the debt I owe to my family with special attention to my mom and dad, both wives, and three children is one that I can never repay. Their support throughout thick and thin gave me the energy to go forward. The commitment to my ultimate success made by all of the teachers, classmates, and support staff of Merryville High School was very important. I felt an obligation to make them proud of me and overachieved to reach this goal. Despite the lack of a degreed education, I never felt that I was not prepared to compete with the Navy's best and brightest throughout my career. This confidence, even if misplaced, is a direct reflection of the commitment these unsung teachers made to each of the students placed in their care. I am forever grateful to everyone regardless of the circumstances that served as my personal heroes.

AUTHORS NOTE: Slightly more than one year after my retirement on 1 September 1995 a formal ceremony was conducted in Pensacola, Florida. The purpose of the ceremony was to dedicate the new Air Traffic Controller and Maintenance School in my honor. CALHOUN HALL is the crowning event of my Naval Career. My selection was symbolic in nature, as I can think of at least fifty personnel, both active duty and civilian, who could have been chosen for this honor. Nevertheless, I am forever grateful to all who made it possible.

Printed in the United States
58427LVS00005B/124-255

9 781413 791587